MEDICAL
MANSLAUGHTER

Gloria J. Yorke

authorHOUSE®

AuthorHouse™
1663 Liberty Drive
Bloomington, IN 47403
www.authorhouse.com
Phone: 1 (800) 839-8640

Published by AuthorHouse June 28, 2018

ISBN: 978-1-5246-9712-9 (sc)
ISBN: 978-1-5246-9711-2 (hc)
ISBN: 978-1-5462-2398-6 (e)

Library of Congress Control Number: 2017919321

Print information available on the last page.

This is a work of fiction. Any resemblance to actual persons, living or dead, businesses, events or locales, names, characters, places and incidents, are purely coincidental. They are a product of the author's creativity, and used fictitiously to create the storyline.

This book is printed on acid-free paper.

Author's Cover Photograph by Legends Photography, Orland Park, IL
Buddy Dow, AH Publishing Agent

authorHOUSE®

GRATITUDE

It is with much Humility, Thankfulness, Love, and profound Appreciation, that I acknowledge the following:

- I am forever indebted to **The Blessed Mother,** for keeping her promise of the Mt. Carmel Scapular, and miraculously informing me that she had protected my beloved husband, Dick, from suffering eternal fire.
- I am extremely thankful to **Archangel Gabriel**, for enlightening me with spiritual guidance throughout this writing.
- I am lovingly beholden to **Archangel Michael**, for protecting me throughout this writing, and during my entire life.
- I am honor-bound to confirm the wondrous deeds shown to me and my husband, Dick, by **Archangel Raphael**, God's Powerful Healer, of Body, Mind, and Spirit.
- A special heartfelt Thank You to **all our Family Members and close Friends,** for your prayers, phone calls, letters, cards, emails, and more... providing me with much consolation.

FOREWORD BY JOE VITALE

Anyone who knows Gloria personally, would have found it so very difficult to witness her anguish, as she ventured through the dark night of the soul, in order to write this book.

She bares all in order to help you, the Reader, understand what can happen in a world we sometimes take for granted, when someone we love is taken from us, because of a hasty human mistake, that is out of our control.

You might read it as a novel, and think it could never happen to you. But think again!

Often, a work of Fiction can unveil the ugly truth, behind what cannot be told otherwise.

I urge you to read this book with an open mind and an open heart. Although entertaining, it provides a valuable, deep-rooted education.

This is one of those rare books, that will stir an awakening in you.

It will surely trigger you, into taking necessary Action. The permanent impression it will imprint upon your psyche, will affect the way you view the Medical Field from this day forward!

Joe Vitale: *Best-Selling World Renowned American Author. Doctorate in Metaphysics. Law of Attraction Guru. Featured in the Movie, "The Secret." Author of numerous Best-Sellers including: The Midas Touch, The Attractor Factor, Zero Limits, Ho'oponopono Practitioner, Instant Manifestation, Anything Is Possible, and The Secret Prayer.*

CONTENTS

PROLOGUE

Medical Manslaughter is based on a TRUE STORY, that you and your loved ones need to read!

Learn from what was actually lived and experienced!

True events that occurred, are now interwoven throughout this Fictional catastrophic medical storyline, of Nicholas and his wife, Gabriella Carcioni. You will find yourself being pulled into the horrendous and mystifying experience of trauma, drama, and miracles; all of which are cloaked within an uncompromising love, that would not give in, nor give up!

As our story unfolds...Nicholas collapses at home, hitting his head several times prior to landing from the fall. He was rushed to a Chicago suburban hospital and placed in Intensive Care. When Nicholas was recovering nicely, he was moved to a regular floor.

DOCTOR ERROR is DEADLY: An egotistical Doctor, made a decision to administer a sleeping pill, even though Nicholas' wife Gabriella, voiced objection. The following morning, Nicholas was found in a Coma.

The Doctor and entire staff, could not rectify this cataclysm. Hence, their recommendation was for Gabriella to, *"Let him die!"* When Gabriella refused, they demanded Nick's immediate Discharge.

Every Nursing Home refused him in his coma state, citing Medicare rules. But finally, *one* accepted him, because they expected him to die in a few days, but...he did not!

After thirty-four days, Gabriella *brought him out of his coma!*

She taught him to speak again. Nearly 100 days later, she brought him home under Hospice care.

Obviously, the names and locations have been changed in this fictional story to protect the guilty! They're not important at this time. What **IS** important is the **WISDOM** that **YOU WILL GAIN, FROM READING THIS ENTIRE STORY!**

LEARN.. exactly what Doctor Error put him in a coma, when he was only a few days away from coming home.

LEARN.. how Gabriella's opinion, as wife and his Power of Attorney for Healthcare, was ignored by the Doctor, as the Doctor fed her own ego.

LEARN.. successful techniques to bring someone out of a coma state.

LEARN.. what being a superior Advocate really means.

LEARN.. that you should meet with, and speak directly to, the attending Doctor often.

LEARN.. what living in a Nursing Home is really like—the mistakes, mistreatments, and being an ignored victim at the mercy of staff members.

LEARN.. what going home on Hospice truly entails, AND be aware there is a *big difference* in Hospice Providers.

LEARN.. that Miracles still do happen, and there is limitless Power in Prayer.

LEARN... THE MIRACULOUS PRAYER TO THE BLESSED MOTHER. (NEVER FOUND TO FAIL!) IT DOESN'T MATTER, IF YOU ARE CATHOLIC OR NOT! SHE IS EVERYONE'S HEAVENLY MOTHER. She hears you, and will help you!

LEARN... to believe in the Supernatural! **DEATH DOES NOT MEAN THAT YOU ARE GONE! Believe it!**

Prepare yourself to be *shocked, angered, mystified,* and yes, *petrified* at what occurred.

It has taken me over three years to write **Medical Manslaughter.**

What kept this project going was You, dear Reader.

You and your loved ones **need** to read this story.

You and your loved ones *need* to know this information, just in case you face an ordeal of similar, or even lesser magnitude. **This was written for *You!***

Much knowledge is intertwined throughout this story, and it will teach you much.

You will learn what Gabriella did right, as well as from what she did wrong. She made mistakes along the way. But, she tried with every fiber of her being, to help and protect her husband from harm, and return him to good health.

Likewise, Gabriella's unwavering and unyielding resolve to bring Nicholas out of his Coma was unshakeable, and through the grace of God, was finally achieved.

May you never have to face what is written here. But, if you do, having read this book, **Medical Manslaughter,** you will be equipped with the knowledge to handle the situation successfully.

Important Note: If you don't have a Living Will or Power of Attorney for your Healthcare, get it immediately! Hospitals and Nursing Homes will ask for it, and you will be *powerless to* be an Advocate, without this necessary information in writing, which is part of any Will prepared by an attorney.

Wishing you Good Health.

God Bless!

Gloria J. Yorke

CHAPTER 1

FACTS

Medical errors are the *3rd leading cause of death in the United States*, after heart disease and cancer!

Approximately 250,000 to 400,000 **PATIENTS *DIE*** *each year* because of medical error, according to a report published in the *British Medical Journal* (May 3, 2016) by Dr. Martin Makary, a professor of surgery and health policy at Johns Hopkins University School of Medicine, and his coauthor, Dr. Michael Daniel.

Their report defines medical errors as, "lapses in judgment, skill or coordination of care, mistaken diagnoses, system failures that lead to patient deaths, or the failure to rescue dying patients, and preventable complication of care."

One could easily add to this list: the limited time Doctors spend with patients, and, in some cases, lack of concern for family members' wishes. The alarming fact is that these estimates are on the low side, because no hospital is proud to report medical errors, fearing loss of good standing, grants, most of all, malpractice suits.

There is no way to sugarcoat this, dear Reader!

The problem is colossal, and thus far, the medical field has been using a Band-Aid to stop the proverbial bleeding, or they have just been sweeping the statistics under the rug, which is costing more people to lose their lives! The policies and practices necessary to alleviate it—and the willingness to alleviate it—at this time, are almost nonexistent.

Yet, it can be rectified. How?

Accountability.

Our government must mandate accountability procedures, so that hospitals keep *honest* and *accurate* records, that can be checked regularly by statistical auditors, who will especially monitor deaths. There should be no more hiding the facts, just so hospitals and other health organizations can get good ratings and funding. Accountability will highlight the magnitude of this fearsome situation, bringing to light the fact that medical error has reached epidemic proportions!

It is only when uncorrupted and ethical facts are chronicled in patients' records, that experts will be able to address the situation in a forthright manner. Those institutions and individuals, who show repeat "error occurrences/deaths" should be subject to interrogation, investigation, and prosecution. No longer will an acceptable excuse for the loss of life—*perhaps your life be—*

"Ooops, I made a mistake!"

Think about it: Presently, who holds Doctors responsible? No one!

Legally, Murder is categorized in four levels: First Degree, Second Degree, Premeditated, and Manslaughter.

Manslaughter is then categorized as voluntary, involuntary, and misdemeanor, all of which are bona fide forms of murder. Intentional or not, murder is murder!

Just because Doctors have several years of schooling, numerous degrees hanging on the walls, and an alphabet of letters behind their names, doesn't mean they know everything.

 **The *Code of Medical Ethics*, of The American Medical Association (AMA), is based on the Goals of the Medical Profession, dating back to the Greek Physician, HIPPOCRATES, who is referred to as the *Father of Medicine*, living in the 5th Century B.C. The now famous OATH that bears his name, surfaced long after his death.**

Every graduating Medical student swears to uphold a form of the HIPPOCRATIC OATH, (classic or modern version), whereupon, in one part of the sacred Oath they declare, (paraphrased): *'They will not be inhibited to utter the outcome of their findings by saying, 'I just don't know...I don't understand the "why." Nor will they be too egotistical to call upon their colleagues for additional advice.'*

Likewise, in taking the Oath, they declare, (partial list) ... *'to keep the patient from harm, not prescribe unnecessary drugs, show no racial bias, protect patient information, and teach their secrets to the next medical generation."* It is indeed, a solemn Covenant.

Therefore, in accordance with the sacred Oath in which they swore, shouldn't they dissect every single possibility, review every possible angle, listen closely to the opinions of the family, discuss cases with their colleagues, and take into full account the ramifications of their decisions, prior to making impetuous judgment calls, or using patients as guinea pigs? Many are not!

And... shouldn't they, as individuals, be held totally responsible for the results of their decisions, with regard to how the outcome affects *the remainder of their patients' lives*? The answer to this question must be, *"Yes!" but,* thus far, many have gone, **"penalty-free!"**

Many Doctors today have put themselves on the same level as God, thinking they know everything and know what is best, even ignoring the opinions and requests of family members. Some don't even confer with their colleagues, to seek various opinions.

IT IS PRECISELY THIS TYPE OF INFLATED EGOTISM, that places their **DEADLY DECISIONS** squarely into the category of **MANSLAUGHTER!** The time has come—indeed it is overdue—for them to be accountable for those decisions!

Obviously, this does not mean to imply that *all Doctors* are in this category. Many Medical Practitioners are caring, conscientious, knowledgeable, and compassionate professionals, who have dedicated their lives to helping others. They deserve our unwavering respect!

However, a multitude of Doctors, are making a multitude of mistakes on a daily basis, so you do the math. Statistics pointing to the number of *"Doctor-Error Deaths"* have tipped the scales tremendously, taking them beyond commonplace and normalcy, into downright alarming!

The siren has sounded, and it screams, *Emergency!*

CHAPTER 2

ATTRIBUTES OF A SUPERIOR ADVOCATE

Being an Advocate for a friend or a loved one, is a full-time job of love and devotion. Trying to absorb and understand modern-day technology and medical procedures, is all-consuming, especially while one is being sucked into the drama of an emergency.

As you look into the eyes of your loved one, you can see exactly what he or she is saying:

"Watch over me, protect me, and help get me well."

From that point on, without a word spoken, you commit to doing anything and everything possible to protect that person. Thus, begins your role as an Advocate, or earthly guardian angel.

You may be thinking: *I have no training in the medical field, so I would not know what to look for.*

This is a reasonable assumption. However, by just being there physically, you will instinctively learn and know, when there is something happening, that is not for the good of the patient.

Don't second guess your "Intuition." This is your alarm button, and it will sound when you need it. Also, you will be amazed at the amount of knowledge you'll pick up just by watching and listening.

Most staff members will be glad that you're there every day, asking questions and keeping watch over your loved one, like, making sure that s/he is not receiving a medication in which they are allergic. Be alert to his or her symptoms: a rash or itchy skin, headaches, irritability, sleep problems, restlessness, anger, irregular bowel movements, and so on. Yes, you will pick up on many important things about your loved one, that the Doctor, Nurses, staff members, or Nursing Home may not notice. They will appreciate your bringing these issues to their attention.

If you encounter a staff member who is not encouraging you to visit daily, see this as a *red flag*, and say to him or her what Gabriella said:

> "He is my whole world. Where would you have me go? He is my best friend. Who would you want me to be with?" This will silence them quickly.

When you're an Advocate, it is not the time to be timid and shy. This is the time to be alert, bold, assertive, and ask questions respectfully. Don't hold back. As an Advocate, you are not there to read magazines and eat bonbons.

Keep a journal and write down what happens every day. Date each page. Later, you will be thankful that you did. Please do not think that you will remember everything. You will not!

Your journal could be your loved one's salvation. Information should include subjects of conversation with the patient; future wishes, reports of pain, conversations with Doctors, Nurses, aids, CNA's, therapists, and other helpers; daily progress of patient; new medications; new staff members; any new events such as side effects, errors, bruises, rashes, signs of abuse.

It's perfectly okay to take a day off; you will eventually need a break. But, be sure there is someone else who will give the necessary time and attention to your loved one. Inform this person of the things to look out for, or questions to ask. If there are several family members, develop a rotating schedule, so that not just one person is carrying the full burden.

Ask all practitioners for their business cards—Doctors, outside Agencies, Hospice representatives, and Specialists—and staple or tape them into your journal. Also include all contact information for family members in the journal.

As you continue to read *Medical Manslaughter,* it will become crystal clear that, as an Advocate, you are no longer to be considered the "odd man out."

You see, dear Reader, the nightmare that Gabriella experienced, is happening every day in Hospitals and Nursing Homes. Yet so very few people are hearing about it. Because so few take the time to address *suspicious* happenings, the problem continues to remain a *well-kept secret, and thus increases.*

Here's some examples that may hit a nerve inside you: Your loved one suddenly becomes severely ill, or worse, dies—in the hospital/nursing home! You are shocked, and say to yourself:

> "What happened...I just talked to him/her? S/he said they were feeling a lot better. Getting stronger every day!"

> "S/he was fine yesterday!"

"I just saw him/her...s/he looked great...eager to go home!"

Unanswered questions burn in your mind, but you say nothing to the Medical staff or the Doctor. You're afraid that they'll get mad at you, or you let it go because you may need them in the future, for your own health issues.

Or, you DO ASK...and are given a succinct, one-sentence explanation....such as 'he died of *old age*.' The reason is glossed over. Your intuition tells you that something isn't right, but you try to quiet that thought for your own peace of mind. Don't! At that point, your Intuition is gnawing at you for a reason. Listen to it! Act upon it!

You will undoubtedly discuss your thoughts with some relatives or friends, but unless you express it openly, preferably in writing, to the Hospital, Doctor, or Government Agency, the actual facts get buried.

Today, with the publication of *Medical Manslaughter*, readers will become more confident, have more backbone to speak up, and suspicions will be placed under the microscope. *Medical Manslaughter* was written to give you the courage to move forward, so that you don't live the rest of your life in regret. Now, you will assume your rightful role as protector of your loved one, and you will defend with fervor, strength, confidence, and determination!

You will now be equipped with knowledge, which is power, and will no longer be looked upon as a nuisance, an intruder, or someone who is getting in the way.

Stand up confidently and speak clearly, respectfully, and precisely, as you *ask all* your questions. There is no such thing as a dumb question. Do not be satisfied until you get clear, concise answers.

Do not be intimidated by any Doctor, Nurse, or staff member. Ask them to clarify all medical language and terminology into layman's terms, so that you understand the entire situation clearly, including the negative aspects, and what could go wrong.

Keep your journal and pen handy, and make notes constantly every day. Again, you will not remember what was said, and you will not remember the timeline, so write it down. Make a list of your questions and concerns.

Staff members, Doctors and Nurses, are there to provide medical assistance and information. They will answer all your questions, if you show you are persistent and respectful, and expect a detailed answer. Ask about everything that you don't understand, and do speak directly to the Doctor for updates.

You have arrived, Advocate Angel, and there is no turning back.

Simply keep in mind...

*What would **you** want done, if **you** were the person in the bed?!*

NICK, AGE 10, IN CUB SCOUTS (top center)

CHAPTER 3

NICK CARCIONI BIOGRAPHY

Nicholas Rocco Carcioni was part of the greatest generation that ever was. Born in Chicago on March 4, 1925, he was true to his sign of Pisces, being tremendously intuitive, artistic, compassionate, and creative.

Nick was born to Italian Catholic immigrant parents, Philomena, born in Naples, Italy, and Rocco, born in Sicily. He had one older brother, Anthony, who was nicknamed Red.

Philomena's Mother, Gizepp, came over from Naples to live with her daughter Philomena, in America, as did her son, Johnny. All six lived in a rented house off Taylor Street in Chicago, but when Nicholas was four years old, they moved to a suburban town, Pepper Patch, Illinois, where most Italians were settling. Soon it was to become known as Little Italy. It was actually Gizepp who bought the three-bedroom, two-story home in Pepper Patch for $2,500 in 1929.

Philomena worked at the Woolworth store, and Gizepp, who spoke very little English, watched Nick and Anthony at home. Often Nicholas would tell stories of how his grandmother raised

**NICK WITH 101-YEAR OLD
GRANDMOTHER, GIZEPP**

them, and he welcomed the intelligence that flowed from her lips, even though she did not have a "formal" education.

Gizepp lived to be 101 years old, and maintained her clear mind. Being well loved by all, on her 100th birthday, the entire small town of Pepper Patch celebrated with music, dancing, and of course, delicious Italian food.

Rocco Carcioni, Nicholas' father, worked in the local steel mill and had various Italian connections, which included a connection to Al Capone. On occasional Sundays, Capone would join the family for spaghetti dinner at noon.

Nick told a story once about one of those meals. Capone liked ricotta cheese on top of his spaghetti, and, while at the table, Nick asked him why. Rocco immediately raised his hand in a gesture to slap Nick's face, and said sternly,

> "You don't ask any questions! Eat and be quiet!" Capone just kept eating, unaffected.

Nick never asked any more questions from that day forward. When Capone was buried, Rocco was one of the two who stood at his gravesite, to insure the burial was complete.

It was Rocco who introduced both children to music. He told them,

> "If you learn to play an instrument, you'll never go hungry."

Anthony became well versed on the accordion, while Nicholas was drawn to the saxophone, first trying the alto sax, but soon learning that he preferred the tenor. Lessons were arranged for

YOUNG NICK WITH HIS TENOR SAXOPHONE

Nick from a black man, who Rocco knew at the steel mill. Each lesson cost fifty cents. Nick learned quickly, as he really loved playing his horn. Later in his life, Frank Sinatra would tell Nick,

> "You play that sax so well, it's like you were born with it in your hands!"

Nick spent his grade school and high school years at Proviso, and some friendships he made there, continued throughout his life. He walked to kindergarten with his good friend, Frank, and they remained friends for 80 years, until they died, only six weeks apart!

Nick loved to sing, and he possessed a natural melodic voice. Almost nightly, he would serenade everyone on the front porch, even at a very young age. His singing was often likened to popular singers during that era, as he constantly listened to the radio, and imitated the singing of Rudy Vallee, Frank Sinatra, Perry Como ---learning all the words to their songs.

He used the opportunity to sing on the porch as a means to rehearse songs, that he would sing in front of his young combo, which he formed with his brother while in high school. With Nick's superb crooning talent, the Nick Carcioni Combo attracted bookings at local clubs and weddings, gaining much notoriety. This included playing lounges, nightclubs, and ballrooms in downtown Chicago and suburbs, during the 1940's.

These were very hard economic years for everyone, and every penny brought into the house was well appreciated and certainly needed. The boys always gave more than half of their earnings, to their parents.

Upon graduating high school, during World War II, Nick went to sign up to join the Navy with his friend, Michael. But as he was waiting among the other recruits, two Marines came into the room and said they needed ten good men to join the U.S. Marines. Nick was very impressed with their crisply pressed navy-blue uniforms, and shot his hand up quickly to his friend's shock.

"Sit down," Michael urged, pulling on Nick's shirt. "The Marines are the first to get killed!"

But, Nick went anyway. After boot camp, the Marines learned that Nick played the tenor sax, and sent him home to get his instrument, so that he could audition for the United States Marine Halls of Montezuma Band. Three days prior to the audition, he heard that he was going to be asked to play "Flight of the Bumblebee," a song with a very fast tempo.

In entering their racquetball court, he set up a chair in the corner, and played the piece over and over, even as other people were playing racquetball. Players grew tired of hearing it repeated, and even began to use Nick as their target, pelting him with balls. But Nick was relentless in his practicing. At his audition, he played the first four bars, and was immediately accepted as first chair and main soloist. Being a member of the band intensified his playing skills, molding him into a truly accomplished artist.

While in the Marines, Nick rose to the rank of Corporal. At one point, a famous jazz tenor sax player from Italy, Vido Musso, joined his barracks. They became very good friends, and Vido even gave Nick his mouthpiece at the end of the war. Nick cherished it throughout the rest of his life.

Additionally, while in the Marines, Nick also played in the Bob Crozby Orchestra. However, Nick and his fellow bandsmen were shocked one morning, when they awoke to learn that Crosby had flown back to the mainland during the night, protecting him from combat. Meanwhile, Nick's saxophone and the instruments of his fellow bandsmen were taken from them, and replaced with rifles!

All band members were trained to reassemble a rifle blindfolded, but were not extensively trained for combat. There wasn't time! Nevertheless, they were shipped out to Peleliu Island in the Philippines, and were sent in as part of the Third Wave, during the Battle of Peleliu. The first two waves had been completely wiped out. As they made their way to land, they were drenched in bloody water, and had to maneuver around floating dead bodies, as bullets flew everywhere, with men screaming in pain.

Arriving on land, they were told to dig in, but were horrified to discover that the shore was made of coral rock, and digging in, was impossible!

Hiding behind a few rocks, they loaded their rifles, but quickly saw that the Japanese were hidden securely in the limestone caves, that had become their fortresses. The Japanese had constructed defensive sliding steel door cave entrances, with openings for their machine guns. The only salvation for the United States would be their flamethrowers, if they could get close enough. After several attempts, the troops achieved perfect timing, and the flamethrowers finally wiped out the Japanese.

Upon going in, the Marines were told it would only take three days to secure Peleliu Island, but unfortunately, it took thirty days, with 1,800 soldiers killed, and 8,000 wounded. The Battle of Peleliu resulted in the highest casualty rate of any amphibious assault in American military history! And it was all done to secure an airstrip, only six miles long and two miles wide!

**NICK IN U.S. MARINE UNIFORM WITH
PARENTS --ROCCO AND PHILOMENA.**

PELELIU   USMC PHOTO

**NICK and the U.S. MARINES...
FIGHTING IN PELELIU**

From there, Nick fought in the jungles of Guadalcanal and Iwo Jima, where he developed Tinnitus (ringing in the ears) as a result of the constant, nonstop bombing and gunfire.

Several months later, toward the end of the war, he developed jungle rot, and was hospitalized, and sent home. The war had ended.

Tinnitus stayed with Nick for the rest of his life. Even medical providers in the finest clinics in America, told him repeatedly that there was no cure. Somehow, even with the Tinnitus, which drives many people to suicide, God still blessed him with perfect pitch for his singing and for playing his tenor sax, which demanded severe concentration. Likewise, he could identify immediately, if someone hit a wrong note in his Orchestra.

During the war, Nick promised himself that, when he got home, he would live his dream and form a Combo again, but his major goal was to front his own Big Band Orchestra. He fulfilled that promise to himself and was extremely successful with both, rising to heights that even he never anticipated.

Nicholas Carcioni was very handsome, with thick black, wavy hair, which in later years became salt and pepper, making him look even more distinguished. His brilliant white smile and effervescent outgoing personality, were his trademark. Always having a joke to tell, he would make people laugh within minutes, as his allure enthralled both men and woman.

By public acclaim, he had the best Orchestra in Chicago. His Big Band Orchestra ranged from 14-40 of the most acclaimed Musicians that Chicago had to offer, some who were with him almost 40 years!

NICK ENTERTAINING ON STAGE IN LAS VEGAS

Often referred to in the newspapers as, "a Chicago Legend," Nick Carcioni lived up to that reputation!

During his expansive 60-year musical career, Nick opened shows and led his Orchestra while fronting some of the biggest named performers in the business—including, *the ORIGINAL Pack Rats* from Hollywood's glamorous entertainment era. The A-list of celebrities, grew extensively, as some left their hearts in San Francisco, while others were the King of the Las Vegas strip. Nicholas achieved his dream, above and beyond!

As if one distinguished career as an Entertainer was not enough, Nick also had a second career that bloomed in the late 1970s. He became General Manager of the Senate Hotel, a 100-year-old hotel on Michigan Avenue, and one of the largest in Chicago, with 1,000 guestrooms and 2,500 employees.

Being one of the most well-known entertainers in Chicago, Nick was recognized with an award from the Chicago Musicians Union, for his numerous accomplishments in the Music and Hospitality Industries. Nick Carcioni was the only musician in the history of Chicago, to become a celebrated Hotel General Manager, and likewise, continue a thriving entertainment career!

His introduction to the Hotel industry came through his music career when, one day, the owner of the Senate Hotel heard Nick and his Orchestra play at another venue. He asked Nick to visit him at his office, which Nick did a few weeks later. He was offered the job to play for high society in the most prestigious hotel supper club at that time, The Music Box.

THE NICK CARCIONI BIG BAND ORCHESTRA
Grand Ballroom in Chicago 1950's

Nick was offered a four-week contract to start. A few years later, Nick was named Director of Entertainment over the ten additional hotels owned by the Senate Hotel chain. Several years passed, and Nick was becoming more and more involved and interested in the hospitality field. After he had been with the hotel for over 25 years, the hotel was sold to another group of investors, and the position of General Manager presented itself.

Nick was very interested in securing this position, as he knew all the movers and shakers in high, powerful positions in Chicago, from Mayor J. Daley on down.

What the new owners did not know, was that Nick had been working in all departments of the hotel during the day, and then entertaining during the evenings on the bandstand—a workaholic for sure!

In having two younger candidates with hospitality degrees to choose from, the owners gave them and Nick specific responsibilities; and whoever did the best job out of the three, would become General Manager. As one month came to a close, the new owners could clearly see that Nick was the perfect man for the job!

Nick used to say, "I started here with a four-week contract, and stayed for thirty-four years!"

Nick had it all—except he had no real love in his life. He had married in his early twenties after the war, but it was not a marriage that lasted. After twenty years, he divorced. Although many women made advances, he was always selective in his dating, and still did not find the perfect one, who would captivate his whole heart—until he met Gabriella.

Although she was twenty-five years younger, their love story was the kind in which fairy tales are made.

Nick would often boast that, the minute he laid eyes on Gabriella, he fell in love with her.

CHAPTER 4

GABRIELLA JOYCE BIOGRAPHY

Gabriella Joyce was an attractive intelligent young lady, of Italian and Polish descent, with an exhilarating personality, who was determined to achieve her goals. Born under the fiery sign of Sagittarius, she aimed her arrows high in the sky, confidently watching them hit the bulls-eye.

Her height of five-foot-seven matched her weight perfectly, as she developed into a full-figure beauty by the age of twenty-two. With shoulder length auburn hair, her deep, soft voice was always uniquely distinguishable, and was matched by her soft brown eyes, that seemed to look into the depths of one's soul.

She was gifted in many ways, and spiritually, she was one of God's chosen. Her razor-sharp intuition, and metaphysical gifts, including the Gift of Discernment, made it easy for her look into people's hearts, and read their true feelings. As her Gifts continued to develop, she became an accomplished Channeler, or as she referred to herself, an Intuitive Messenger, enabling her to communicate with various Spirits.

Devout in her Catholic upbringing, she had always felt a closeness with Jesus and The Blessed Virgin Mary. Although it was completely unexpected, she began Channeling them at a young age, and conversations continued throughout her life!

Yes, God was sending someone very special to his son, Nick, and deservingly so.

Gabriella Joyce was born in Canonsburg, Pennsylvania, to Catholic parents Virginia Rose and Edward Paul.

Being born on December 11, just two weeks before Christmas, she received her name because her parents said the Angel Gabriel had announced Jesus's birth, and her birth brought them such joy. Gabriella had three siblings.

Gabriella's paternal grandparents, Sophie and John, were from Poland. They resided in a small mining village of Muse, Pennsylvania, with their nine children: Helen, Edmund, Ann, John, Genevieve, Edward (Gabriella's father), Roland, Henry, and Wanda Therese.

Gabriella's maternal grandmother, Gelsamina, (who everyone called Gessie), was born in Naples, Italy; her maternal grandfather, Antonio, was born in Pittsburgh, Pennsylvania. When they married, they settled in the small town of Canonsburg, Pennsylvania, as many Italians did, raising five children: Angeline, Mary, Virginia, John, and Lena Marie.

**WEDDING PHOTO
VIRGINIA ROSE AND EDWARD PAUL**

Virginia Rose, Gabriella's Mother, was a sensuous beauty with an alluring, warm smile and an outgoing personality. Born under the sign of Aries, she radiated a fiery exuberance and optimism. Many declared that she was *'the most beautiful woman in Canonsburg,'* shapely with long brunette hair, a loving personality, and a warm heart to match.

As a homemaker, Virginia excelled in cooking and baking, following every recipe to the letter, as there was no room for error. Of course, she prepared homemade Italian and Polish meals daily. Every Sunday was Pasta day, covered in her homemade delectable Neapolitan sauce.

Desserts were a part of every meal, producing vast batches of cookies, cakes, pies, pizzelle, kolacky, and other baked goods, to satisfy the entire family on a regular basis.

A warm houseful of relatives and friends was a regular occurrence, especially during the holidays. Baking commenced a month in advance, sometimes with the help of Virginia Rose's sisters, Mary, Angeline, and Lena Marie.

In the fall, dear friends Helen and Rosalie came to assist with making Piccalilli, utilizing the green tomatoes and onions, from their huge garden. Nothing went to waste.

Always anxious to learn new and delicious recipes, Virginia Rose was the only one in the family, who mastered making a very soft buttery-flavored Polish bread, a recipe she learned from Edward Paul's Mother. It was a meal in itself, and most indescribably delicious!

Being extremely organized in her motherly duties, Monday was reserved as "wash day," using a two-tub Maytag machine with attached wringer, as she utilized several outside clothes lines, as her dryer. Tuesday was "ironing day." Every pillowcase, underwear garment, blouse, shirt, pair of pants, skirt, dress, and handkerchief was ironed meticulously.

Of course, a clean home was an absolute must. Virginia Rose deplored clutter, and would repeatedly tell her children clutter-babies to, "Clean up!"

For Virginia Rose, her husband, children, and her home were her life! She was indeed the "heart" of the family, who enjoyed and instilled much laughter, and generosity. Her true happiness was in making a loving and comfortable home for her family— as she never asked for much. Everyone who ever met Virginia Rose, immediately liked her.

When wished Happy Mother's Day, she would always smile and reply,

> "Every day is Mother's Day!"

Virginia Rose was a phenomenal Mother, and an exceptional woman!

GABRIELLA AND PARENTS
VIRGINIA ROSE AND EDWARD PAUL

Edward Paul, Gabriella's Father, was an extremely handsome man—six feet tall with wavy brown hair and blue eyes. Of course, all the ladies wanted to win his heart, but Edward Paul was very particular, waiting patiently for his perfect soulmate.

Born under the sign of Leo, he truly was king of his castle. He was a man of few words, but when he spoke, he was blatantly honest, and his rich, loud voice was heard above the rest.

Listening to his favorite record albums on the stereo, was a past time he truly enjoyed, while singing along in his own rich modulated voice to the likes of Mario Lanza, Perry Como, Nat King Cole, Al Martino, and always leading the family in singing Christmas Carols and Happy Birthday.

Edward Paul was physically fit, with strong arms and huge hands. But, those mighty hands would turn ever-so-gentle, when attending to Gabriella's scraped knee, tying her Buster Brown shoelaces, fixing her broken baby doll, or picking a bouquet of lilacs. Yes, it was in her Daddy's arms, where Gabriella always found love, healing, and safety.

Weather permitting, you could find him sitting on his front porch, enjoying the fragrance of the huge Azalea, and surrounded by his wife, children, and pedigree collie, Goldy, (Lassie bred), eating butter pecan ice cream, or one of Virginia Rose's homemade desserts.

Planting his annual homegrown garden of Beefsteak tomatoes, lettuce, onions, radishes, and parsley, with just his pitchfork and muscle, provided many bountiful salads throughout the summer and fall.

Edward Paul worked for 11 years in the Coalmines, before and after World War II. During the war he served 4 years in the U.S. Army/Air Force at various posts. The last year of the war, he was stationed in Okinawa, Japan aboard a Gunner Ship.

One day, he and fellow miners experienced the collapse in the mine. Although the whole thing landed on top of them, luckily, by the grace of God, they survived. Edward Paul came home that day on crutches with bloody clothes, shocking his young wife, with two infants in her arms.

Shortly after the mine collapse, Edward Paul was hired as a Steel Worker at Forbes Steel, one of the main factories in Canonsburg, working 3 rotating shifts for 32 years! Although he disliked the job, he knew he had responsibilities, and he took them seriously. He was an excellent employee, laboring in an unheated and uncooled mill. It was bitter cold in the winter, and as hot as an oven in the summer, with the constant deafening clang of the wire machines 24/7, that eventually took their toll on his hearing.

His paycheck provided a moderate income, and he supported his family of six on a strict budget, always approaching his job earnestly and living by the motto, to always give your boss more than what he expects. Edward Paul was extremely thankful and grateful for being able to walk to work, as he did not own a car all his life, although he knew how to drive, having learned in the Army. The family members took the bus or a cab when necessary; otherwise, they walked. As Edward Paul explained to his grumbling children,

"Walking is great exercise for your legs!"

A strict Catholic his entire life, he quoted the Bible in using it as a guideline for raising his children. One inspirational Gospel Parable, in particular, he used when the children decided to take something, that what wasn't theirs.

He would reprimand sternly: *"As your Parent, it would be better that I cut off our hand, rather than see you go to hell for stealing!"*

Other Words of Wisdom included:
"In Life, you reap what you sow!"
"Take off your rose-colored glasses...face reality!"
"Wake up and smell the coffee!"
"Protect your name. Once your reputation is ruined, it's ruined for life!"
"You better straighten up and fly right!"
"It isn't going to get done, by looking at it!"

Often laughingly he'd remark, *"Everybody wants to go to heaven, but nobody wants to die!"*

Edward Paul provided great leadership, and set an excellent example for his children. He expected them to follow the rules, and if his children ignored those rules, they met with "the belt." His strictness was always bred out of love, guidance, and protection...never cruelty, as his children meant everything to him and Virginia Rose.

In 1967, Edward Paul, was coaxed by the Canonsburg political powers-that-be, to run for Councilman of the 3rd Ward. Not having political aspirations prior, he discussed it thoroughly with Virginia Rose, and then finally decided to accept the challenge.

Every day, before going to work his shift at Forbes Steel, he dressed in a suit and tie, and went knocking on every door, asking for their Vote.

His efforts paid off, and he Won the Election, serving several productive years as Councilman!

Thankful that he did not see combat during the war, he promised The Blessed Mother, that he would pray The Rosary daily, if he got home safely. The Blessed Mother answered his prayer, and Edward Paul kept his promise. He prayed the Rosary daily with Virginia Rose and all the children. No excuses to miss prayers were acceptable.

Edward Paul possessed a passionate deep love for his Family, and his Country.

He was, indeed, a giant of a man!

###

**FIVE-YEAR-OLD GABRIELLA RETURNING
FROM SUNDAY MASS (far right)**

Growing up in Canonsburg, Gabriella enjoyed the small community where neighbors were friendly, everyone knew everyone's name, and catching lightening bugs, or sitting on the porch each evening were the perfect ways to end the day. It was a close-knit neighborhood, where the neighbors kept an eye on all the children as they played, and would be quick to offer correction, if they saw wrongdoings. Gabriella was taught respect for her elders and always referred to each of them as Mr. or Mrs.

Throughout her life, when planting flowers, Gabriella fondly remembered Mrs. Mastic, an elder neighbor next door, who taught her about various flowers, planting, and how to knit.

In her childhood, Gabriella was extremely athletic, trim, and quite the tomboy, although very quiet and shy. She was a quick learner when it came to riding a bike or scooter, jumping rope, roller skating, riding horseback, or playing badminton and softball. All games and activities were of little challenge. She won the neighborhood hula hoop contest, arranged by neighbors, Mr. and Mrs. Osinski. The prize was a new yellow hula hoop, which Gabriella cherished, as she didn't have one of her own. She had to borrow her sister's, in order to enter the contest.

Like most little girls, Gabriella enjoyed playing house. She and her sister played with their baby dolls, while dressing in their mom's clothes and heels and sampling her lipsticks. Curiosity always led her to asking the "why" of things. Being inquisitive and mechanically inclined, she enjoyed taking items apart—a broken iron or sweeper—just to see if she could get it working again. To her mother's amazement, sometimes she did!

Writing was always the best communication for shy Gabriella, who was a very good listener. Since her Daddy worked different shifts, she would often write him notes outlining the day's happenings for him to read, when he got home from work. Needless to say, she excelled in English and Language Arts in school. By the time she was in the third grade, she was already a published author, having her poem, "Halloween," published in the school newspaper.

Raised in a strict Catholic upbringing, she attended St. Patrick's Church on Sundays, all Feast Days, and Holy Days of Obligation. Catholic grade school at St. Patrick's, taught by the strict, but caring Franciscan nuns, for seven years was expensive. But Gabriella's parents felt it was worth their sacrifice for all the children, and it did indeed provide a profound spiritual base.

Public high school followed at Canon McMillan, home of the Mighty Big Macs.

Upon attending college, Gabriella quickly found that she became impatient with the need to carry a variety of subjects when, indeed, she just wanted to focus on learning specifics. Actually, Gabriella's thirst for knowledge was never satisfied, and never would be. So, upon leaving college in its early stage, she gained employment, and opted to attend night classes on subjects that interested her, along with weekend seminars and conventions for her continued education.

After five years in the workforce, as Secretary to Principal Quincy, at Canon McMillan, she learned that a new Marriott Hotel was being built in Pittsburgh, and she quickly applied, as a means to expand her horizons. Physically attractive, and having good secretarial skills, she was hired immediately.

Tony, a hard-working, dedicated General Manager of the Hotel, quickly saw that Gabriella's charm, appearance, and outgoing personality, would be better suited in the Sales Department, instead of the secretarial pool. Upon telling her that she was being moved, Gabriella cried, as she thought she was being demoted. He laughingly told her that the move was a definite promotion and would include her own office and, of course, a raise. Upon hearing that, her tears dried quickly! She later was named Marriott Employee of the Year.

Gabriella loved the Hospitality business. She enjoyed meeting new people daily. She would work all day in sales, and many evenings invite potential clients to come for dinner and a tour, in order to secure their business. As a diligent hard worker, she emerged very successful.

After leaving the Marriott, she continued her climb up the Hospitality ladder by working for various chains. A few years later, she secured a position at a beautiful Resort in Ohio, on Lake Huron. Months later, the parent company then moved her to their popular Chicago suburban Resort. She was hired as the first female General Manager of a 150-room Ramada Inn at the young age of twenty-six. As a zealous over-achiever, Gabriella turned the hotel around, and made it a revenue producer. Thus, she was promoted to Corporate Director of Marketing, over 12 hotels located throughout the United States and Virgin Islands.

Still single, she often thought about moving to downtown Chicago, so that she could not only expand her career, but hopefully meet her soul mate. One day, Gabriella saw a newspaper ad for Director of Sales at The Senate Hotel in Chicago, so she and her friend, Beverly, took the train to go apply.

While she was there completing the application, the Personnel Director, Joe, asked her what position had sparked her interest. When she said Director of Sales, he immediately ushered her into his office.

Hurriedly he went to get the General Manager, who was just leaving for lunch, saying he would have to see Gabriella at another time. Joe insisted that this was the only day she would be in the city, as she worked in the suburbs. The General Manager still persisted that a friend was waiting for him, and he had to leave. But Joe would not give in.

"Just five minutes. That's all it will take," he pleaded. "She's exactly what we're looking for!"

"Okay ... okay," the General Manager relented. "Five minutes."

He went immediately to Joe's office, quickly introduced himself to Gabriella, and rattled off about six questions for her to answer. Gabriella answered quickly, because she knew the hotel business inside and out. The General Manager was very impressed. He looked at Joe and said,

"Hire her!"

Then, looking back to Gabriella he asked,

"When can you start?"

Gabriella had not really prepared for an offer, but she quickly replied,

"Two weeks."

"Great. We'll see you in two weeks."

Joe and Gabriella were ecstatic! They sat and hashed out salary and benefits.

When Gabriella returned to her job at the Resort the next day, she had a meeting with her boss, Harry, the Vice President.

At the conclusion of the meeting, she slid an envelope toward Harry on his desk. "What's this?" he asked.

Gabriella smiled, as Harry opened the envelope, and read the word *Resignation*.

"You're resigning?" Harry looked at her puzzled.

"Yes." Gabriella smiled and said happily, "I have been offered the Director of Sales job at The Senate Hotel in Chicago."

Harry immediately ripped up the resignation, threw it in the wastebasket, and said, "No, you're not resigning!"

Gabriella was shocked.

"Yes, I am, Harry. It's time for me to expand my horizons, both personally and professionally."

"No, you're not resigning, Gabriella! Now get out of my office," replied an angry Harry.

Gabriella left in a huff. In returning to her office, she was disappointed that resigning was not going to be as simple as she thought. Calling the General Manager of the Senate Hotel, she told him that she needed another week, and could be there in about 3 weeks, fully expecting him to be agreeable and understanding.

Instead, his reply was,

"Gabriella, start in two weeks or don't come!" And he hung up the phone.

Gabriella sat there holding a dead phone, with her mouth wide open. She called her friend, Beverly, for an opinion.

"You don't want to work for a tough guy like that! Don't go!" responded Beverly.

But Gabriella thought about it, and concluded,

"No, I like a man who knows what he wants, and he wants me on his staff. I'm going! Tomorrow, I will hand Harry another resignation letter, and that will be final!"

The next morning, Gabriella entered Harry's office. She sat down quietly. He knew she was there, but he just kept writing. Finally, he raised his head, leaned back in his chair, and just stared at her.

"So, you want to leave and move to the city?" he asked.

"Yes, Harry. I have to go. It's time for me to move on. The suburbs are filled with married men, and I really would like to meet someone special. I'll miss you, but it's time."

Harry cared about Gabriella, and knew she was right.

"Yeah, I hear you. You're right. But, you know … if it doesn't work out, you can always come back. You know that, right?"

"Thank you, Harry. You've always been wonderful to me, and I'll never forget you! I can give you only one week's notice, but all my work is up to date. Any questions ever, just call me. I have to take the second week, to find a new place and move in. I haven't even found one yet. I'll have to get set up quickly before I start my new job. It's a drastic leap, but I feel I'm ready for it!"

Harry forced a smile.

"I understand, Gabriella. I wish you a lot of good luck. Give me a hug."

Gabriella felt so much better having Harry's blessing. He had always been good to her, protected her, and advised her. She truly loved him.

Gabriella called her friends, Beverly and Joan, who knew the city very well, and that Saturday they went down to find an apartment for Gabriella. As luck would have it, the very first condo they looked at, was for rent in a secure high-rise building, and she grabbed it. The rent was more than she had been paying in the suburbs, but it was worth it, as safety and security were the number-one concerns in any city, especially Chicago. This had been reinforced by Joan and Beverly.

Gabriella packed up her suburban apartment, contacted movers, and disposed of extra items that she could not sell.

She worked tirelessly to make this her new home. In not liking the paint color in the condo bathroom, so she painted it a bright refreshing green. Bought area carpets for the bedroom, cut them to fit, scrubbed all the cabinets, floors, sinks, and tubs before she started to empty her boxes. Her nails were broken, and her hands were scratched. She organized her closet, carefully putting away clothes, shoes, and jewelry that she would need for work.

Walking in the door, on her first day at The Senate Hotel, she was pleasantly greeted by the General Manager.

Upon seeing her, he smiled.

> "Good morning, Gabriella! It's so good to see you. How about some breakfast?"

> "Okay, that sounds good," she replied with a smile. As she ordered a Danish and coffee, she kept her hands on her lap, under the table, as she did not want him to notice her broken nails and scratched hands.

> "So, what have you been up to these past two weeks?" he asked, making conversation.

Gabriella unabashedly proceeded to give him a litany of all her chores, including the decluttering, moving, painting, cleaning, and organizing.

> "Wow! You did all that in two weeks! You know, if you needed more time, you really could have called me," he replied with a huge smile.

> "Yeah, right!" Gabriella smirked. "It seems to me that I did call you, and that went over big, didn't it!" she laughed.

Then he got serious. Putting his hand on her arm, he said,

> "Gabriella, I really wanted you to join us here. You're exactly what we were looking for. I was afraid you were going to string me along, and play me against your current employer, and then not show. Really. So that's why I was so stern on the phone."

Gabriella looked at him in a new light.

> "Well, thank you for sharing that with me. Now I know you're *not* a tyrant!" they both laughed. She continued…
>
> "I didn't expect my resignation at the Resort to be so difficult initially. But I'm happy to say that it all worked out, and we're all still good friends. So here I am. Ready to start my new job and my new life!"
>
> "Great! I'm so glad," the General Manager replied.

Gabriella did an excellent job for The Senate, and stayed for two years until she received another offer: Area Director of Sales over three Holiday Inns in the suburbs. This was indeed a major promotion.

Gabriella submitted her resignation to the General Manager, who regretted her leaving. Still single, she returned to suburban living, but learned that she truly did enjoy living in the city, too. The city had taught her much. She enjoyed the hustle and bustle, the arts, the museums, Lake Michigan, the variety of excellent restaurants. Yes, it had been an eye-opening experience for her, and had greatly added to her maturity.

About six months later, she was at a Hotel Association cocktail party. Many hoteliers from the city and suburbs were there. All of a sudden, she heard a familiar voice.

> "Well, look who's here!" the voice called out laughingly. As Gabriella turned, she saw it was the General Manager from The Senate Hotel, Nicholas Carcioni.
>
> "Nick Carcioni. How are you? I can't believe we got you to leave the city," she joked.

"It doesn't happen often, Gabriella, but sometimes, on rare occasions ..." He laughed.

There had always been a friendly rapport between them, so they spent the rest of the evening getting caught up, chatting, and laughing, sipping cocktails, and enjoying each other's company—until they noticed the party was over.

Then Nick asked her,

"I'm going to my boat on Sunday. Would you like to come?"

"What time?" asked Gabriella.

"About noon."

"Hhmmm ... I'm still in church then. Sorry."

"Well, this is a first!" laughed Nick, scratching his head. "I've never had a woman turn down a date with me, because she had to go to church. What time would you be able to go?"

"I could be ready by one thirty," Gabriella quickly responded.

"Great. I'll pick you up at one thirty."

Happily, Gabriella gave him her address.

When Gabriella was exiting church on that Sunday, she heard a car horn repeatedly blowing, but with all the traffic, she ignored it. Finally, she heard her name. Looking up, she was pleasantly surprised to see that it was Nick. He had come to the church, and waited for her to exit.

"Get in, my princess," he commanded with a smile, as he got out and opened her door.

And that, folks, was the beginning of the fairytale love story between Gabriella and Nick Carcioni.

"My tears provide the Ink, for all that's written here."

Gabriella

CHAPTER 5

RUSHED TO THE EMERGENCY ROOM

Early on Sunday morning, July 22, 2012, ambulance sirens blared through the Chicago suburban town of Arapaho Woods.

"Where we headed?" Emergency Attendant, Gage asked driver, Devin.

"One-Thirty-Eight Geronimo Trail. Not too far from here."

"What's the problem?"

"Man collapsed in his house and hit his head several times. His wife just called in … extremely upset."

"Okay. Concussion undoubtedly."

"Yep. Bring in the stretcher and helmet guard."

"We're here. What's their names?"

"Nick and Gabriella Carcioni."

When the Emergency Medical Technicians entered the home, Gabriella quickly ushered them to the dining room where a flight of stairs led to the second floor. At the top of the stairs, Nicholas sat, leaning against the wall.

Gabriella quickly informed the EMT what had transpired.

> "Mr. Carcioni, can you hear me?" asked Devin.

> "Yes," responded Nick softly.

> "Please help me. I have severe pain in my head. It's killing me!"

> "Yes, sir. We'll get you to the hospital as fast as we can."

> "Give me something for this pain, please!"

> "We need to get you to the hospital so they can evaluate your condition, before giving you something for the pain, Mr. Carcioni." replied Devin.

The men quickly brought the stretcher to upper-level hall and gently placed Nick on it. They placed a helmet on his head and strapped him down to keep him as still as possible.

> "We'll need a list of his medicines, ma'am," said Gage to Gabriella.

> "I have a list of all his medicines. I'll give them to you at the hospital," Gabriella responded.

> "Wonderful, most people aren't as organized as you, and that could lead to complications."

"Yes, it's good for all of us to carry a list of our meds in our wallets because ... well, you never know," replied Gabriella softly as she collected Nick's meds.

Upon seeing the ambulance in the driveway, a few neighbors gathered inside the Carcioni house. They began asking each other what had transpired.

After they put Nick in the ambulance, Devin noted that the closest hospital was Community, and they would be taking him there.

"Don't worry, darling," Gabriella said, kissing Nick's forehead, "I won't be far behind."

"My head ... it hurts so bad. I have never had a headache like this before in my life!" said Nick moaning.

Telling neighbors that she would keep them informed, Gabriella quickly locked the front door and proceeded to the garage. She backed out in her Hyundai just in time to follow the ambulance down the street. Having never done this before, she felt it would be good to keep pace with them, so she started to go through yellow lights to do so. Not far up the road, the ambulance pulled off to the side, and Gage came running back to her car. Gabriella sat there petrified, thinking something had happened to Nick.

Rolling down her window, she said.

"What's wrong? Is Nick okay?"

"Yes, ma'am, he is, but we *cannot* have you following the ambulance so closely, and *do not* go through yellow and red lights with us," scolded EMT Gage. "You're going to get into an accident! You know where we're taking him—Community Hospital on Canyon Drive. So just take your time, and get there safely. Mr. Carcioni needs you in one piece. Right?"

"Yes, of course," an embarrassed Gabriella answered. I'll meet you in the Emergency Room, correct?"

"Yes."

With that he rushed back to the ambulance, and they took off. Gabriella still proceeded to get there as quickly as possible, but she did so at a safe speed, and followed the traffic signals safely.

Upon entering the Emergency Room, she ran to the desk and asked for Nick. She was taken to a draped area. Nurse Kyla entered, saying they would be taking a CAT scan immediately. When asked about his medications, Gabriella handed her the typed list that she always kept in her purse, listing Nick's medications, dosages, and allergies to medications. Additionally, she had listed the name and phone number of his Primary Care Doctor.

"This is perfect. Glad you brought this," Nurse Kyla remarked, smiling.

"Can I have something for this head pain?" Nick winced.

"Not yet, Mr. Carcioni. We have to see what is going on inside your head, and if there's any damage. After that, we'll be able to give you something to ease the pain."

Two aides pulled back the curtain as they prepared to wheel Nick out.

"Okay. Let's go. They shouldn't be too long," Nurse Kyla informed Gabriella. You can wait here or in the waiting room."

"No, I'm going too!" replied Gabriella.

"You won't be permitted to enter the CAT scan area," Nurse Kyla responded quickly.

"That's okay. I'll go as far as I am permitted. Then I'll wait till he comes out." Kissing Nick's forehead and grabbing his hand she stated, "Let's go!"

With raised eyebrows, Nurse Kyla consented with a smile.

Promptly, they ushered Nick in for the CAT scan, which took about a half hour. When finished, they wheeled him back to the Emergency Room area. As they approached, Gabriella spotted two of their closest neighbors, Les and Pamela, waiting near the desk. Gabriella smiled and remarked,

"Hi, neighbors. I told you that I'd call you. You didn't have to come to the hospital."

"I know," said Pamela, "but Les insisted on coming to see his buddy and make sure that he's okay." The two guys strongly shook hands.

"We just came from having a CAT scan," said Gabriella. "Hopefully, they'll let us know soon. This place is a mad house. Look—every room is filled!"

"I see that. Wow!" remarked Pamela. "Nick do you feel nauseous?"

"No, it's just that my damn head is killing me!"

Pamela shook her head.

"We'll say a prayer for him tonight. Let's go, Les. Nick needs to rest." She turned to Gabriella.

"Call us later with the results, okay?" as she tried to usher Les toward the exit.

The guys shook hands again.

"Take care, Nick. I'll see you at home soon," said Les smiling.

"Yeah, you take care too, my friend. God Bless!" replied Nick sincerely.

"Thank you. You're going to be okay."

"I hope so, Les. I hope so!"

As Les and Pamela departed, Gabriella remarked,

"That was nice of them to come, wasn't it, Darling?"

"Yes, that Les is such a good guy and friend. They're both very nice people. Glad we have them as neighbors. When she bakes cookies during the day, Pam brings some out for me to eat while I'm working in the yard. She's really a good baker!" Nick responded.

"I think I remember you saving me at least *one* recently." Gabriella laughed.

"Yep. Only one." Nick laughed. Then quickly grabbed his forehead "Oh, hon, my head hurts so bad."

"I'm going to get you a cold cloth to put on it. I'll be back," said Gabriella, and she quickly exited.

"Please hurry!" Nick moaned.

Although the nurses' desk was extremely busy, Gabriella was able to get Nurse Kyla's attention, and she quickly retrieved a cold pack.

Nick said the coolness felt good, but it didn't relieve the pain.

Enter Radiologist, Dr. Ayden...

> "Mr. Carcioni, I have the results from your CAT scan, sir. You have traumatic brain injury and blood on all sides of your brain. We do not have a Neurological Department here, and you need to be sent to a hospital that has one. Your choices are Bridgeville or Asclepius."
>
> "Asclepius is the closest. Bridgeville is farther? Is that right, Doctor?" asked Gabriella.
>
> "Yes, that's correct," replied Dr. Ayden.
>
> "Okay. I think we should go to the one closest in the neighborhood, don't you Nick?"
>
> "Yes, that makes sense. That way you won't have to travel too far every day, Gabriella."
>
> "But, is their Neurological Department reputable?" asked Gabriella.
>
> "Yes, years of experience there."
>
> "Okay then. Let's transfer Nick there. How soon can we do it?" Gabriella asked.

"First, I have to call them and see if they have any room in ICU. He needs to be where they can watch him carefully for the next few days. I'll do that now."

About a half hour later, Dr. Ayden returned to say Asclepius Christian Medical Center could take Nick, and he arranged transportation within a half hour.

In ICU at Asclepius Christian Medical Center, Nick was constantly monitored by a friendly staff. Several CAT scans were given to him over the next few days. By the third day, they started to see the blood slowly going back into his body, which was a good sign.

Early on the third morning, Raynin Rose, a sweet young Licensed Practical Nurse (LPN), brought Nick several Cadbury and Hershey bars, because he had mentioned the day before that he really had a taste for some chocolate. Even in his painful state, Nick had a warm personality, and all the staff enjoyed his company.

Raynin Rose had a particular fondness for Nick, especially after she learned that he had his own Big Band Orchestra. She played the piano and sang, and so they endlessly talked music when she attended to him. On that day, she even serenaded Nick, singing "*Memories,*" from *Cats*. Nick being very impressed with her voice, told her to pursue a career in music, as she had the talent.

For his head pain, Nick was given strong doses of a narcotic called Norco. It helped somewhat, but he was told the pain would not ease totally until all the blood left the brain area. The drug made him very sleepy. He just kept saying he was very anxious to get up, get out of there, and get well.

On the fourth morning, Dr. Brandon came to examine Nick. In looking at his latest CAT scan, taken the night before, he had seen that the blood was starting to go back into Nick's body. He felt that Nick should get up, and get some exercise, as soon as possible. He recommended that Rehabilitation start soon, and Nick could be moved that very day out of the ICU. Gabriella and Nick were so delighted with the good news!

At 10 a.m., he was moved to the 8th floor, into Room 804.

Not having much of an appetite since his collapse, he had hardly eaten while in the ICU. A luncheon tray was brought into Room 804, but Gabriella was only able to get Nick to eat the chicken broth and gelatin.

For the remainder of his first day in Room 804, Nick rested as best he could, and they continued giving him Norco for his head pain, along with all his normal meds that he'd taken for years, that were prescribed by his Primary Care Doctor. Blood was drawn several times, and a variety of nurses stopped by to do their various jobs, hooking up machines, and getting acquainted.

Gabriella completed the menu questionnaires, listing food that Nick liked, hoping that she could get him to eat more.

> "If you don't eat soon, my love, I am going to smuggle you a Buona Beef sandwich," she joked, knowing Nick's favorite fast food.

> "Now, that sounds good to me!" Nick responded quickly with a smile.

> "Great. I'll do it tomorrow!" she said with a smile.

It was a busy day, all in all, getting acclimated to the eighth floor.

As usual, Gabriella stayed with Nick all day and departed at about 9:00 p.m. for home. He always called her to make sure she got home safely, and to once more to say Goodnight.

CHAPTER 6

NURSING DIRECTOR ASSESSES GABRIELLA

My name is Helen Sargento, Nursing Director at Asclepius Christian Medical Center for thirty-five years. I've seen a lot in my days here at Asclepius, as well as at several other hospitals where I've worked. I'd like to think I've seen it all; at least that's what I tell my team of young nurses.

But then along came Gabriella Carcioni, and this teacher reverted back to being the student. Gabriella was a young, very attractive, intelligent woman. She had an eagle eye and a sharp wit. I listened to her ask questions of my staff. Actually, she questioned everything that was—or would be—connected with the care of her husband, Nicholas. She was one hundred percent devoted to that man. There was a drastic age difference between them. My staff members told me that twenty-five years separate them. Wow!

After observing her, I purposely took charge of overseeing Mr. Carcioni's care, so that I could evaluate the situation more clearly. I must say, I was tremendously impressed with the love and attention that she showed toward him. They seemed to enjoy each other's company so very much. They laughed together at private jokes, discussed upcoming travel plans, all while she showered him with her undivided attention, giving him kisses, brushing his hair, asking him if he was comfortable or wanted anything, checking and rechecking every detail of his bed and room.

"You know I'm a germ fanatic," she said to both of us.

"Are these sheets changed every day?"

I nodded and replied, "Yes."

She called him, Darling. He usually called her, Honey.

Yes, anyone could see that the love between them was deep, genuine, and all consuming. It also became apparent how she brought the "youth" out in him with her affectionate ways. One day, for example, she brought him a dozen of gorgeous yellow roses, and arranged them in a vase. She then reminded him of how many times he had bought these for her, knowing it was her favorite color rose. He would bring these home to her for no particular reason—just that he loved her. Sweetly smiling, she took them over to his bedside so he could sniff their heavenly fragrance. He nodded with much approval and satisfaction.

Beneath that delicate nature was a strong-willed woman. That I could tell for sure! Perhaps it was her positive attitude and constant smile that led me to this assessment. She didn't seem to let much rattle her, and her main focus was to keep Mr. Carcioni calm. She did this by remaining calm herself.

However, I believe she hid a lot of inner fears behind that smile, although she would not let on that anything was frightening her. It was evident that she was taking charge of this situation regarding his health, and was going to scrutinize every detail till he was completely well. Likewise, he seemed very pleased in knowing that.

The intensity of her love was something that one does not witness every day. I know, because I have seen many families around a supposed loved one's bedside, and many times it isn't a pretty site. But Gabriella was unique. She took her role seriously, and her goal was to get him the best care and get him home in good health, as soon as possible. It was obvious that he was her whole world.

Yes, I had gained much respect for her. I and my other nurses took note of her standing at his bedside for ten or more hours a day, alone, not even leaving the room to take lunch. I wondered why she choose to be there alone with him, not inviting friends or family members, but I did not ask.

When his food tray came, she fed him his soup. Even though he said he was not hungry, she was always able to force him to accept a few forkfuls of sliced beef and mashed potatoes. She just kept asking him various questions, trying to keep his mind occupied, so he would eat more. *Smart woman*, I thought. He knew what she was doing. I could tell he was no dummy. But he went along with her anyway. He seemed to love how she treated him as if he was her "baby." Finally, he said,

"Enough!"

She could tell by the tone in his voice that he meant it, and so she stopped immediately as a smile graced her lips. She had achieved her goal, and so they were both satisfied. When he asked her if she wanted anything on his tray, she politely said, "No thank you."

It was obvious that she was used to eating in fine restaurants with upscale service. I would say she was particular, yet not pompous. I respected her in many ways, and therefore I willingly did what she asked of me, and instructed my staff to do the same.

I felt confident, that this was one story that was going to have a very happy ending.

Chapter 7

"HELP ME! SOMEONE PLEASE!"

On Thursday, July 26, 2012, Nick's second morning in room 804, he awakened to a shocking reality. He could not move his arms. The hospital had tied his wrists with straps to the side bars! That morning, as Gabriella exited the elevator to the eighth floor, she could hear him screaming from down the hall.

"Help! Someone please untie me!"

"Oh my God," she thought. *"That's Nick!"*

Immediately she took off running down the hall toward him, dragging her belongings behind. As she entered his room, the shock of what she saw made her drop everything on the floor as she rushed to his bedside. Both of his hands were tied to the side bed bars. Nick was yanking furiously to get untied, but to no avail as he cried in desperation.

"Oh, Gabriella! Where have you been? I've been calling for you all morning!"

His nose was running, and tears flowed down his face.

"Help me!" he pleaded.

Gabriella was horrified.

> "Nicky! My God, what has happened here to make them tie you down?"

She grabbed some tissue and wiped his face.

> "I don't know. Please just untie me!"

The tie-down belts were made of a thick scratchy material that did not slide easily, which served their purpose well. Immediately she started to yank on the straps.

> "Yes, yes, I will. Stay still! Please Relax. I'll untie you!" she reassured.

Gabriella yanked and pulled, but the straps would hardly budge. Finally, she grabbed a butter knife from the food tray sitting there. As she loosened one restraint, an alarm went off at the nurse's desk.

Male Nurse, Gregory, came running in.

> "What are you doing, ma'am?" he scolded.

> "I'm untying my husband's hands! He's not an animal! Why was this done?"

Male Nurse, Gregory, quickly responded,

> "It's for his own good. We didn't want him to climb out of bed."

"Climb out of bed!" reprimanded Gabriella. "He has these high bars that keep him in! Do you tie all your senior patients?"

"Ma'am I'm going to have to insist that you let me retie him." He stated emphatically, as he grabbed the manacle from Gabriella's hand.

"No! No!" Nick cried out in a frightened tone.

Gabriella looked at his wrists and saw that they were all black and blue and cut from his struggling. Becoming infuriated, she snatched the belt back from Male Nurse, Gregory, stating,

"I am his wife. I will not permit him to be tied up like an animal. Am I making myself clear? I want that to show on his record that he is *never* to be tied down again! *Never again!*" she repeated in a loud voice. *And*, I'm keeping these tie-downs."

With that, Male Nurse, Gregory, stated abruptly, "I'm reporting this!"

"You do that," Gabriella replied. "And I want to see your Supervisor."

"Oh, hon," Nick cried, "Thank you!"

Gabriella proceeded to untie the other wrist.

"You're okay now. Just calm down and relax. They'll never do that again, baby." As she hugged him in her arms, she continued,

"I still don't understand what pushed them into doing this. Did you make any threats that you were leaving?" Gabriella asked.

"No, but I did say I would like to get up and walk around. I'm very tired of lying in this bed!" replied Nick in self-defense.

"Nicky, I can understand how you feel. However, you must promise me that you will *never* try to climb out of this bed on your own—*never!* They're trying to protect you from yourself and keep you safe. They cannot watch you every minute, and if you abide by the rules, they will not tie you again. Understand, sweetheart? You can ask them to get you up, but you must wait for them to assist you, okay?"

"Yes, of course. I know that!" Nick responded strongly.

"I didn't try to get out myself. But I did tell everyone who came in here, that I wanted to get up for a while. But nobody would help me. They just said they would tell my nurse."

Gabriella proceeded to roll both straps of coarse material into a ball. Nick's wrists were bruised, cut, swollen, and black and blue, and this caused him to complain of much pain. Shaking her head in disgust, Gabriella left the room briefly to ask for ice packs. Upon returning, she applied them to his wrists till he fell asleep. When he awoke, he moaned,

"I'd like to get up and get out of this bed. Can I please get up for a while? I'm sick of lying here all day, every day."

"Hmmm, well let me see if I can get someone to help us," Gabriella responded as she stared out the eighth-floor window, to the pounding rain, lightening, and thunder... as she hoped they wouldn't lose electricity.

"Why don't I just adjust your bed so you can sit up straight, and we'll watch TV?" she suggested.

"No, Gabriella, I really need to get out of this bed for a while. Please," he pleaded.

"Okay, let me go ask for some help at the Nurses' station."

Approaching the Nurses' station, she was surprised to find no one there. Proceeding further down the hall, she looked into various rooms, but still found no nurses. They must all be on break, she thought. That's strange.

When she returned to Nick, he asked if help was coming.

"No, I couldn't find anyone." Gabriella looked around the room, trying to decide if she could handle Nick by herself, knowing that he was weaker than even he knew.

"Please, Gabriella," Nick continued with his pleas.

Then she noticed the reclining chair in the corner, about three steps from Nick's bed.

"Okay," she finally blurted out. "Here's the plan. I'll help you out of bed. You try to stand with my help, and let's see if you have the strength to even stand, because you've been in bed for almost a week. Incidentally, how's your head pain—your headache. Is it gone?"

"No, my head still hurts." He moaned and rubbed his forehead.

"That's because you still have blood on all sides of your brain. You're taking the strongest pain medicine they have, so it will just take time, babe. Be patient."

Be patient, she half chuckled to herself, knowing full well that patience was not one of his strong suits.

"Now, let's take this one step at a time. We're not going to hurry, Nicky. Let's take it slow. Okay?"

"Yeah."

Gabriella raised his head to a sitting position and then lowered the entire bed as close as she could to the floor.

"Okay, sweetheart, come on. Turn towards me!"

She helped Nick swing his legs around as she held his back to support him in a sitting position with his feet dangling off the side of the bed.

"Just sit like this for a few minutes. How's that feel? Are you dizzy?"

"No, I'm good."

"Great! You see that chair?" She pointed to the blue chair about three feet away.

"Yes"

"Nicky, I'm going to help you stand up. Let's see if you have the strength to do so. When you're standing, tell me if you get dizzy. If you don't, then put your arm around my neck. I'll be holding you around your waist. Then we'll take steps toward the chair, and sit you down there. Okay?"

"Yeah, okay," he replied softly as he concentrated on standing.

He was a little shaky, but nonetheless, he was able to stand. Gabriella held him tightly around the waist, and he put his arm around her neck.

Watching him closely, she prayed silently that she would have the strength to handle him.

"Ready to take that first step?" Nick nodded.

He was determined to do this, and determined to get well.

"Okay, Nicky, move your foot. Good. That's one step. Okay … next step. Two! Great! Now … three steps! One more, babe. Yeah! You're doing great!"

They were now in front of the blue chair.

"Now the hard part. Let me turn you around slowly. Ready? Plop!"

With that Nick collapsed into the chair.

"Great job, darling! I'm so proud of you. How did that feel?"

Nick was smiling with pride. Gabriella could see the satisfaction on his face, that he had been able to accomplish such a feat.

"Felt good! I'm a little weak, but I did it," he confessed.

"Well, it's good for you to know that, and it was great for you to get a little exercise too. You're my superman, Mr. Carcioni."

She smiled as she laughingly kissed him all over his face, which got him laughing too. Gabriella pulled up a chair next to his, resting her head on his shoulder, as she held his hand. She reached over, took a blanket from the bed, and covered both of them as they watched TV.

After Nick dozed on and off for about forty-five minutes, she suggested that he get back into bed, as that had been enough exercise for one day. He agreed. However, she soon discovered that getting him up out of the recliner chair was not as easy, as getting him into it. His arms and legs were not really strong enough, to support the upward momentum that was required.

"Can you get up? Can you push harder with your legs, babe? Come on, babe ... push," she encouraged.

"I'm trying! My legs are weak!" he said in disgust.

"Okay. Okay. Stay calm." She grimaced as she tried to think of a solution.

"We have a little unexpected situation here. Now let's see, how can we remedy this? We'll get you up, don't worry."

Eyeing the walker across the room, she rose, grabbed it and placed it in front of Nick. She got down almost to her knees and backed into him. She instructed Nick to put his arms around her neck as she held on to the walker for support.

"I'm going to try to stand and bring you with me. All you have to do is hold on! Don't let go, and don't fall! As soon as you're standing, I'll grab your waist. You put your arm around my neck like before. Got it?"

"Okay. That sounds good."

"Again, hold on *tight* to me!" She reminded him sternly.

"Here we go! *Push!* Come on, again! *Push!*"

"I *am* pushing," Nick grimaced.

"Harder, sweetheart. Push harder. Let's go."

As Gabriella lifted with all her strength, she commanded,

"Stand! Nick! Stand! Yes! Finally, Alleluia!"

Third time was a charm. Nick had got himself to stand.

"Great job, baby. I've got you. Hold on to me. You're doing great!"

Gabriella quickly turned, grabbed him around the waist, and helped him put his arm around her neck.

"Now, let's walk to the bed. Come on, walk. One step. Two steps. Three. Four steps. Wonderful!" she encouraged.

Upon reaching the bedside, she slowly turned him around, and down they both tumbled onto the bed. Nick first, then Gabriella on top of him, both laughing at their success, as they kissed and hugged each other.

Just then, Nurse Barbara Jo entered to check the machines and record his blood pressure and pulse.

"You two look like you're having fun," she quipped.

Still laughing, Nick replied,

"Yep, we're having a ball!"

Gabriella proceeded to get him comfortably situated in the bed. As she covered him with a sheet, Nick grabbed Gabriella's hand, pulled her toward him, and looked into her eyes. With a serious tone in his voice, he said,

"Gabriella, I love you so much. You're my heartbeat! I mean it! Don't ever leave me!"

Gabriella became teary-eyed. Fighting back her tears, she said,

"Don't worry, my love. I won't, and don't you ever leave me!"

Nick lowered his eyes.

"Nothing lasts forever, sweetheart. Everything comes to an end. I'm much older than you. It only stands to reason that God will take me first. And, honestly, I hope and pray he does. I sincerely couldn't live without you!"

"I don't want to hear that, Nick," Gabriella replied. She laid her head on his chest, as tears ran down her cheeks.

Stroking her hair, Nick whispered,

"Don't cry. You know I can't stand it when you cry. Come on ..."

After a few minutes, in order to lighten the mood, he asked cheerfully,

> "So, anything still left on that breakfast tray?"

Gabriella chuckled, wiped her face, and arose to go look at the tray.

> "Let me see. Oh, boy, we have scrambled eggs, fruit, and a cookie."

> "Sounds great. I'll have the cookie. You take the rest."

> "No, Nicky. You have to eat. You have hardly eaten in the last three days. Come on—just a little of each. I'll feed you."

> "Okay. Okay. Just the fruit. I'm really not hungry."

> "I know, sweetie, but you need your nourishment."

> "Okay, give me the fruit. Did they bring tea?"

> "Yes, hot tea."

> "That will go good with my cookie." He laughed.

Just as he finished eating and started to sip his tea, a slender beautiful young woman in her late twenties with long, dark-brown hair entered the room.

> "Hello, I'm Supervisor Jessica. I understand you wanted to speak to me about Mr. Carcioni being restricted today," she said in a sweet soft voice.

Immediately, Gabriella's mood turned severely defensive, as she wiped Nick's lips and put the napkin down.

"Yes, there was a gross misunderstanding here, Supervisor Jessica!"

"My husband is not an animal. Therefore, he should never have been tied down in his bed against his will. Earlier, I told Male Nurse, Gregory, that I want it put on his chart, that he is *never* to be tied with those belts again. Did you receive the message?"

"Yes, I did, Mrs. Carcioni, but I want to explain to you why we did this. Mr. Carcioni kept asking to get up and out of bed. We don't think he is strong enough to do that, and we didn't want him to hurt himself. At that time, we were too busy to assist him. So, in this case, we thought it best to keep him subdued to protect him—only until rehab could come up and evaluate him."

"Well, for your information, I got him out of bed this morning."

"What? You did WHAT?" asked a shocked Supervisor Jessica.

"That's right. I got him up, and he walked, with my help, to that blue chair. Then he walked back to bed. You are right. His legs are not very strong at this time. But how are they going to get strong if you keep him a prisoner in that bed every single hour of every single day! He will never get strong enough. Exercise is what he needs. He desperately wants to get well, and I expect you to do all you can to get him well as fast as you can so he can come home!

"Starting tomorrow, I want to hear about an exercise schedule devised for his progress. Do you see my point?

This is the reason he was sent up to this regular floor from ICU—to get Rehabilitation, per Dr. Brandon. They said he could come home in about three days. Did they not tell you?"

"Yes, I see that was the recommendation, stated Supervisor Jessica, but Rehab must come up and evaluate him. I am waiting to hear from them. Either today or tomorrow."

"Why do we have to wait so long?"

"Our Director is on vacation."

"Are there no other staff members who evaluate?"

"Yes, there are, but normally she does the Eval scheduling. I really would prefer that she assign someone, but I'll meet with her assistant later, to see if we can possibly expedite it."

"Yes, please do. We would greatly appreciate that. He's anxious to get home. And again, *no straps!* Look at his wrists. Look at how black blue and swollen they are!" Gabriella stated firmly, as they both looked at Nick.

"You call that *'for the good of the patient'*? I think not! I sincerely hope we have an understanding Supervisor Jessica? Really, take a look at him now. Look how happy and calm he is. Why? Because I treated him with dignity and respect! It's so upsetting to see any patient, let alone a senior, treated this way. No one came in to answer his cries for help! Everyone just ignored him. What kind of a hospital is this? I thought you had a good rating. I'm shocked at your heartless lack of concern! I'll look forward to seeing rehab today or tomorrow," Gabriella concluded shaking her head.

Not wanting to leave on a negative note, Supervisor Jessica again reiterated in a sweet tone,

> "This *is* a good hospital, Mrs. Carcioni. Our rating for a Chicago suburban hospital is one of the best. We have many patients who come here from the suburbs and the city too, with a multitude of injuries. It is most difficult to give prolonged attention to just one. Additionally, we take extra precautions, that a lay person may misinterpret."

Gabriella interrupted.

> "I'm not misinterpreting those black-and-blue swollen wrists, Supervisor Jessica. Look, don't get me wrong. I understand that you have a large number of patients, but to ignore his cries for help and assistance, is cruel in my book. I have no idea how many hours he lay here crying to get free!"

Gabriella sighed...

> "Okay, enough talk about that. It upsets me too much! I do thank you for coming in, and permitting us to have this conversation, and I do trust we have come to a better understanding now. Am I correct?"

> "Yes, Mrs. Carcioni," Supervisor Jessica responded in agreement. "Our staff here prides themselves on being empathetic to all patients. Mr. Carcioni will soon be well and back home again," she added, smiling as she touched his foot tenderly.

"We all look forward to seeing excellent results regarding his health. I'll contact Rehab and see how soon they can come up."

"Thank you so much, Supervisor Jessica," said Gabriella as Jessica departed.

Nick just kept smiling at Gabriella.

"I love how you handled that. You're my baby!"

"No, you're my baby!" she said with a chuckle.

"No, you're *my* baby!" He laughed more heartily, adding, "I'd like another cookie."

Gabriella laughed.

"Mr. Carcioni, you're just too adorable. Time for more kisses."

CHAPTER 8

NICK'S REHABILITATION EVALUATION

Nick spent the remainder of the morning resting comfortably, knowing that Gabriella was watching over him and he was safe. At 11 AM, a man and woman entered his room with pleasant smiles.

"Hi! We're here to see Mr. Nicholas Carcioni," the female greeted.

"I'm Rosemary and this is Joseph. We're occupational therapists from the Rehab Department."

"I'm Mrs. Carcioni. Nick is sleeping now, but we can wake him. It's been an eventful morning for him."

"Is he feeling okay?"

"Oh yes! Now he his! When I came in this morning, I found him sobbing because they had tied his wrists to the bed rails, and he was trying to get loose."

"What? Why?" asked Joseph.

Gloria J. Yorke

"I talked with Jessica, the Floor Supervisor, and she said they were trying to protect him from harm. It really didn't make much sense, and it upset Nick so very much. No one wants to be tied down like an animal, especially if there's no cause for such drastic action!

They both looked at each other and frowned.

"We're glad that is all straightened out now, right?" said Rosemary.

"You better believe it! I have given strict orders. He is never to be tied down again!" responded Gabriella as she nudged Nick to wake up.

"Wake up, sweetie. You have company." Nick opened his eyes and smiled. "This is Rosemary and Joseph from Rehab. They're here to evaluate you."

"Oh Hi," a groggy Nick responded.

"How are you, Mr. Carcioni?" Rosemary asked.

"Good. I feel good. Still have some head pain ... but good," he responded.

"That's great! As your wife said, I'm Rosemary and this is Joseph. We are here to test your cognitive, communication, and behavioral skills. Sounds like a mouthful, doesn't it?" She laughed.

"Yeah, it sure does," replied Nick with a chuckle.

Joseph moved in closer.

"Can you tell me your name?"

78

"Nick Carcioni."

"When's your birthday, Mr. Carcioni?

"March 4, 1925."

"Where do you live?"

"Arapaho Woods."

"Who's this woman?"

"That's my heartbeat."

Joseph and Rosemary smiled at each other.

"What's her name?" Joseph continued.

"Gabriella."

"What's her relationship to you?"

"What do you mean? She's my wife!"

"Who's the President of the United States?"

"Is it still Obama?" Nick asked looking at Gabriella, who nodded.

"What day is it today, Mr. Carcioni?"

"Monday ... Tuesday ... Gabriella what day is it?" Nick asked.

Gabriella smiled.

"It's Thursday. You've been too busy to read the newspaper, sweetie," she responded chuckling.

"Yeah," he agreed.

Joseph then stated,

"How many fingers am I holding up?" He showed eight, four, and then ten, and Nick answered correctly each time.

"You're doing real good, Mr. Carcioni."

Rosemary then changed places with Joseph near the bedside.

"Mr. Carcioni, can you touch your nose with your finger?"

"Sure." And he did.

"Can you raise your right arm?" He did.

"Can you raise your left leg? Your right leg? Both arms in the air?" Nick accomplished all.

"Now, shake my hand. Wow! That's a good grip you have, Mr. Carcioni." She smiled.

"You're shaking hands with a U.S. Marine, Rosemary," Nick responded.

"Great job!" added Joseph.

"I can even stand for you, if you want," volunteered an assertive Nick.

"What! You can? Show us," remarked Rosemary, as she looked at Gabriella for confirmation.

Gabriella smiled and nodded as she proceeded to his side.

As she lowered the bed, she began to explain to them that, with her help that morning, he had, indeed, stood for a very short period.

"Wonderful. Let's see," coaxed Joseph.

Gabriella helped Nick get his legs off the bed and held his back for support. Slowly he sat at the edge of the bed. When she slipped her arm under his, she whispered to him, "On the count of three, okay?"

"Yes!" Nick responded.

"One, two, three—up!" Nick stood as Gabriella held him.

"That's fantastic!" Rosemary exclaimed as both she and Joseph clapped their hands.

"Thank you. Thank you," joked Nick, giving a small bow.

"Okay, sweetheart. You can sit back down now. That was fabulous!" whispered Gabriella in his ear.

Nick sat back on the bed, and Gabriella helped move his legs back so he could lie down again.

"You have passed our test with flying colors, Mr. Carcioni. We'll see you in therapy as early as tomorrow, and you should be home in a few days. We can tell you're going to progress quickly!" said Joseph.

"It was such a pleasure meeting both of you," added Rosemary.

They departed with smiles, and Gabriella turned to Nick.

"I'm so proud of you, Darling."

Nick lay there smiling, too.

"I knew I would pass that test. No problem."

"Yes, you aced it! I must say though, when you said you could stand, my heart skipped a beat. I was hoping you could duplicate what you did this morning. And you did!"

"Yes, but only because *you* helped me," responded Nick.

"I did nothing. You are so strong willed. I love that about you!"

"Yeah. I'm really exhausted now. I think I could sleep a little bit." He yawned.

"That's fine. Go ahead. You're done for the day. No more tests for you, my love."

CHAPTER 9

"MY NAME IS DR. HILDA GERMAN"

Having just completed his rigorous Rehabilitation evaluation test, Nick fell asleep as Gabriella started to make notes in her journal. Into the room walked a woman in her early fifties with brown hair, about 5 ft. 5 in, wearing a white coat with a stethoscope around her neck.

"Hello. I'm Dr. Hilda German," she proclaimed with a foreign European accent.

"Oh, hello, Doctor. I'm Mrs. Carcioni. Nick's wife. He's sleeping now. He just completed the Rehab Evaluation, and he passed it with flying colors!" Gabriella smiled with pride.

"Yes, I know," Dr. German responded, devoid of enthusiasm. "I've been assigned to be his Doctor, and in looking over his chart, I'm going to make several changes in his medications."

"Oh, like what, Doctor?" asked a concerned Gabriella.

"I'm going to change his Blood Pressure medicine. I will give him a different one. I'll also decrease his Diabetes meds. We'll keep giving him the Norco, with a few other minor modifications. And *tonight*, I'm ordering him a sleeping pill."

"A sleeping pill!!?" questioned a shocked Gabriella. "He doesn't need a sleeping pill, Doctor. He's sleeping just fine—look at him."

"Yes, yes. But I want him to be rested for Rehab tomorrow.

"Doctor, Is that his chart in your hand?" Gabriella asked.

"Yes, it is."

"Did you read it?" questioned Gabriella.

"Yes, I did."

"Well then, Doctor, you know that he has blood on all sides of his brain from a fall just a few days ago. I have always heard that you don't want someone with a Concussion to sleep. You want him to stay awake! And I'm not even a Doctor! I don't agree that giving him a sleeping pill is right, Dr. German."

"Mrs. Carcioni, I know what I'm doing!" responded Dr. German adamantly, as she abruptly turned and walked out of the room.

Wow! thought Gabriella. *That is one egotistical Doctor!*

I'm the Wife. I'm allowed to voice my opinion about my husband's care, and it should be accepted! I have to pray on this. I'll say my Rosary. It just doesn't sound like the right thing to do—give him a sleeping pill. I'm going to call my sister, and see what she thinks.

Meanwhile, Nick kept sleeping as Gabriella dialed her cell. Reception was not the greatest in the hospital, and Gabriella hoped she wouldn't have to leave the room. Finally, the call went through.

CHAPTER 10

"WHAT HAVE YOU DONE TO MY HUSBAND?"

By Friday, July 27,2012, it had been raining hard for four consecutive days, and this morning was no exception. Buckets of rain and high winds had created overflowing rivers/streams and flooded streets, which had caused numerous traffic accidents and airline cancellations. It had been a nightmare for all travelers.

However, none of this was going to be a deterrent for Gabriella Carcioni, who robotically swerved in and out of traffic, desperate to reach Asclepius Christian Medical Center where her husband, Nicholas, had been hospitalized five days earlier.

"Move it!" yelling through the closed windows. "Don't you know how to drive?"

Traffic was bumper to bumper. Red brake lights flashed on and off every second, tires squealed, and people's nerves frayed. Gabriella's vision was blurred from the tears that streamed down her face, dissolving her makeup. It was a constant battle to keep her clammy hands from slipping off the steering wheel, as her entire body broke into a cold sweat.

"Please, dear God. Please let him be okay," she pleaded repeatedly. Oh, Nicky, I love you so much!"

All along she kept replaying questions in her mind—*Was he going to be all right? Why would the Doctor even think of giving him a sleeping pill? She totally discounted my viewpoint...* thought Gabriella.

> *I'm the wife, damn it! And that sarcastic Nurse Destini last night ... Oh my God...Wait till I see her!"*

Perspiration ran down her back, saturating her clothes and undergarments. Even the air conditioner at full blast provided little to no relief.

> "Breathe, Gabriella," she kept repeating to herself aloud, practicing a meditation method to calm herself down, but it didn't help.

When she reached the Asclepius Christian Medical Center parking garage, the line of waiting cars stretched around the corner. Men in drenched raincoats blew their whistles, waving their arms, desperately trying to move the traffic into the garage.

> "Please let there be a space for me inside the garage, dear God." She whispered.

Closer and closer she crept. Finally, it was her turn to enter, and she was motioned inside.

> "Thank you, Lord," she said, as she advanced quickly.

As if by a miracle, one space opened near the door on the second level. Not wasting a moment, she parked quickly, grabbed her roller carry-on luggage, purse, and small shopping bag filled with goodies. At a hurried pace, pushing through the doors, she made her way to the reception desk on the first floor to validate her ticket.

> *So many people here this morning,* she thought. *Hope I don't have to wait long for the elevator.*

Ding! Finally, a set of elevator doors opened, and the crowd moved forward quickly like a herd of animals. Although it was almost filled to capacity, she was determined to squeeze in to be the very last one. With passengers packed like sardines, the elevator took its time, stopping at every floor. No one was exiting.

Is everyone going to the eighth floor? she thought, as perspiration ran down her forehead.

Finally, two people departed on the seventh floor, giving everyone a little bit of breathing room.

The elevator stopped again.

> "Eighth Floor. Out please," Gabriella voiced. People shuffled to let her exit. Quickly she departed, trying to juggle it all—arms full, and a carry-on dragging behind.

After taking a few steps, suddenly she stopped dead in her tracks. Frozen. It was as though she had hit a glass wall. Gabriella always had a strong Sixth Sense. Even as a child, she'd been able to sense more than the average person. As she matured, her Psychic abilities had strengthened, enabling her to communicate with Spirits in other dimensions.

Standing there, she stared down the hall. Room 804 was only four doors away, and yet it seemed like a journey of a million miles. Fear gripped her. A veil of deep dread draped over her, as she stood there in a trance oblivious to everything happening around her. Something was drastically wrong, and a spiral collapse was about to unfold. Her inner tower of strength was in the process of complete destruction. She bowed her head and started to cry, as she prayed that her intuition would be wrong this time. Her hands and feet suddenly were ice cold. Fighting desperately to free herself from this negative stronghold, she forced herself to take steps to move toward Room 804.

> "All will be well. Nicholas is fine. He is waiting to say good morning to me. Get in there!" she reaffirmed herself, again and again. "All will be well. Nicholas is fine …"

Proceeding slowly, she finally arrived at his door. Wiping her eyes, she straightened her shoulders and pasted a fake grin on her face, as she entered with bravado.

> "Good morning, darling," she sang as she went to place her things on the table in the corner. Still not looking at him, she called out again…

> "Nick, darling, Good Morning. Gabriella is here!" she chimed.

Hearing no answer, she turned her head slowly to look at him in bed. There he lay, eyes shut as though he was sleeping. There was no movement. No reaction to her loud greetings. This was not normal, as he was a light sleeper. Quickly she ran to his side.

> "Nick, I'm here baby. Wake up. Nick, do you hear me?" she asked frantically. Grabbing his face, she repeated her pleas even louder.

"Nicholas Carcioni, wake up! *Please*, my darling, wake up!"

Tears streamed down her face. She scooped him up into her arms, rocking him back and forth. "Nicky, baby, *please* wake up!"

Gently, she tried raising his eyelids as she continued to call his name, but he did not react.

Hysteria overtook her. Running out of the room, she looked to the left, then to the right, but saw no medical staff. Frantically, she called out,

"Hello someone, anyone!" but no one answered.

Suddenly, she spotted a nurse sitting at the computer at the end of the elongated hallway. Down the hall she went running... screaming and choking on her tears.

"What have you done to my husband? Oh, my God! What have you done?"

People in neighboring rooms came out to see what was wrong, but Gabriella ran past them, as she focused on the vision at the end of the long hall. Now that she was closer, she recognized it was Nurse Ann, Nick's nurse from yesterday, a woman in her fifties.

"What have you done to my husband, Ann?" a breathless Gabriella choked out. "Nicholas Carcioni. What have you done to him? He will not wake up!"

Nurse Ann sat there staring at Gabriella, without emotion. Other nurses came and stood in nearby doorways. Finally, Nurse Ann, replied in a calm manner.

"I've done nothing to your husband, Mrs. Carcioni. I went to give him his pills at five this morning, and couldn't get him to wake up. He's just in a deep sleep. So, I just let him sleep, and planned to see him again, later this morning."

"No! He's not in a deep sleep, Ann. There's something wrong!" Gabriella retorted. "Get that Dr. German up here immediately! She did something. Call her and tell her I want to see her immediately! Something is drastically wrong with my husband, and it's *her* doing!"

"What do you mean?" Nurse Ann asked, as she started to become very concerned.

"I don't have time to explain the story to you, Ann! Just get her up here, *now!*"

"Okay, I'll page her." Nurse Ann grabbed for the phone.

Gabriella continued to yell out....

"Tell her to come immediately, and I mean immediately! Oh my God, how could this be happening? I told her, No!" Gabriella added as she turned to hurry back to the room.

Nurse Ann started dialing immediately.

Gabriella ran back to Nick's room, while others in the hallway tried to stop her, to ask what was wrong. Not stopping for a second, she just yelled out,

"Something's wrong with my husband. He will not wake up, and it's Dr. Hilda German's fault!"

Upon returning to the room, Gabriella continued to try to awaken Nick, but to no avail. She dampened a washcloth with cold water and dabbed his face, pleading for him to wake up.

Within fifteen minutes, Nurse Ann came to Nick's room, saying that she had gotten no response to her Page, but had left word for Dr. German to come as soon as possible, emphasizing there was a problem with Mr. Carcioni. While in the room, Nurse Ann also tried to arouse Nick from his sleep, calling out his name and tapping his face. She told Gabriella that she wanted to check him again herself. Gabriella interrupted and asked for the name of the sleeping pill prescribed by Dr. German the night before.

"It was Trezidone," Nurse Ann responded.

"How many milligrams?"

"Fifty."

"Is that a strong dosage?" Gabriella quizzed.

"Yes, that's the strongest!"

"Oh my God!" screamed Gabriella.

Standing over Nurse Ann like a hawk, Gabriella watched her lift Nick's eyelids and call out his name, louder and louder, but there was no response.

"Is he in a coma?" Gabriella finally asked in a shaky voice.

Nurse Ann just clinched her lips and did not reply. Obviously, she did not want to make a snap decision, and felt it was up to Dr. German to diagnose. In checking the chart over and over,

Nurse Ann noticed that Dr. German had changed the dosage of his medicines, and even switched his normal medications to other medications. This also surprised her!

What was this doctor thinking? she wondered. Not wanting to upset Gabriella any further, she finally said,

> "He's obviously in a deep sleep. When the doctor calls back, I will emphasize for her come immediately."

As Nurse Ann departed, a tall, very attractive Doctor around thirty years old, with light brown streaked hair, entered smiling cheerfully.

> "Good morning, "I'm Dr. Cristina, Director of Rehabilitation. I've come to meet Mr. Nicholas Carcioni, as we would like to start Rehab today."

> "Oh, Doctor, there is something drastically wrong with Nick this morning," Gabriella cried out.

> "What? My staff evaluated him yesterday afternoon and gave him a glowing report."

> "I know. I'm his wife, Gabriella. I was here when they evaluated him. He did it all--- counted to ten, even stood for them. But then ... Oh, my God!" Gabriella broke down and buried her face, crying in Nick's sheet.

> "Oh my, Mrs. Carcioni, What's happened?" Dr. Cristina said as she rushed to her side.

> "Sit down. Let me get you a glass of water. What's going on?"

Dr. Cristina positioned two chairs next to each other and sat down next to Gabriella. As Gabriella regained her composure, she told Dr. Cristina the entire story about Dr. Hilda German.

Dr. Cristina shook her head in shock and disbelief over what she was hearing. When Gabriella finished, she asked Dr. Cristina to call Dr. German, as Nurse Ann got no response.

>"Please inform her that Nick is unconscious, and tell her to come up here immediately. *Please.*"

>"Yes, I will do that. Take it easy. He'll wake up. I just want to look at him before I make that call."

Dr. Cristina went to Nick's bedside and called out,

>"Mr. Carcioni, wake up. It's Dr. Cristina, Director of Rehabilitation. Come on, Mr. Carcioni, I need to talk to you! Wake up!"

She slapped him gently on his face, trying to get a response, but none came. She grabbed his hands and lifted his arms, even jiggled them. All the while she kept calling out his name, and still Nick did not wake up. Finally, shaking her head, she turned to Gabriella.

>"Yes, there is something *definitely* wrong. He's *nothing* like he was yesterday, according to my assistants' report. I'll go call Dr. German now!"

Placing her hand gently on Gabriella's shoulder, Dr. Cristina softly whispered,

>"I'm sorry, Mrs. Carcioni. Oh, my!"

Approximately twenty minutes later, Dr. Cristina returned.

"Mrs. Carcioni, I just spoke with Dr. German, and she'll come up in a little bit. However, I must say, even though I explained his condition, and that your husband would not awaken, her reply to me was astounding. She said she'll give him **only 20 mg** of that medicine tonight, instead of 50 mg."

"*What!*" yelled Gabriella. "Did you explain that he's unconscious?" Did you explain that he doesn't respond, and doesn't open his eyes? Is she fucking nuts?!"

Dr. Cristina nodded her head and replied,

"Yes, I did explain the situation clearly. I don't understand her reasoning either, and I suggested she come up as soon as possible to see for herself, before prescribing any more medication. I emphasized that something was *drastically* wrong!"

Then shaking her head and shrugging her shoulders she said,

"I have done all I can do here, Mrs. Carcioni. I'm so truly sorry. I just can't get over what has happened here. Such a drastic change from just yesterday! I did tell her that you wanted a CAT scan today, and she said she will order it. They'll be coming up shortly, as I just got off the phone with them too."

Gabriella moved from around Nick's bed and walked toward Dr. Cristina. Speaking with all the firmness she could muster, she looked into her eyes stating,

"Dr. Cristina, I want to speak to the President, Superintendent, or Director of this hospital. Please call that person and tell him or her that I want to meet with them TODAY! I want another Doctor. Dr. Hilda German is insane*!*

I don't want her to be my husband's doctor anymore! She is *not* to prescribe any more medications for him!" Dr. Cristina saw the fire in Gabriella's eyes and knew this was not going to be swept under the rug.

This woman is going to demand answers, and rightfully so! she thought.

"Yes, I will call Patient Advocacy. That's who you have to speak with. I'll tell them you want to meet with them, immediately."

Just then, the aides came to take Nick for a CAT scan. Gabriella stepped out of the way, but warned them to be careful as he was in a delicate state. The aides were very understanding.

Gabriella proceeded to walk down the hall holding Nick's hand, telling him he was going for a CAT scan, and that everything was all right. Nothing to fear. She assured him that he was doing fine, and this was routine. As they waited for the elevator, she kissed him gently on the forehead, and told him repeatedly that she loved him so very much.

"Soon you will be home, darling. You just rest," she whispered and kissed his lips, never letting go of his hand.

CHAPTER 11

GABRIELLA DEMORALIZES DR. GERMAN

Upon reaching the lower floor where Nick would have his CAT scan, they exited the elevator, one in a bank of several. All the elevators seemed to open at the same time, causing some congestion. Just at that moment, out stepped Dr. Hilda German from the next elevator. Surprised to see Gabriella standing there with Nick on the gurney, she stopped immediately, blocking the doorway to her elevator.

"Oh, Mrs. Carcioni, Hi," Dr. German exclaimed in a somewhat frazzled tone.

"Hi? Is that all you can say!?" responded a furious Gabriella loudly. "Look at what you've done to my husband!" She pointed to Nick.

"I brought him in here in relatively good condition. He had all his senses. He was awake and alert. And you have turned him into this—a vegetable state!"

Dr. German started to stutter, as people just stopped and listened.

"He'll be okay," she said. "He'll awaken by tomorrow. He's just sleeping. Don't worry!"

"He'd better be wake up tomorrow, Doctor, or I will OWN this hospital!" a fiery Gabriella retorted loudly, with her finger pointing in the doctor's face.

People in the elevator gasped, looking at each other in shock, but no one moved to exit. This was a confrontation that people rarely see take place, and they were staying till the conclusion.

Gabriella continued,

"Oh, and what's this about you wanting to give him *more* medication tonight? No! You will *NOT* give him any more medication. Is that clear, Doctor?"

"Yes, of course," Dr. German responded quickly. "I didn't know he was unconscious. Now I see the state he's in."

"Yes, you did know, Doctor! Stop your lying! When Dr. Cristina called you a few hours ago, she made it perfectly clear to you on the phone that he was unconscious, and you still insisted on wanting to prescribe more of that sleeping medication! I can see now that you don't know what you're doing! Seriously! You really don't!"

"He'll be okay, Mrs. Carcioni. Don't worry! He's just sleeping!" Dr. German kept insisting.

A teary-eyed Gabriella interrupted,

"I pray to God that you know what you're talking about, Doctor! All I can say to you is, he had *better* wake up tomorrow. Meanwhile, you are NOT to prescribe anything further for my husband. Understand? Nothing!"

"Yes, of course not." Dr. German consented.

Gabriella was so furious, she was shaking all over. Then she motioned to the aides.

"Come on. Let's get this CAT scan done."

Then adding,

"I'll see you tomorrow, Doctor. Bright and early!"

Gabriella turned abruptly and walked away leaving an embarrassed Dr. German to stand speechless, in front of horrified onlookers, whispering among themselves.

Nicholas was ushered thru a locked door area that was reserved for CAT scans, into a curtained area where there were several other patients lying in beds. The aides departed. Gabriella stood there observing several Nurses checking stats on the computer, and going in and out of the various partitioned rooms. It was a very busy place with a huge staff. As with everything in the hospital, the wait time was over an hour before the technicians could do the scan. Then there was another waiting period when it was finished, while they checked the scan to make sure it was okay and they didn't have to do it over again.

Finally, over two hours later, Nick's scan was completed, and he was sent back to Room 804.

Gabriella stood there looking at the love of her life—so fragile, so innocent. Taking his hand, she kissed him on his forehead, as tears welled in her eyes. She talked to him, hoping he could hear her.

"Nick, I love you so much! You're my entire world, darling, and I cannot make it without you! I need you. I need you so very much. You know that! It's always been Nick and Gabriella ... Gabriella and Nick. Just you and me. Just us! Like we always tell people—no kids, no pets, just you and me!"

She kissed his face.

"You always said that I am your heartbeat. Well, darling, you're *my* heartbeat! You're my *everything*! Return to me, my love. Please! You must return to me!"

She dried her tear-stained face, trying to hide the fact that she was crying. Taking a deep breath, she mustered up a half smile and stated positively,

"You rest now, my love. You've had a hard day with everyone wanting to talk to you, and then going down for that test. Wow, you must be exhausted! Tomorrow morning when I come in, I look forward to finding you awake. I want to hear you singing out my name with a cheerful 'Good morning, Gabriella', as you always have in the past. I need to hear your voice again, my darling. I'm here watching over you! I won't ever leave you! Don't worry about anything! I am here!" she assured him, while trying to reassure herself!

It was now almost 5:30 p.m. and dinner trays were being distributed. Aide Kathleen brought in Nick's tray, and Gabriella remarked that he didn't need a tray, because he was not awake. Kathleen replied that he was paying for it, so perhaps Gabriella would like to eat it. Gabriella smiled, and at first was going to refuse, but because she had not eaten all day, she decided to just take a look.

Gabriella had always had a phobia about hospitals, and had found it extremely difficult to enter one as a visitor. In all her years, she had never been admitted into a hospital, and was very thankful to be in good health. Seeing any kind of needle—especially the intravenous cannula in a patient's hand or arm—made her extremely squeamish, almost to the point of fainting. Of course, she would not touch anything, being fearful of germs. Most of the time, she would wait till hospitalized family members and friends went home, before she visited them. Because she kept this fear to herself and never explained, some people simply thought that she lacked compassion.

When her Daddy had been hospitalized several times over a six-year period of illness, she was forced to overcome that fear, so she could visit him. Also, in later years, when her Mother was in the hospital for three solid months until her death, Gabriella flew in several times, to be by her bedside. Her deep love for her Parents surpassed any fear that presented itself, and of course, she had her Nick to lean on and hold her hand. Nick was always there to give her support! He had never let her down. Never!

Slowly, she approached his dinner tray.

> "Well, let's see, Nicky. What did they bring you here?" she questioned aloud.

> "Oh, this looks delicious," she remarked, shaking her head.

> "Looks like sliced beef, vegetables, mashed potatoes, applesauce, and gelatin for dessert. Yum, Wake up, darling. Time to eat. I'm starving! You must be too!"

Looking over at him and seeing no response, sadly she lifted the fork as she tried to decide what to sample. *The beef doesn't appeal to me*, she thought. *Mashed potatoes look good.* She brought a small bite to her lips.

> "Oh, they're barely warm!" She cringed.

> "Okay, babe, it looks like it's going to be applesauce and gelatin for my dinner." She was pleasantly surprised to find that she enjoyed the applesauce. She scooped it up quickly, and followed it with the gelatin.

> "That was delicious, sweetheart. I really needed that. Tomorrow you'll have some delicious food to eat too, *and* I'll bring you that Buona Beef sandwich with sweet and hot peppers that you craved. Yum, Yum!"

Then, remembering she had potato chips in her bag too, she scrambled through her carry-on to find them. Ripping open the bag quickly, she complimented herself for bringing them.

Gabriella returned to Nick's side and continued talking to him, always believing that he could hear her.

> "Nice people here. You're in a good place," she said, half believing her own words.

> "When you wake up tomorrow, all this good food will be waiting for you. Yum, Yum! Get ready to dine in style, baby! And yes, I'll be here to feed, my li'l angel."

She spoke positively with tears running down her face.

Gabriella kept showering Nick with a million kisses. She wanted him to feel her love. She always had demonstrated her affections openly, and Nick loved the fact that she was not inhibited about hugging or kissing him, no matter where they were. She felt sure he could hear her, so she allowed only positive words to be spoken. She believed wholeheartedly in the Law of Attraction. If he could hear her—and she truly felt that he could—she didn't want him to think that something was drastically wrong with him, or that he might not recover. Oh no...it was tremendously important for him to believe that he was recovering, and would be home soon. She believed it, and so should he!

Staring at him, she thought,

> *I must believe that Dr. German knows what she's talking about. After all, she is a Doctor!*

Gently, she took Nick's face in her hands and kissed it repeatedly.

> "I love you, Nicholas Rocco. Keep resting. You're doing great!"

CHAPTER 12

PATIENT ADVOCACY RESPONDS

Around 6:00 p.m. an attractive woman in her late fifties entered Nick's Room. Dressed in a navy-blue pantsuit, she carried a notebook and silver-plated pen. Gabriella could tell she was meticulous, with her manicured painted nails, delicate bracelet watch, and a large marquis diamond wedding ring.

"Mrs. Carcioni?"

"Yes."

"Hello, I am Yvonne Falonzo, Patient Advocacy Director. I was told by Dr. Cristina that you wanted to speak with me regarding your husband, Nicholas Carcioni."

"Yes, I did!" Gabriella replied sternly. "I brought him in here because he had fallen at the house. He had his senses, and now ... look at him!" She began to cry.

"He's in a coma—all because of Dr. Hilda German!"

Director Yvonne quickly interrupted,

"Please Mrs. Carcioni. Let's sit down. Please start from the beginning. Give me a chance to take notes. I want to hear the entire story and get all the facts. Exactly what day did he enter our hospital?"

"All right," Gabriella took a seat.

Inhaling and exhaling deeply, she grabbed for some tissue. With both ladies seated, Gabriella began...

'My husband was brought by ambulance to ICU on Sunday, July 22. He was sent from Community Hospital, because they said the CAT scan revealed he had blood on all sides of his brain, and even inside the brain...and he required a hospital that had a Neurological Department. After three days here in ICU, his only complaint was the tremendous head pain that he was experiencing, so they gave him Norco. He knew me and could move his arms and legs, but was confined to the bed. Because the blood started to go back into his body, which was a good sign, Dr. Brandon stated that he should be moved up to a Regular floor for Rehabilitation as soon as possible, and said he should be home in about three days. He was moved to this room in the early morning of Wednesday, July 25th.

She took a deep breath.

'He ate some lunch—just a little— around noon. Rehab came up on Thursday at 11 a.m. to evaluate him. Even with his strong head pain, he pushed to answer their questions and do the tasks they asked. They had him lift his arms and legs, touch his nose, answer several current event questions, and then he volunteered to stand for them. They were shocked, but let him prove himself to them. They were most impressed. At the conclusion, they said he was doing great and they would definitely get him to Rehab first thing the next morning, and yes, would probably go home in just a couple of days! Of course, Nick was exhausted from the test, and he was still suffering with that strong headache. He fell asleep quickly!'

Director, Yvonne gave Gabriella a nod of encouragement, so Gabriella continued.

'Then Dr. Hilda German walked in carrying a chart and told me she was assigned to be his Doctor. The first thing Dr. German said was that she was going to change all his medications—his blood pressure pills, his diabetes medicine, the dosage of Norco they were giving him for the severe head pain.'

And then she said,

'And tonight, I am going to give him a SLEEPING PILL!'

I, of course, stopped her abruptly and asked her if that was Nick's chart she was holding. She said it was, and I asked her if she'd read it.

She said she had. Being skeptical, I reiterated that Nick had blood all over his brain—on all sides! I told her I didn't think a sleeping pill was the right thing to give him. I mean, I have always heard that you want to keep a person awake, who has had head trauma. Right? She agreed with that, but she said she wanted him to have a good night's rest, before he went to Rehab the next day. I again pointed to him, reminding her that he had no trouble sleeping, and reaffirmed my opinion, that he didn't need any sleeping medication.

Her response to me was sharp and curt.

'I know what I'm doing!' she blurted. And then turned quickly on her heels and stormed out of the room. This was around two thirty in the afternoon.'

Director Yvonne looked up from her notes frowning, not saying a word. She had been listening intently, and she nodded for Gabriella to continue.

"Yvonne, I'm not a doctor," said Gabriella, "neither do I have any medical training, but I've always heard that when people have head trauma, you try to keep them awake, not put them to sleep! Then, I prayed on it, and asked my sisters and brother in Pennsylvania, and a few friends for their opinion, and everyone thought that a sleeping pill didn't sound like the right thing to do. Of course, we all said that Dr. German *is a Doctor,* and should know what she's doing. And yet, even knowing she was a Doctor, my intuition said otherwise about this treatment! Obviously, I couldn't get it out of my mind all day. I just kept praying for the right answer to come, and knew I had time, as he didn't get his pills till 10 p.m."

Gabriella continued with her story.

"Nick kept sleeping on and off all day, only being awake for short periods. He would awaken just long enough to see I was here, smile, and tell me he loved me, then apologize for sleeping. Back to sleep he would go. As the day progressed, I made up my mind, that I would not permit him to be given a sleeping pill! Usually, I leave him in the evening around 9:30 p.m., but that night I wanted to find his Night Nurse, to inform her that I did *not* want him to get any sleeping pill, with his other pills at 10:00 p.m. I wanted it written on the chart in front of me.

"At 8:00 p.m. I woke him up and told him I was going home and I would see him the next day, first thing in the morning. He smiled, kissed me good night, told me to drive carefully, and I left to find the Nurse. Unfortunately, there was *no one* at the Nurses' station, so I walked up and down the hall looking in the various rooms. No Nurses were on the floor. I knew that it was still early, and his pills were not given until 10 p.m., so I thought I would leave, and call in a half hour when I got home."

"To my surprise, as I entered the house shortly after 8:30 p.m., the phone rang. It was Nick, making sure I had arrived home safely. I smiled and thought to myself, how lucky I was to have such a loving husband."

He said the Nurse was there and had dialed the phone for him. I asked him to put her on, as I needed to talk to her. I told him to get a good night's sleep, and that I'd be there early in the morning. I told him tomorrow, he'd be going to Rehab, and then he'd be home in a couple of days. He was so happy to hear that, and said that he would get a good night's sleep.

The Nurse took the phone and identified herself as Nurse Destini. I proceeded to tell her that Dr. German had mentioned giving Nick a sleeping pill tonight, and I told her I disagreed. I absolutely did *not* want Nick to get that sleeping pill with his ten o'clock pills. Her response to me was abrupt, and with a smart mouth she responded,

'Well, too late. I already gave it to him!'

Chills immediately covered my entire body, causing an uncontrollable shiver.

'No!' I yelled. 'He gets his pills at 10:00 p.m.!!

Nurse Destini replied,

'This pill might take a little longer to take effect, so I gave it to him early, along with his other pills. Doctor wants to make sure he gets a good night's sleep—'

'I interrupted her, and told her I hadn't been able to find any Nurses, before I left tonight, and I definitely DID NOT want him to have any sleeping medication. She coldly told me that it was her job to follow the Doctor's orders. She abruptly said good night, that she had other patients she needed to attend to, and then hung up the phone.'

'When I came in this morning at around 8:00 a.m., this is how I found him! He is unresponsive to me and everyone. He doesn't move, doesn't make a sound. I believe he's in a Coma. Nurse Ann said that she couldn't even give him his pills at 5:00 a.m. because she couldn't wake him!'

Gabriella grasped Yvonne's arm.

"Yvonne, listen to me...I absolutely positively do NOT want Dr. German to be my husband's Doctor anymore. She is off the case! Gone! Do you hear me? I want a *different* Doctor immediately! I have lost *all* confidence in her ability. Actually, I think the woman is insane."

Gabriella sat back momentarily, but then resumed her erect posture.

> "Oh, and then to add insult to injury, listen to this. You won't believe it, but it's true. She told Doctor Cristina, Rehab Director, that she would give him only 25 milligrams of Trezidone tonight, instead of 50...and this was <u>BEFORE</u> she even *saw* the state he was in today!
>
> *"Dear God, he's in a Coma*! He should *never* have been given that sleeping medication in his fragile condition!"
>
> *"Get me another Doctor immediately!"* Gabriella's voice started to rise. The more she recalled the story, the angrier she got!

Director Yvonne put down her notes and looked at Gabriella with much concern.

> "I will meet with my key staff members, including Dr. German, and I will get her side of the story. But most certainly I will get another Doctor, assigned to your husband immediately! I'm so sorry, Mrs. Carcioni! We will do everything we can to get Nicholas awake, and back to good health, as soon as possible. I promised you that!"

Walking over to Nick's side and taking his hand, Gabriella responded,

> "I brought him here with all his senses and *all h*is faculties working. He hit his head when he fell, and he had head pain. That was all! But he knew me, he could think and talk, he had use of all his bodily functions, he could walk. The main thing wrong was that he had

severe head pain, which was because of all the blood all over his brain, but it was going back in his body, which was good. Otherwise, ICU would not have sent him up here! Now look at him," Gabriella cried.

"He doesn't even move. He won't wake up! Oh God!"

Yvonne tried to comfort Gabriella.

"Mrs. Carcioni, please calm yourself. Again, I am so sorry," the Advocacy Director said as she placed her hand on Gabriella's arm.

"Would you like the Chaplin to come and talk with you?"

Gabriella shook her head.

"No. I don't need to talk to a Chaplain. I need my Nicky!"

How to recite the Holy Rosary

1. SAY THESE PRAYERS...

IN THE NAME of the Father, and of the Son, and of the Holy Spirit. Amen. *(As you say this, with your right hand touch your forehead when you say Father, touch your breastbone when you say Son, touch your left shoulder when you say Holy, and touch your right shoulder when you say Spirit.)*

I BELIEVE IN GOD, the Father almighty, Creator of Heaven and earth. And in Jesus Christ, His only Son, our Lord. Who was conceived by the Holy Spirit, born of the Virgin Mary, suffered under Pontius Pilate; was crucified, died, and was buried. He descended into Hell. The third day He rose again from the dead. He ascended into Heaven, and sits at the right hand of God, the Father almighty. He shall come again to judge the living and the dead. I believe in the Holy Spirit, the holy Catholic Church, the communion of saints, the forgiveness of sins, the resurrection of the body, and life everlasting. Amen.

OUR FATHER, Who art in Heaven, hallowed be Thy Name. Thy kingdom come, Thy will be done on earth as it is in Heaven. Give us this day our daily bread, and forgive us our trespasses, as we forgive those who trespass against us. And lead us not into temptation, but deliver us from evil. Amen.

HAIL MARY, full of grace, the Lord is with thee. Blessed art thou among women, and blessed is the fruit of thy womb, Jesus, Holy Mary, Mother of God, pray for us sinners, now and at the hour of our death. Amen.

GLORY BE to the Father, and to the Son, and to the Holy Spirit. As it was in the . . .

2. IN THIS ORDER...

3. WHILE TOUCHING THESE BEADS TO KEEP TRACK OF YOUR PROGRESS...

INTRODUCTION
1. IN THE NAME...
2. I BELIEVE IN GOD...
3. OUR FATHER...
4. HAIL MARY...
5. HAIL MARY...
6. HAIL MARY...
7. GLORY BE...
8. O MY JESUS...

THE FIRST DECADE
9. ANNOUNCE...
10. OUR FATHER...
11. HAIL MARY...
12. HAIL MARY...
13. HAIL MARY...
14. HAIL MARY...
15. HAIL MARY...
16. HAIL MARY...
17. HAIL MARY...
18. HAIL MARY...
19. HAIL MARY...
20. HAIL MARY...
21. GLORY BE...
22. O MY JESUS...

THE SECOND DECADE
23. ANNOUNCE...
24. OUR FATHER...
25. HAIL MARY...
26. HAIL MARY...
27. HAIL MARY...
28. HAIL MARY...
29. HAIL MARY...
30. HAIL MARY...
31. HAIL MARY...
32. HAIL MARY...
33. HAIL MARY...
34. HAIL MARY...
35. GLORY BE...
36. O MY JESUS...

THE THIRD DECADE
37. ANNOUNCE...
38. OUR FATHER...
39. HAIL MARY...
40. HAIL MARY...
41. HAIL MARY...
42. HAIL MARY...
43. HAIL MARY...
44. HAIL MARY...
45. HAIL MARY...

4. AND SILENTLY MEDITATING ON THESE "MYSTERIES", OR EVENTS FROM THE LIVES OF JESUS AND MARY...

On Monday and Saturday, meditate on the "Joyful Mysteries"
First Decade (Steps 9-22): The Annunciation of Gabriel to Mary (Luke 1:26-38)
Second Decade (Steps 23-36): The Visitation of Mary to Elizabeth (Luke 1:39-56)
Third Decade (Steps 37-50): The Birth of Our Lord (Luke 2:1-21)
Fourth Decade (Steps 51-64): The Presentation of Our Lord (Luke 2:22-38)
Fifth Decade (Steps 65-78): The Finding of Our Lord in the Temple (Luke 2:41-52)

On Thursday, meditate on the "Luminous Mysteries"
First Decade: The Baptism of Our Lord in the River Jordan (Matthew 3:13-16)
Second Decade: The Wedding at Cana, when Christ manifested Himself (Jn 2:1-11)
Third Decade: The Proclamation of the Kingdom of God (Mark 1:14-15)
Fourth Decade: The Transfiguration of Our Lord (Matthew 17:1-8)
Fifth Decade: The Last Supper, when Our Lord gave us the Holy Eucharist (Mt 26)

On Tuesday and Friday, meditate on the "Sorrowful Mysteries"
First Decade: The Agony of Our Lord in the Garden (Matthew 26:36-56)
Second Decade: Our Lord is Scourged at the Pillar (Matthew 27:26)
Third Decade: Our Lord is Crowned with Thorns (Matthew 27:27-31)
Fourth Decade: Our Lord Carries the Cross to Calvary (Matthew 27:32)
Fifth Decade: The Crucifixion of Our Lord (Matthew 27:33-56)

On Wednesday and Sunday, meditate on the "Glorious Mysteries"
First Decade: The Glorious Resurrection of Our Lord (John 20:1-29)
Second Decade: The Ascension of Our Lord (Luke 24:36-53)
Third Decade: The Descent of the Holy Spirit at Pentecost (Acts 2:1-41)
Fourth Decade: The Assumption of Mary into Heaven
Fifth Decade: The Coronation of Mary as Queen of Heaven and Earth

You are encouraged to copy and distribute this sheet.

www.newadvent.org

beginning is now, and ever shall be, world without end. Amen.

O MY JESUS, forgive us our sins, save us from the fires of Hell; lead all souls to Heaven, especially those in most need of Thy mercy. Amen.

HAIL HOLY QUEEN, mother of mercy; our life, our sweetness, and our hope. To thee do we cry, poor banished children of Eve. To thee do we send up our sighs, mourning and weeping in this vale of tears. Turn, then, most gracious advocate, thine eyes of mercy toward us. And after this, our exile, show unto us the blessed fruit of thy womb, Jesus. Pray for us, O holy Mother of God, that we may be made worthy of the promises of Christ. Amen.

O GOD, WHOSE only-begotten Son by His life, death and resurrection, has purchased for us the rewards of eternal life; grant, we beseech Thee, that by meditating upon these mysteries of the Most Holy Rosary of the Blessed Virgin Mary, we may imitate what they contain and obtain what they promise, through the same Christ our Lord. Amen.

ANNOUNCE *each mystery by saying something like, "The third Joyful Mystery is the Birth of Our Lord." This is required only when saying the Rosary in a group.*

46. HAIL MARY...
47. HAIL MARY...
48. HAIL MARY...
49. GLORY BE...
50. O MY JESUS...

THE FOURTH DECADE
51. ANNOUNCE...
52. OUR FATHER...
53. HAIL MARY...
54. HAIL MARY...
55. HAIL MARY...
56. HAIL MARY...
57. HAIL MARY...
58. HAIL MARY...
59. HAIL MARY...
60. HAIL MARY...
61. HAIL MARY...
62. HAIL MARY...
63. GLORY BE...
64. O MY JESUS...

THE FIFTH DECADE
65. ANNOUNCE...
66. OUR FATHER...
67. HAIL MARY...
68. HAIL MARY...
69. HAIL MARY...
70. HAIL MARY...
71. HAIL MARY...
72. HAIL MARY...
73. HAIL MARY...
74. HAIL MARY...
75. HAIL MARY...
76. HAIL MARY...
77. GLORY BE...
78. O MY JESUS...

CONCLUSION
79. HAIL HOLY QUEEN...
80. O GOD, WHOSE...
81. IN THE NAME...

CHAPTER 13

REPLACEMENT: DR. BOBBIE EDWARD

After Patient Advocacy Director, Yvonne Falonzo departed, Gabriella sat next to Nick's bedside, and started to pray The Rosary aloud.

> "Pray with me, darling. The Blessed Mother is listening, and she will help you get well! She never lets us down! We love saying the Rosary, don't we my love, because it brings us such peace and comfort. Remember how many times we would pray it together in the afternoon? Yes ..."

She then started to bless herself...

> "In the name of the Father, and of the Son, and of the Holy Spirit. I believe in God, the Father Almighty ..."

About an hour later, a distinguished tall man with salt-and-pepper hair and a wide smile entered the room.

> "Hello, Mrs. Carcioni, I'm Dr. Bobbie Edward. I'm your husband's new doctor." He spoke with a pleasant English accent.

"Oh, I am so glad to meet you, Dr. Edward!" Gabriella jumped to her feet.

"Mrs. Carcioni, I've been somewhat briefed on what has happened to Mr. Carcioni, but I would like to hear it from you. Let me check him first, and then I would like you to bring me up to date and give me more specific details."

He moved to Nick's bedside and checked him over thoroughly from head to toe, listening to his heart and lungs, lifting his eyelids, checking his feet, calling out his name, asking him to squeeze his hand and hoping for a response. None came. When he finished, he made notes on Nick's chart. Dr. Edward looked at Gabriella with intense hazel eyes, as though he could see through to her broken heart.

"I would like to know the entire story, Mrs. Carcioni. What exactly happened at your home that morning when Mr. Carcioni fell?" his charming accented voice showed grave concern.

Gabriella responded,

"If I may, Doctor, I have a few questions for you first."

"Please, what would you like to know?" Dr. Edward nodded.

Gabriella smiled.

"I hear an accent. Where are you from? How long have you been a Doctor? And how long have you been in the United States?"

"I'm from the UK," Dr. Edward responded. "I've lived here for eight years, and came here from Northwestern in Chicago two years ago."

"How long have you practiced medicine, Doctor?"

"Twenty-five years, Mrs. Carcioni. I promise you, I will do all I can for Mr. Carcioni. He will have my undivided attention."

"Have you ever been sued, Doctor Bobbie ... I mean Dr. Edward?"

With a smile on his face he responded,

"No, Mrs. Carcioni, I have not, and you can call me by either name, and I will respond."

A blushing Gabriella responded,

"Please forgive me for being cynical, Doctor. It's just that I have lost faith in this hospital presently because of Dr. Hilda German, and I know I shouldn't judge everyone else by her inadequacy, but this man here is my entire world, and there is no room for doctor error! Understand? Please, I have faith that you will help us, and bring my Nicholas back to me. Honestly I do!"

"You have my word, Mrs. Carcioni. I will do everything in my power! Kindly remember, I am just a Doctor. I am not God!"

"Thank you! Yes, of course. Okay. You wanted to hear the entire story of what happened at our home," said Gabriella.

"Yes, as detailed as you can get. I need to know exactly what happened. It will help me assess exactly what happened to him," replied Dr. Edward.

"Yes, that makes sense, Doctor. We both awoke simultaneously at around 5:00 a.m. on Sunday morning, July 22. Nick said he was going to go to the bathroom, and he jumped out of bed quickly and headed for the hall on his way to his bathroom. I got up too, and as I was walking into the master bath, I heard three loud thumps banging against the wall. I called out to Nick, but he didn't answer. So, I yelled louder and asked if he was okay. Still no answer.'

'I went running into the hall and found him on the floor staring straight up at the ceiling, mouth open, with his arms and hands outstretched in the air. I dropped to my knees and immediately cradled him in my arms, rocking him back and forth screaming his name, asking him if he was okay and what had happened. In my panic, Doctor, I didn't even realize that he wasn't answering me at all. I was just rocking him back and forth and pleading for him to speak to me. As I recall it now, I believe I brought him back from somewhere.'

Finally, he started to moan, repeating...

'Oh, my head! My head hurts so *bad!*' He said it was the worst he'd ever had in his life, and he asked me to help him. I sat him up and leaned him against the hall closet door, and ran to get a chair so he could grab it, and together we could get him up. He has implants in both knees and can't really kneel on them easily. With the chair and my assistance, I finally got him standing and walked him to the bed, but he kept screaming that his head hurt so bad. He pleaded for me to give him something for the pain. I ran and got him an Aleve, which I take for headaches, and gave him one. About two minutes later, he pleaded again for something for the pain. Of course, I told him that I had just given him something, and knew instantly that something was very wrong with him. He didn't want to lie down on the bed again, so I let him lean against the headboard. I ran into the bathroom for a cold washcloth to put on his head. Then, I ran into the other bedroom, called the ambulance, and got dressed quickly. I then started to dress him with underwear, socks, pants, and shirt. I got him to the hallway again, and that's as far as he said he could go. I sat him at him at the top of the steps and leaned him against the wall. All this time he was complaining about his severe head pain.'

Dr. Edward nodded, and Gabrielle continued,

'The ambulance came quickly, and I ran down to open the front door. They came in and put a helmet on his head and laid him carefully on a gurney. They asked for a list of all his medicines, which I said I would bring with me. I kept a current list for his Doctor's visits.'

"Did he see his Primary Care Doctor on a regular basis?" Dr. Edward inquired.

"Yes, he saw Dr. Kastoris at least once a month, if not more. He felt close to him; in fact, Nick and I often went out to dinner with Dr. and Mrs. Kastoris."

"Has Dr. Kastoris been here to see him since he was hospitalized?"

"No. When Nick was taken to ICU, I called Dr. Kastoris and told him what had transpired, and he said to keep him informed. Sincerely, Dr. Bobbie, with so much happening, I felt that Dr. Kastoris should have taken more of an interest. He should have come to see Nick during the first three days of his hospitalization. I didn't have time to keep calling him with updates. I am very disappointed in him. It's not as though Nick was just another patient, that he saw once a year! We even invited him and his wife to several of Nick's shows that featured Nick's Big Band Orchestra. I'm disappointed in him, and truly hurt!"

Dr. Edward shook his head.

"Yes, I can understand that. Please continue. The ambulance brought him here?"

"No, they took him to the Emergency Room at Community Hospital, because they said it was closer, and they felt it necessary to get him to a hospital fast! The staff at Community did a fine job. Immediately they took him in for a CAT scan. After the Doctors got the results, they made the recommendation that Nick to be transported to either here, or to another hospital in the vicinity. It was necessary to go to one with a neurological department. I selected Asclepius Christian Medical Center because it's the closest to the house, and I thought it had a good reputation. He was in ICU Sunday, Monday, and Tuesday. Then he was transferred to this room early on Wednesday morning. He was evaluated by rehab and passed their tests with flying colors on Thursday morning, and they said he would be home in a few days." Gabriella shuddered and broke down into tears.

"And then on Thursday afternoon, in walked Dr. Hilda German, stating she wanted to give him a sleeping pill! How insane! That's it, Dr. Edward. It's the sleeping pill that did this to him! I know that! Don't you agree, Doctor Edward? I mean, a man in his state … you wouldn't have prescribed a sleeping pill, would you?"

Dr. Edward offered no response! His eyes stayed glued to Nick's chart. Instead he asked,

"When was the last time Mr. Carcioni ate?"

Gabriella tried to think.

"He has not had a good appetite for the past five days—just a few forkfuls of this and that. Hardly anything."

"Okay, then. He needs nourishment badly," Dr. Edward stated as he made more notes on the chart. "I'm going to order a Feeding Tube because he obviously needs nutrition. Also, I will have a Filter put into his lungs later today, just in case a blood clot forms. The Filter will stop it from going to the heart, which would be fatal! Let's get that going, and hopefully he will awaken very soon. You should eat regularly, too, Mrs. Carcioni. When was the last time you had a good meal?"

"I don't know. Probably six days ago. I munch during the day."

"Do you have any friends or family members who could stay with you?"

Gabriella shook her head.

"I don't have any family close by; they're all out of state. And I am not permitting any visitors here. That's on the chart. No visitors! There is nothing here for anyone to see. I know Nick wouldn't want to have people gawking at him, while he's in this state. No, I'm here alone. I'm doing fine. And this way, I don't get distracted. I watch everything that is going into him, or happening to him. I trust nothing. I do talk to family members and several close friends almost daily. Also, I email, friends and family members every few days, giving them updates on his situation. They all want to hear about Nick, as he is so well loved by so many, and they are praying for him."

Before leaving, Dr. Edward added,

"On Monday, I'll also have the Head of Neurology look at Nick's CAT scans and MRIs. We'll get the entire team involved in this, until we find out why this has happened!"

"Thank you, Dr. Edward. Thank you!" Gabriella couldn't help repeating herself.

At the doorway, Dr. Edward added,

"Neurology will probably order more tests next week. Hopefully Mr. Carcioni will wake up tomorrow or very soon. That's what we must hope for now. Till then, we will do all we can. May I suggest that you take care of yourself, too, Mrs. Carcioni? Make sure you eat and get some rest."

"Yes, I will. Thank you, Doctor."

CHAPTER 14

FEEDING TUBE INSERTED

Shortly after Dr. Edward left the room, aides came to take Nick downstairs to have the Feeding Tube inserted. As always, Gabriella walked alongside the gurney, holding his hand and explaining to him what was transpiring. Down to the first floor the elevator descended, to the same place area where they had gone for the CAT scan. There they waited for about twenty minutes, and finally the aides wheeled Nick into a private room, Gabriella at his side.

Soon, attractive, blue-eyed Nurse Rachel entered and proceeded to administer some anesthesia.

"Wait!" Gabriella blurted. "What are you doing?"

Stunned, Nurse Rachel replied,

"I'm going to give him the anesthesia required for the feeding tube insertion."

"No, Wait!" Gabriella placed her hand over Nick's arm. "We have a dreadful situation here. He was given a sleeping pill last night, which he *never* should have been given, and now we cannot wake him! He does not need any more medicine to keep him calm or knock him out!

No. Absolutely not! I want to see the person in charge here. Please, get your Supervisor here!"

Nurse Rachel left quickly to get her Supervisor. A few minutes later, a striking brunette with long flowing hair entered.

"Mrs. Carcioni, I'm the Supervisor, Johanna. What's going on?"

Gabriella repeated what she had said to Nurse Rachel.

Supervisor Johanna was baffled.

"Oh my, this is awful. I must say I have never been confronted with this situation before."

She leaned forward to Nick's face and called out his name loudly several times, asking him to awaken. There was no movement, and no reply.

"Mr. Carcioni, wake up! This is Supervisor Johanna. Mr. Carcioni!"

Upon seeing that Nick was not responding, she shook her head.

"This is an extremely unusual. I am so very sorry about this, Mrs. Carcioni, but I am bound by certain regulations, and we *must* sedate him. We cannot take a chance that he will wake up during the operation. You understand. That would be very traumatic for him. You wouldn't want that. I know you wouldn't. I'm very sorry!"

Shaking her head, she asked,

"How long has he been like this?

Gabriella began to ramble almost like a tape recorder,

> "Since last night. He was given a sleeping pill last night
> on the orders of Dr. Hilda German even though he has
> blood on all sides of his swollen brain. I told her I didn't
> think it was the right thing to do, but she ordered it,
> and the nurse gave it to him last night before I could
> stop her. Dr. German said she knew what she was doing.
> However, at this moment, I don't think she does!"

Supervisor Johanna shook her head in disgust.

> "Oh my, such a shame! But, you see, he must be given
> the anesthesia! I know this will *not* help his situation,
> but we have procedures that must be followed."

Then, nodding to Nurse Rachel, she motioned to give him
the anesthesia, and in departing she touched Gabriella's arm
saying,

> "I do hope that he wakes up tonight, Mrs. Carcioni. Poor
> guy. I'm so sorry!"

When finished, Nurse Rachel remarked,

> "I'll say a special prayer for him tonight. And for you,
> Mrs. Carcioni. We'll be in shortly to get him."

Over an hour passed while they performed the procedure, and
finally Nick was wheeled out with the tube in place. He was
soon back upstairs to his room with Gabriella holding his hand.

At around 6:00 p.m, the dinner trays were being delivered
again. In walked the aide, leaving the tray for Nick. Once
again, Gabriella had not eaten all day so she went eagerly to

see what had been delivered. As she lifted the lid to each dish, she remarked aloud for Nick to hear,

> "Wow! Look at this, Nicky. Chicken noodle soup, cornbread, and mandarin oranges for dessert. Perfect. Come on, babe time for dinner. You say you're still not hungry...Okay, I'll sample it for you, and see if it is up to your standards. I'm kind of hungry!"

When she finished, she walked over to Nick's bedside and began talking to him as she had done on days previous, thinking it was good for him to hear her voice. She kissed his hand and lowered his bed so it would almost match the height of the chair, which she pulled up close to the bed. Then she put an extra pillow next to his shoulder. She laid her head on the pillow and grabbed his hand, snuggling as close as she could as she repeated how much she loved him and how much she missed him.

> "I need you to wake up, darling," she whispered.

> "Drove your car today. Yep! She purrs like a kitten. I'm taking extra good care of her for you, babe, and believe it or not, I could tell your car misses you. That's right. It was as if the car was saying to me, "Who are you? Where's Nicky?'" She tried her best to be cheerful. "Please follow my voice, sweetheart, and come back to me. You're lost in there somewhere, and I desperately need for you to come home to me. Follow my voice, baby. It'll bring you back to me!"

She wiggled around to get more comfortable, still holding his hand.

> "Today, you have a *new* Doctor. His name is Dr. Bobbie Edward. Tall, nice looking, from the UK. He seems

very knowledgeable. You'll like him. He has a strong English accent, but you'll understand him—no worries. He ordered your Feeding Tube because he feels you need some nourishment, and that's why you keep sleeping. You need food, sweetie. It makes sense, doesn't it? Yeah, I think we are on the right track now. You'll wake up tomorrow because you'll have had all this food going into your system all night. It's chocolate, your favorite flavor. Yummy! Once you're awake, you'll go back to eating regularly, so no worries about that. I plan to make all your Italian favorites—Braciole, Raviolis, Italian garlic Pork Chops with peppers and potatoes, and of course we have to have our weekly Italian beef sandwiches with sweet and hot peppers at the Stand. Come back, baby, I need you."

She spoke softly as her face was being washed by unstoppable tears.

Gabriella thought endlessly about ways to help Nick wake up. She played CD's of Nick's Combo and Big Band Orchestra every day, all day long, so he could hear his own singing and his Orchestra. Likewise, she brought other CDs of popular singers that Nick had worked with throughout his career. She was determined to do everything possible to reach his inner mind.

Playfully she announced,

> "And now, ladies and gentlemen, we have a big treat for you! Mr. Nick Carcioni and his Big Band Orchestra are here for your listening enjoyment," and she hit the play button.

> "Yes, ladies and gentlemen, relax and enjoy Nick Carcioni's melodic singing. And listen to that sexy sax

sound!" She stroked Nick's brow. "Oh, how I love your singing and sax playing, my Darling," she said sincerely. "Everyone loves you!" After listening to Nick's Big Band CD, she replaced it with the Nick Carcioni Combo CD. The first song to play was "Apples and Bananas," a cute bouncy tune that Nick had released as a single in the late '50s.

"Apples and Bananas" sold nearly 100,000 copies and sales were continuing to climb. However, a well-known Big Band TV personality, heard the tune and put it on his newly released album, and so people stopped buying Nick's version. Nick had told Gabriella that "Apples and Bananas" had become a turntable hit, especially in Chicago. Surprisingly, even though it had been about thirty years since it was released, when people saw Nick and Gabriella at a restaurant or party, the first thing they would smile and say, "Hi, Nick! Apples and Bananas!"

Nick's Big Band Orchestra performed for over 60 years, and ranged from 14- 40 musicians, depending on the celebrity performer he was fronting. Additionally, Nick had his own Combo for smaller gigs. His Combo CD featured a beautiful love song called "Always Together," which Nick referred to as *their* song. When Nick was on stage, he would always announce before singing it,

> "This is for my lovely wife, Gabriella," and the crowd would applaud.

Sitting by his bedside, listening to the CD, Gabriella stared at him and began singing along as she choked on her tears: "Always together...."

> "Sing with me, Nicky. Sing to me, just one more time," she cried.

It was now nearing 10:00 p.m., and there was no change in Nick's condition. Gabriella thought it was probably too soon, but she was still hopeful that he would at least moan or move his arms or legs, or even a finger! But no, he continued to lie still. Even though it was late, Gabriella waited for the staff members to come to insert the Filter.

Hope they didn't forget, she thought.

Meantime, another patient was being admitted in the second bed in Nicky's room. The curtain was drawn between them, so she could not see who was there, but it sounded like a young man and older woman.

Could be his wife or mother? she thought.

The woman was making sure that she completed the patient's meal selections so that they would start promptly the next morning. She was asking the aide questions as the aide helped the man out of bed to use the bathroom.

Concerned that Nick's music was disturbing them, Gabriella stood up and moved the curtain back slightly.

"Is the music bothering you?"

"Oh, no," replied the woman joyfully. "We're loving it. I just love that music!"

"Yeah," said the young guy.

Gabriella opened the curtain further so she could see them. She introduced herself.

"Hi, I'm Gabriella, and my husband is Nick. He's in a Coma so I'm playing his CDs to help him come out of it. That's his Orchestra playing behind him as he sings."

"Wow, really! He has such a lovely voice ... a lot like Sinatra."

"And we were listening to you sing. You have a lovely voice too," she noted.

"Oh, thank you," replied a somewhat embarrassed Gabriella. "What's your name?"

"I'm Donna, and this my son, Daniel. What happened to Nick?" she asked.

"He fell at our house about six days ago and hit his head. He was in ICU for three days, and now that the blood that is all over his brain is starting to go back into his body, they moved him up here. He was supposed to go to rehab and be home in a few days, but Dr. Hilda German, the doctor who was assigned to him, ordered a sleeping pill for him, even though I didn't think it was right, and I told her so ... But, she went ahead and gave it to him anyway. That pushed him immediately into a Coma during the night! He won't wake up. He doesn't moan. He doesn't move. He doesn't respond to anyone or anything."

"Oh, my God, I am so very sorry! How devastating!" Donna expressed, and Daniel nodded in agreement.

"How awful! What does the Doctor say now?" Donna asked.

"Oh, I insisted she be removed. She is NOT his Doctor anymore! I don't want her anywhere near my husband! Starting today, I have a new doctor, Dr. Bobbie Edward. He seems very knowledgeable, and he ordered a Feeding Tube and lung Filter for Nick immediately. We are all praying that the nourishment will help him to awaken by tomorrow."

She turned to Donna's son.

"What's wrong with you Daniel?" Gabriella asked, changing the subject.

"Well," replied Daniel regretfully, "I've been on drugs for several years, and now I'm having bad side effects! I passed out at Mom's house the other day, and that's how I ended up in here. They think it's my heart," he answered candidly. "I get the shakes, have hallucinations and nightmares. I've lost most of my teeth. I've tried to quit many times, but the habit keeps drawing me back in. They say they will try to help me in one of their programs here. I hope so. I tried to quit many times, but it's *extremely* hard. I seem to always fall right back into the habit again. I hate it! I'm so sorry that I ruined my life like this. I have two little adorable boys, who love me. I'm divorced. She doesn't want me around the kids, while I am on drugs. I agree with her, but I do miss being with them so much!"

Daniel continued...

"I want to see my boys grow up, and I definitely want to stress to them *'don't do drugs!'*

"My liver and kidneys are screwed up now, too."

"What drugs did you take?" asked Gabriella.

"Mostly heroin, but you name it, I tried it—meth, marijuana, cocaine."

"I'm sorry. I'll pray that they can help you, Daniel. You're so young! You have that going for you," added Gabriella sadly.

Donna nodded, looking down at her knitting, which she had in her lap.

"Gabriella. Such a beautiful name," she said softly. "I will say a prayer for your husband tonight when I say my Rosary."

"Thank you," Gabriella replied.

Daniel quickly added,

"And she *will!* When she says she is going to pray for someone, she does!"

"Thank you. That's so good to hear," Gabriella said. "I'll keep you both in my prayers. And that *you* can count on!"

"Thank you," whispered Donna. "We sure need it!"

As Gabriella placed the CD and player back into her carry-on, she said,

"Well, it's nearing 10:30 p.m. so I think I'll call it a day. I look forward to seeing you both tomorrow."

Returning to Nick's bedside, she bent over and gave him kisses, saying,

"It's late, darling—10:30 p.m.—so I am going to head home and go to bed. I'll be back tomorrow morning, bright and early, and I'm looking forward to you shouting, "Good morning, Gabriella!"

She held his hands and kissed them.

"For now, you rest and dream of us together in Vegas on vacation. "I wuv you," she said with a smile. He used to always respond, "I wuv you more!" and she would respond, "No, I wuv *you* more!" So, she pretended as though he was saying that to her now, and said, "No, I wuv *you* more! Good night, my love! See you early tomorrow morning. A million kisses ..."

Gabriella walked out into the hall and went to the Nurses' station to ask about the Filter to be inserted in Nicky's lungs.

"My husband, Nicholas Carcioni, is supposed to get a Filter inserted in his lungs tonight. Do you know what time that is going to happen?" she asked a Nurse.

"Nick who? What room is he in?" she asked quickly.

"Nicholas Carcioni, in Room 804."

"Let me look at his chart. Yes, I see Dr. Edward ordered it. I'll call downstairs and see if I can find out for you."

"Thank you." Gabriella noticed the nurse's name tag—Monica—as the young woman dialed the phone. *Seems to be a new Nurse here every day*, she thought.

"This is Nurse Monica on the eighth floor. Mr. Nicholas Carcioni is supposed to get an IVC Filter. Do you have any idea when that might happen? Okay. I'll tell his wife. Thank you." She turned to Gabriella.

"They said about midnight."

"Oh, that late!" Gabriella responded with a sigh. "Is it a long procedure?"

"No, it's routine. Half an hour at the most," Nurse Monica replied, as she continued pulling files.

"As I understand it, the Filter prevents any blood clots from going to the lungs, right?"

"Yes, that's right. If he developed a pulmonary embolism, it could be deadly," she stated. "This will prevent that." placing her files on the counter.

"It's late, and you've been here all day, Mrs. Carcioni. Go home, because when they say midnight, it could be three in the morning! Go. Get your rest," Monica coaxed.

An exhausted Gabriella took her advice and went home.

Note: *Two weeks later, Gabriella noticed that Daniel no longer occupied the other bed. When she asked, she learned that he had died in his sleep the previous night. Rest in peace, dear Daniel! May your sons grow up in a drug-free America!*

Illegal drugs infiltrating America have killed more of our youth, than in all wars.

CHAPTER 15

DAY 2: NICK STILL IN A DEEP SLEEP

It had been a long unsettling night! Gabriella looked at her bedside clock, reading 11:30p.m.

"Still Friday, Gabriella. Get some sleep," she murmured.

Her mind kept replaying the horrendous shock of seeing Nick in his motionless sleep state, so helpless and mentally devoid. It was a picture that was burned in her mind, and would not give her the peace or rest that she craved.

"Dear God," she prayed aloud, "Is he going to be all right? Will Dr. Edward be able to awaken Nick, and will he awaken tomorrow as Dr. German keeps promising? Is he in a Coma? I am the *only* one using the word, *Coma*. The Doctors keep using *deep sleep*. It's as though they are deliberately avoiding saying the word, *Coma*. They are probably fearful that I will sue them and the hospital...and they may be very right! Oh, Jesus, help me. Bring him back!" She sobbed.

I can't stop blaming myself, Gabriella thought as she tried to get comfortable in the bed. *I should have been more forceful,*

134

when the doctor mentioned the sleeping pill. I should have put my foot down and told her forcefully, "I'm the wife, and I said no sleeping pill!"

A remorseful Gabriella screamed from her lonely bed,

> "I will never forgive myself! Never! Oh, Nicky can you ever forgive me!"

As she drown her tears in her pillow, she recalled what Dr. Cristina had said to her earlier that day:

> "You are not a doctor. You have no medical training. How can you presume to know if the sleeping pill was right or wrong? You had no other alternative but to have trust in Dr. German. All you had going for you was your gut feeling—your instinct, your intuition—which may have been right, or it may have been wrong! You will never know. Think of it this way—if you had stopped the sleeping pill from being administered, and he ended up in this same condition, you would have blamed yourself for that also. Gabriella, it's not your fault!"

With tears burning her eyes, she choked,

> "Dear God, please let him wake up tomorrow, and be back to normal! Please don't let him be in a Coma! I need him so much!"

Tossing and turning, she experienced nightmares throughout her sleep. Finally, she awoke and got out of bed at 5:00 a.m. She was still exhausted, she grabbed her robe, walked downstairs to make a cup of coffee and take her blood pressure pills. At the bottom of the stairs, she looked around and felt the loneliness in the deserted house, almost too much to bear. Standing in the kitchen, in a trance state, she put the coffee on, and then forced down her medicine, accompanied by a few crackers. Grasping onto the hot cup of coffee with both hands, she got lost in a million thoughts. Deeper and deeper she sank into depressive thinking, that soon resulted in intense anger and fear.

What would I do without him? she asked herself. *I can't imagine life without him. I don't want to think about life without him. I need him to hold me, to give me one of his strong hugs. In his arms is the only place I find comfort. That's the only place I feel safe! He's my best friend, my lover, my protector, my knight in shining armor. Oh, God, he's my everything! I can't live without him. I don't want to live without him!*

"Stop it, Gabriella!" she reprimanded herself out loud.

"Stop thinking negatively! Change your thinking! Think positive thoughts. You must realign your thinking. Remember the Law of Attraction!"

I must think Positively, she thought. *He IS going to wake up today. Yes, today will be a glorious day. We both will be talking and laughing and planning things again. Get dressed. Get over there. Your Nicky is waiting for you!*

Quickly, she snapped back to reality, carried her coffee upstairs, and proceeded to get dressed.

"Have to look pretty for my angel," she remarked as she looked in the mirror. "Don't want to scare him to death without my makeup," she half joked trying to smile, as negative thoughts fought constantly to enter her mind. She repeated,

"He will awaken. He will be okay. He will return to normal. I will not let negativity grip me. I am only going to think POSITIVE thoughts! My Nicholas will awaken today!"

Dressed and ready to go, she opened the garage door. The sight of Nick's white Cadillac DeVille stopped her in her tracks. Staring at it for a few moments, she then touched the hood saying,

"He'll be home soon," as if it could understand her.

I think I'll drive his car again today, she thought. *It makes me feel closer to him. Besides, he will probably ask me if I ran his car recently.* She chuckled. *Typical guy. He takes such good care of his car! It will put his mind at ease to know that I have been running it until he gets home, to keep the battery charged.*

Stepping back inside the house, she grabbed his car keys from the nut dish, where he had laid them near the door just seven days ago. The nut dish was an antique wooden dish that Gabriella's parents had owned all their married lives, for over 50 years. They used to have it on the dining room table, and it was always overflowing with various nuts, especially during the holiday season. When her parents passed away, Gabriella took the dish as a memento, as it brought back many vivid happy memories of family gatherings. The dish was now placed on the foyer table of their home, and Nick would always put his car keys in it, when he entered the house.

With the garage door open, she stood there staring at the pouring rain. Lightning and thunder vibrated the area. *Another rainy day,* she thought.

How very appropriate. Even the sky is crying for you, Nicky. I must be extra careful in my driving today.

Upon entering the car, she started to familiarize herself with it again.

Where are the wipers? No. They're on the left side. This car is so different from my Hyundai. "Dear Lord, keep me protected, as I drive this car," she prayed.

When she reached Asclepius Christian Medical Center, the line of cars going into the parking garage was exceptionally long, just as it had been every day before.

"Please let there be a space for me when I get to the entrance," she whispered. *I have way too much to carry, and it's pouring buckets,* she thought.

Once again, God answered her prayer, and there was one space available within the covered garage. "Thank you. Thank you," she said aloud.

Rushing into the hospital and into the elevator, she could hardly wait to reach the eighth floor. In her rush, she even forgot to stop and get her ticket validated. *Must remember to do that before I leave today,* she thought. The elevator was almost full again, but she insisted on being the last one to squeeze in. Finally, the eighth-floor button lit up. The instant the doors opened, she had one foot out, as she dragged all her possessions behind her. Down the hall she raced. "Good morning!" she called out to the nurses at the nurses' station.

"Good morning," they replied automatically, preoccupied with their work, not even looking up.

Entering Room 804, she made as much noise as she possibly could, slamming the carry-on and shopping bag onto the table and her purse onto the chair.

"Good morning, Nicholas my darling," she called out loudly, purposely not looking at him.

Silence!

Oh, No! Come on, Nicky, please! Thoughts screamed in her head.

"Good morning, Sweetheart. Gabriella's here!" she called out.

Again, only silence.

She turned and ran to his bedside instantly.

"Nick, it's me, Gabriella. Please wake up, sweetheart!" Fear and trepidation started again to grip her!

"You *will* wake up today! You *have* to wake up today. The Doctor said you would!" Oh, Nicky, I'm begging you ... Wake up!" she wailed, burying her head on his chest. Putting her face close to his, she kissed his lips gently, and softly said, "I love you!"

No response. No movement. Her tears dripped down onto his face.

"Hey, baby," she insisted,

"I *need* you to wake up. I *need* you to look at me. I *need* you to tell me *you love me* again! Please, darling, open your eyes. You've been sleeping long enough. Time to wake up. *Please*, Nicky!"

139

"You know I'm going to do everything to get you well again, right? You know I won't give up on you! I won't let you down. You're my entire world. Don't you dare think about leaving me, Nicholas Carcioni! You're not leaving me, till I say you can leave! Do you understand me? Do you? My God, I love you, and I need you so much. You're my angel from heaven!" she sobbed uncontrollably, collapsing once again onto his chest.

In need of tissue, she rose to wipe her face, and then inserted his Big Band CD into the player. Pulling up a chair to his bedside, she lowered the bed and laid a pillow next to his chest. Resting her head next to him, she held his hand in hers, kissing his fingers.

"Your singing is so beautiful, and your Orchestra is the best! Wake up, sweetheart, and sing to me again."

Shortly thereafter she drifted into a comfortable sleep, thinking how much this man meant to her. Suddenly, the feeling of someone being close to the bed, roused her from her sleep.

"I'm sorry," said a Nurse she did not recognize.

"Who are you? And what are you doing?" Gabriella asked hastily.

"Hi, I'm Nurse Cammi. Sorry. Didn't mean to scare you."

"Oh." Gabriella sat up in a dazed state. "What are you doing?"

"I just need to take some blood," Nurse Cammi replied.

"Okay. More tests? Who ordered more tests? Dr. Edward?"

"Yes. How's your husband doing?" Nurse Cammi asked.

"He still won't wake up."

"What happened to him?"

"Dr. Hilda German gave him 50 milligrams of Trezidone—a sleeping pill—two nights ago, when he had blood on all sides of his brain, due to a fall at our house. What you're seeing here is the result! I say he's in a Coma, but she won't admit to that! She keeps saying he's in a *"deep sleep."*

"Oh, my God!" responded Nurse Cammi.

"We're taught in our first year of Nursing school that you try to keep a person awake when they had a recent head injury—and blood all over his brain! Wow, that doesn't make any sense—" She suddenly stopped in midsentence, obviously thinking she was saying too much.

"That's what I was always told," Gabriella said in disgust.

"Thank you, Nurse Cammi. This conversation was exactly what I needed to wake me up fully. I have so much anger toward Dr. German, and I'm waiting for her to walk in her this morning. She said my husband would wake up *today,* and so far, she's *wrong again!* I'm beyond furious with her! I truly believe the woman is insane! I insisted on a new Doctor, and Patient Advocacy sent Dr. Bobbie Edward. He's from the UK. Do you know him?"

"Yes, he's wonderful! Very knowledgeable, and handsome too. I think he's one of our best."

"Well, that's good to hear. Thank God!" Gabriella replied.

"Although Dr. German is not his Doctor anymore, I'm waiting for her to step in here one final time to check on Nick. I'm looking forward to telling her exactly what I think of her, and that I'm privy to her Agenda, for even prescribing that sleeping pill."

"Agenda, Mrs. Carcioni?"

"Yes, Nurse Cammi. She had a reason for prescribing it, and it *wasn't* to benefit my husband," answered Gabriella.

Nurse Cammi just shook her head and whispered softly,

"I'm so sorry." as she departed.

CHAPTER 16

"GET OUT, AND DON'T EVER COME BACK"

Distraught and alone, Gabriella sat by Nick's bedside recalling happy memories of their 33 years together. She looked around the room through tear-blurred vision, asking,

> *"How could it end this way? How could a man who was so health conscious, a regular visitor to his Primary Care Doctor, a man who read countless books on staying healthy, daily took his vitamins ... how could be caught in this unforeseeable web of malpractice?"*

She reached for her tablet and began writing another email to their friends and family members. The numbers kept growing, as many people had been asking to be added to the list. She refused no one. She wrote:

> Nick is still in a "deep sleep" for the second day! No! I'm so sorry to inform you that he did not wake up, as Dr. German said he would! I'm trying everything possible to stir his mind and arouse him back here to reality. It's so extremely difficult to watch him in this lifeless state. As you all know, Nick was such a dynamo, always running, promoting his Big Band, making phone calls, arranging

luncheons with friends, always on the move! The fire and spirit inside him has been removed completely, and I will have my say with Dr. Hilda German. Guaranteed. I promise you! Chaplain Roxanna stopped in today and tried to console me. I asked her to pray for Nick. She said she would put him on their prayer line. I am grateful. My Aunt Kay in Lexington, Kentucky, is putting him on their Prayer Line, who I call The Angels of Kentucky, because they always seem to work miracles."

As she continued writing, Gabriella heard footsteps enter the room.

"How's he doing?" said a familiar voice.

Gabriella recognized the voice to be that of Dr. Hilda German. Slowly, she looked up from her tablet.

"My husband still has not awakened, Doctor German! Look at what you've done! You are no longer my husband's Doctor, and not permitted in this room after this visit! I made that perfectly clear with Yvonne Falonzo of Patient Advocacy."

Gabriella spoke with intensity, as she rose from her seat.

Dr. German was quick to reply in an apologetic tone.

"I'm upset that you don't want me to be your husband's Doctor anymore. I wish you would reconsider, Mrs. Carcioni."

Gabriella walked from around the bed. Staring Dr. German in the eyes, she stated emphatically,

"*No!* I will *not* reconsider. Look at him!" she said pointing to Nick. "My husband is in a *Coma* thanks to you. I don't want you anywhere near my husband, do you understand? You're out! You're fired!"

"We have a *new* Doctor, and he seems to have some intelligence. I just pray he's not too late! I told you specifically the day you walked into this room, and announced that you were Nick's doctor, that he did **not** need a sleeping pill, and that he had blood on all sides of his brain. But, no, you wouldn't listen. You said,

'I know what I'm doing!' Well, I'm here to tell you, you do *NOT* know what you are doing, Dr. German! You had no right to ignore my opinion. I'm his *wife*, damn you! My hatred and anger toward you at this moment is intense, and you have succeeded in making me hate myself too!" Gabriella stated firmly.

"What? Why, Mrs. Carcioni?" asked the perplexed doctor.

Turning quickly to wipe her tears, Gabriella answered,

"Because, Doctor, I should have *demanded* that you *not* give him that pill!"

"I should have walked with you to the desk, and watched you write it on his chart, 'No sleeping pill, per his wife!' But, I didn't, did I? I will never forgive myself for the rest of my life, if he doesn't come out of this. I swear! All thanks to you, Dr. Hilda German. You're an egotistical maniac, Doctor! I should have stood up to you, Doctor or not. I should have overridden your suggestion with force. It makes no sense to anyone who hears what you did. Even your own staff here, are completely baffled by your thinking! You should be prosecuted for your stupidity and arrogance!"

In her defense, Dr. German interrupted.

"Mrs. Carcioni, You don't know, that it was the sleeping pill that did this!"

Gabriella took a step toward Dr. German, raising her voice...

"*Yes, I do! And,* on top of that, you prescribed the highest dosage! *And,* to add insult to injury, when Dr. Cristina called you and told you of his coma state, you said you would only give him 25 milligrams instead of 50 last night! *You hadn't even seen him yet!* The man is in a Coma, and you still are prescribing medicine. *You're insane ... truly insane!* You did all this to a man who was in a very delicate condition—swollen brain, blood on all sides."

Then, Gabriella took a step closer to the doctor, looked her squarely in the eyes, and stated the profound truth,

"And I know exactly why you did it, Doctor!"

Dr. German tensed up, frowning.

"What? What do you mean, you know *why* I did it!"

Nodding her head, Gabriella replied,

"That's right. I know exactly *why* you did it. It wasn't that you wanted my husband to get enough rest, so that he would have energy for Rehab the next day. No, that wasn't it at all. You didn't care one iota if he was rested or not!"

Dr. German stood there frozen, and didn't say a word.

Gabriella continued...

"You gave him that sleeping pill because you cared more about the Nurse on the night shift, than you did about my husband! She didn't want to be bothered with him. She wanted to sit on her fat ass all night. That's how you silence patients—you give them sleeping pills!"

Dr. German's mouth opened in shock, but Gabriella hadn't finished talking.

"How shallow you are, Doctor. I see right through you. I even know the name of the nurse, who didn't want to be bothered that night. Yes, Doctor German! I see right through you *and* Nurse Destini."

Dr. German gasped, but Gabriella would not be silenced.

"This is not over, Doctor. Not by a long shot. Pass that on to Nurse Destini too! I will have the *last word* regarding this fiasco. This I promise you! Now, get out!" demanded Gabriella, pointing to the door. "And don't ever step foot in this room again—you or Destini!"

Both women stared at each other in silence, for what seemed like an eternity. Dr. German spoke not a word, as she could see the fire in Gabriella's eyes, and a rage that would not even permit Gabriella to blink. Clearly, Dr. German was shaken by all that Gabriella had surmised, and knew she was spot-on in her thinking. Dr. German's facial expression clearly conveyed her thoughts.

> *How did she figure this out? Had someone here told this woman? How?*

Tears began to well in Dr. German's eyes. She had no more defense to offer. With eyes lowered to the floor, she swiftly exited the room, never to be seen again on the eighth floor.

Normally, Gabriella had always been a soft-spoken person, and one who did not want to make waves. She held much inside behind her smile. Always described as reserved, classy, and quite intelligent, she bottled up many opinions. It was her Nicholas who constantly preached to her, that she should speak up, and not hold anything inside.

"If you have something to say, speak up!" he'd advised.

"Don't be a closet talker."

This was easy for Nick to say, as he was forthright and direct. He always said what was on his mind, no holds barred. And he never pulled any punches. At times, people may not have liked what he said, but in the end, they respected him for his honesty. People always knew where they stood with Nick.

Finally, today, Gabriella had summoned the courage and fortitude she needed to speak, in a fashion that her Nicholas would have been proud. If only he could have heard—and maybe he had.

Now that he was unable to speak for himself, she gained the words that he would have spoken. Her entire demeanor changed dramatically, never to be the same again. She became like a lioness defending her cub, and came out of the gate at rapid speed. Her senses were keen, as she promised to watch every single thing from that point on, regarding her beloved Nicholas. She would view everything with much scrutiny. From this day forward, she would question every administration of medicine, and stay by his side all day and into the night, to protect him from further harm.

Nicholas Carcioni was her entire world, and she was not going to listen to any lame excuse, as to why this had to happen to him. She vowed to him, at his bedside, that she would do everything possible in her power, to bring him back from the edge of mental darkness, that was draining his life. She would not be deterred. She would never give up on him!

Gabriella believed, with every fiber of her being, that it was the sleeping pill prescribed by Dr. Hilda German, that had taken her Nicholas away. No one would ever convince her of anything different! Ever!

CHAPTER 17

FRIENDS STILL IN SHOCK

Gabriella left the hospital numb from a day of shock. That morning, she had tried to muster some optimism that Dr. German's prediction would be correct, and Nick would awaken that day. However, her tears flowed continually, as she soon realized that Dr. German did not know when, and even, *if* Nick would ever awaken. Exiting the elevator, in a depressed state, she walked into the ever-busy garage.

As she looked at her cell, she saw that her neighbor, Pamela, had left a message of concern, so she decided to stop by their house, on the way home to give them the horrendous news. It was Pamela and Les who had come to the Community Hospital on Sunday, when Nick was rushed there by ambulance. Because of their close rapport, Les wanted to make sure his buddy was going to be all right. Les was from Poland, and though he'd been in America for several years, he still had a very strong Polish accent. He didn't associate with many other neighbors. Pamela was a college professor.

One day, Nick had started a conversation with Les, telling him one of his favorite jokes. Les couldn't stop laughing, and that was the beginning of their close friendship. Each time they saw each other outside, they always had lengthy conversations. Les used to compliment Nick on how young he looked for his age, how he looked to be in such good health, and how active he remained. Nick always attributed his youthfulness to Gabriella.

Every year, Les planted a bountiful vegetable garden. He was obsessed with every detail of the garden, insuring that the rows were perfectly straight, and that the selection of delicious vegetables was varied. Often Les and Pam would send over a bag of tomatoes, cucumbers, zucchini, and peppers from the garden. Gabriella and Nick would relish these homegrown delicacies for several meals.

Gabriella thought to herself,

> *Thank you, dear God, for sending these kind people to be our neighbors. Nick and I are so tremendously grateful, for their loving friendship!*

Gabriella pulled into her neighbors' driveway. She hadn't spoken to them all day, because of all the drama surrounding Nick. They were so happy to see her, and of course, they were expecting good news about Nick's recovery. Pamela said she had called earlier, but there had been no answer, so they were a bit concerned.

"You look exhausted, Gabriella!" she remarked.

"Yes. It's been a trying day. Let's sit down. I have much to tell you." They moved to the living room.

Les immediately offered some brandy, and Gabriella accepted. When everyone was seated, Gabriella told them about Nick's drastic change, emphasizing that the doctor believed he was only "sleeping," and no one in the hospital was using the word, *Coma.*

Even so, when Dr. German visited today, she could not predict if, or when, Nicholas might wake up. It was painfully obvious, that she had no idea the lasting effect that sleeping pill was going to have on him! She had run out of options, ideas, and excuses.

Shaking their heads, they both started to cry.

> "I've never heard of anyone getting a sleeping pill with a recent brain injury. It doesn't make sense, and I'm not even in the medical field," voiced Pamela.

> "Oh my God," cried Les. "My good buddy! He's got to get well. He must get well!"

Without hesitation, Les jumped up, saying they had to go to the Grotto of The Blessed Mother, located in the next town, to plead for Nick's recovery.

> "Pamela, we're going there first thing tomorrow morning! I will get on my knees and beg for him to get well!" he cried.

> "Yes, Les, let's do that! We'll bring some flowers from the garden too," agreed Pamela.

The tears continued to flow, and they each tried to come up with some positive thoughts, regarding when Nicholas might awaken, and the severity of the dosage. All they could do was pray that tomorrow Nicholas would awaken. Gabriella did not stay long. Exhausted, she left, saying she would be in touch the next day.

> "Pray, dear friends. Pray hard, please!"

Vowing to do so, they both hugged Gabriella. They were all in tears as they said Goodnight.

When Gabriella got home, she immediately sent an email to friends and family members with the same disappointing news. As she typed, Marty, Nick's good friend for 40 years and a member of his Big Band Orchestra, phoned and was so distraught.

> "I'll pray on my prayer mat immediately," he said. "Nick *has* to get well! He just *has* to!"

CHAPTER 18

"WILL YOU MARRY ME?"

"Cause there's something in a Sunday, that makes a body feel alone,' sings Johnny Cash.

The hospital was especially quiet on this Sunday, July 29, 2012, as most of the doctors were off, or making a few rounds very early in the morning. It truly was a different kind of day—a peaceful day for reflection, and an extremely lonely day, when your loved one is comatose.

As Nick's CDs played, Gabriella couldn't help but recall so much about Nicholas, this marvelous, kind man with the sensual voice, and loving heart. Her mind drifted back 33 years, as she reminisced about how they met. Yes, they'd had had their ups and downs, as all married couples do. Marriage is never a cakewalk. But their strong loving bond, gave them the strength to get through many challenges.

In touching his knee, as he lay there, she recalled the two knee replacement surgeries he went through within 5 years. How he suffered with unbearable pain. After his operations, Gabriella slept on the expanded window sill, in his hospital room, to keep him company all night.

A slight pain suddenly went through her chest at that moment, reminding her of the night she swallowed a duck bone, and started to choke, while she began eating her dinner at their favorite restaurant. Seeking help at a nearby hospital, they admitted her, but the doctor did not come until morning, to remove the bone. He was not told of the seriousness of the emergency. All night Gabriella sat up, gasping for air, knowing she could not lay down. Nick sat with her all night and watched over her, as Gabriella worried about him being a diabetic, and not having eaten.

Yes, there were several distinguishable dramas. But, Gabriella had said often, that she would not change one thing about their time together. Meditating on these and many other occurrences, she pondered how fate maneuvered its finger, pushing them to connect like pawns on a chessboard, knowing they were perfect for each other.

In recalling their first date on his boat, and the many laughs they shared, drew a chuckle even now, as she sat there by his bedside.

Many people had thought their relationship would never last, and many thought it shouldn't have started in the first place, because he was so much older than she was. But Gabriella and Nick proved them all wrong.

When they first started to date, Gabriella, 29, mentioned that when she married, she wanted to have a child. Actually, all her life she had hoped to have 6 children, but she didn't share that part with Nick.

Nick, 54 years of age when they met, told her frankly, when the subject of children arose...

"You should have children. You would make a good Mother. But I'm too old for raising a child. So, if that is really a dream of yours, you should find someone else— someone much younger, around your age. I love you, but I am beyond that stage."

Gabriella was really surprised by Nick's reaction, but appreciated his candor, as always. Over the next several weeks, she thought long and hard about it and decided...

How can I give up being with this wonderful man, in exchange for having a child, which may or may not occur?

After coming to that conclusion, she never mentioned wanting a child again.

Nick was a romantic lover. He was always thinking of ways to surprise Gabriella. On the night he proposed marriage, they were having dinner in Nick's hotel suite, where he lived while being the General Manager, and where Gabriella stayed many nights.

She was treated as queen when she was in his hotel—daily maid service, housekeeping service, any meal she desired was cooked for them to perfection. Nick would ask her every night what she wanted for dinner—steak, chateaubriand, lobster, caviar...anything her heart desired; there were no limitations or restrictions. Nick would then have his Purchasing Director buy it, and the Chef would gladly prepare it.

On this particular evening, the waiter brought shrimp cocktail served on shaved ice as an appetizer, which Nick had ordered. Gabriella had told Nick that she wasn't that hungry, and just wanted some prime rib and a salad.

"Oh, have some shrimp cocktail, Gabriella," he coaxed, pointing to the shrimp dish, which was covered.

"No, I don't think I have a taste for that, Nick," she answered to Nick's chagrin.

"Just have a few pieces. That's all. It's so fresh. Chef Frank sent it especially for you to try."

"Oh, okay. I don't want to hurt Chef Frank's feelings. I'll have just one or two."

That was the cue for the waiter to lift the cover, which he did.

Gabriella, however, was not paying close attention to the food display in front of her. She began to ask Nick about his day.

Nick was shocked that she did not even see the huge ring with twenty-six diamonds surrounding one huge, three-carat diamond in the center. The ring was sitting in the middle of the ice! He could barely keep his thoughts on answering her about his day. But, he finally muttered,

"Oh, it was good. How was yours? This shrimp is delicious, isn't it? Have another."

"Yes," replied Gabriella. Looking down to sample another shrimp. Then she noticed the ring!

"Nick, look … what's this?" she exclaimed, picking up the ring with a wide smile.

A relieved Nick laughed and got up from his chair. He kissed her and said,

"Will you marry me, Gabriella? It took you long enough to see that ring. You scared me!" He laughed.

Gabriella laughed and was truly embarrassed.

"Yes, I didn't notice it at first. Sorry. It's gorgeous. It's so big. Maybe it's too much, Nicky."

He slipped it onto her finger, saying,

"You wear it for a few weeks, and if you feel it is too big, you let me know and we'll go get you another one, okay?"

Tears flowed down Gabriella's face.

"Oh, Nicky. I love you so much. Yes, I'll marry you!"

Everyday Gabriella wore the ring, and everyone seemed to notice it. It was truly impressive. Nick said he had helped design it with a jeweler friend. He wanted something truly different. It was designed in the shape of a pyramid, as Gabriella was his Cleopatra. Needless to say, she kept the ring.

Gabriella had never been married prior to meeting Nick. However, Nick had married in his early twenties, and had now been divorced for over thirty years.

Like all little girls, Gabriella had always dreamt about walking down the long isle of the Catholic church on her Daddy's arm. Most of their friends now were in the Chicago area, so it was only feasible for the wedding to take place in Chicago instead of her hometown of Canonsburg, Pennsylvania. In thinking of convenience for her family members and friends who would attend, Gabriella made arrangements in reserving a huge air-conditioned motorcoach, that would transport them to Chicago in comfort.

**GABRIELLA, 30, AT HER AND
NICK'S ENGAGEMENT PARTY.**

Nick and Gabriella often frequented St. Mary's Catholic Church, a small church in the Loop, and over the years, Nick became very good friends with Fr. Heinz, the Pastor.

Because Nick was so well known, a grandiose wedding was being planned at the Senate Hotel, where Nick was General Manager. Gabriella was in full agreement.

He suggested cocktails and hors d'oeuvres to be served in the Gold Room, where musicians would serenade guests with violin and harp music. The Gold Room was like no other room in the city of Chicago. The ceiling was painted to resemble the ceiling of the Sistine Chapel in Rome, Italy. The walls were adorned with crystal sconces along with angel cherubs holding numerous candle lights. The room was painted in a very soft golden hue, and the carpet was a rich burgundy pattern. The elegance of the room captivated everyone who saw it.

A scrumptious seven-course dinner would be served in the Great Hall, which seated comfortably 1,500 guests.

Of course, Nick's Big Band Orchestra would provide music throughout the evening. Hundreds of huge deep red and golden yellow rose combinations (Gabriella's favorites) were to be draped over the balcony of the Great Hall.

All the arrangements were coming together beautifully for their fairytale October wedding. Nick was sparing no expense for the princess of his dreams. Gabriella started to peruse several bridal magazines in search of the perfect gown. Nothing was exciting her until, all of a sudden, she turned a page in the Bridal Magazine, and there was *the* perfect gown for her—a white satin gown with long champagne lace sleeves, and a sweetheart bodice. Without saying a word, Gabriella contacted the shop manager, who said she had one in stock in size twelve. Gabriella left immediately, as she was so excited to try it on.

When she entered the shop, the manager greeted her and offered assistance, but Gabriella said she preferred to be alone. When she emerged from the dressing room, everyone in the shop just stopped what they were doing, and stared at the vision of her loveliness. Gabriella had swept her hair up on top of her head with a barrette, which added to the elegance. The shop manager exclaimed,

> "Gabriella, you look gorgeous—like a fairytale princess! You're the first person to try that gown on, and I must say, it was made for you!"

Other people in the shop all joined in with numerous compliments. Another bride-to-be burst out saying...

> "I want that gown too!" as everyone in the shop started to chuckle.

The manager even suggested a crown tiara for her head, and an extra-long veil.

> "You'll be a sight to behold on that day!" she exclaimed.

Gabriella was so extremely happy, as she knew Nick would be very pleased too. She paid the deposit, and left for home.

Meanwhile, Nick had an appointment with Father Heinz that very day to secure the church. He, too, had kept his appointment a secret, thinking to surprise Gabriella.

He and Gabriella had planned to meet at the end of the day at her condo for dinner. Gabriella could hardly wait to tell Nick, that she had purchased the most gorgeous gown, and she knew he would love it. When Nick arrived at the Condo, she could see instantly that he was distraught about something.

Gabriella immediately poured Nick his J&B Scotch with a lemon twist, on the rocks. They both sat on the sofa, she sipping her glass of Christian Brothers – Ruby Port, as he began to tell her about his appointment with Father Heinz, who had become very good friends of Nick's over the years. Anytime Father had friends coming into town, Nick would always put them up gratis at the hotel. Additionally, Nick was a very generous donor to the church.

> "Gabriella, I went to see Father Heinz today to confirm our wedding date."

> "Fantastic! It was available, I hope," she replied, holding her breath and crossing her fingers.

> "Yes, honey, it was available. But when I told him that I was married before over 30 years ago, and have been divorced, he said that I had to get an Annulment.

> "Ohhh? What's that involve?" Gabriella asked hesitantly.

> "See this Form?" Reaching into his suit coat pocket, he brought out a Form printed on legal-size paper. As he showed it to her, she realized the Form consisted of six double-sided pages.

Nick continued....

> "I must take this form to my ex-wife, and ask her to complete it. She has to state what kind of a man I was, and what she thinks caused our divorce, and she must add other comments about me. Then, I have to do the same thing to my Best Man and the Maid of Honor, who

must also complete this form. When all is completed, I return it to Father, and he sends it to the Vatican for approval. It may take up to one year to get their decision! And they could deny us!"

"I love you, sweetheart, and I will do this if you want. I haven't spoken to my first wife in many years, but I will do this, if it will make you happy."

Gabriella could hardly believe her ears! Tears started to well in her eyes. Sitting there in stunned silence, a barrage of thoughts exploded in her head:

I was born and raised a Catholic and have been faithful all my life. I've received all the sacraments. I've gone to Catholic school, and I've gone to church every Sunday and on Holy Days of Obligation. I've fasted during Lent. I've done all that they have asked of me over the years. How can they deny me the happiest day of my life? Why must they make it so difficult for me to get married in the Catholic Church? Divorced people are not bad people! We are good people, Nick and I. It may take a year for a decision? I could be dead in a year!

Nick kept staring at her. He was anxious for her reaction. Obviously, this had been a shock to him, too.

He had asked Father Heinz if he would just marry them based on their friendship, and everything Nick had done for the church, but Father replied,

"No! I can't, Nick! I love you and Gabriella, but if anyone found out, I would be excommunicated!"

Gabriella got up and stared out the window, as her mind raced with a million thoughts. She finally turned to Nick and held out her hand, asking to see the form. He handed it to her and, in a rage of anger, she ripped it up into several pieces.

Nick jumped up in shock.

"Gabriella, that's my only copy!"

"We won't need it, Nick! I love you, and I don't need your first wife's approval or anyone's approval to marry you! I don't need a piece of paper, to tell me that our hearts are married, and will always be merged as one!"

"*AND*.... I don't need anyone to confirm that you're a good man. I *know* you are! Forget about getting married in the Catholic Church. Forget about the Catholic Church totally! I'm sick to my stomach. My heart is shattered!" she cried in Nick' arms.

"Gabriella, I will do it for you, Honey. Honest," Nick insisted.

"No, Nick. What they're asking for is not right. Forget it!" She continued to cry.

"Sweetheart, we can get married in a non-Catholic church. I have many friends, as you know. There's Reverend Laverne at the Lutheran, Reverend Buddy at the Methodist. Either of them would be glad to marry us!"

"No, Nick. Please let's not talk about a wedding now. I'm too devastated."

As the weeks went by, Nick kept occasionally bringing up the wedding, but Gabriella was just too heart broken, and didn't even want to discuss it.

> "Erase the date out of the book at the hotel, Nick. Please. I don't want to think about it. Maybe next year, or the year after. I don't know."

Nick nodded, even though he didn't like Gabriella's state of mind. He even asked some friends, to have their girlfriends take Gabriella to lunch and talk it out, which they did gladly. They tried to convince her it didn't matter what Church she got married in—just get married, they coaxed. But no one could help Gabriella get over this betrayal that she felt from the Catholic Church. Maybe it was because she had been so devoted. Maybe it was because she was so spiritual. Maybe it was because she'd dreamt of her wedding in a Catholic Church all her life. She felt as if her best friend, had stabbed her in the back, and left her there drowning in her sorrow!

Gabriella never mentioned the beautiful gown that she had ordered. Only she and the people in the bridal shop that very day, ever witnessed the vision of her loveliness in that particular gown. The next day, she called the Manager of the bridal shop and cancelled the gown. It was not normal policy for them to return the deposit, but the Manager liked Gabriella so much, and she could hear how depressed she was, and thus quickly issued the refund.

This major devastation ate away at Gabriella like a cancer. Nick noticed. It was as if someone had blown out the candle, that once had been the fire that lit Gabriella's soul. She was totally different. Depressed. Broken hearted.

Gabriella, of course, shared her feelings with her Mother and Father. Her Mother's feelings were the same as those of Gabriella's friends.

"Get married in any Church. God is present in every Church, Gabriella!" coaxed her Mother.

Gabriella's Father had a different feeling. He liked Nick—everyone did—but he really thought Nick was too old for Gabriella, and he knew she'd always wanted children, which he knew would not happen with Nick. He concluded,

"Maybe it is happening for the best, Gabriella."

To which a distraught Gabriella quickly responded,

"No, Daddy. It's not!"

CHAPTER 19

GABRIELLA CHALLENGES THE CATHOLIC CHURCH

A few months later, while shopping at the local grocery store, Gabriella noticed the front page of one of the gossip magazines at checkout. It showed the picture of a very prominent married President of a billion-dollar company, who was known worldwide. Then it showed the younger lady with whom he'd been having an affair, for a few years. The headline read, "Just Married!" Gabriella picked up the magazine and started to read the story. The young lady was a Catholic, and although he was recently divorced, they had gotten married in a Catholic Cathedral in San Francisco.

> *What!* thought Gabriella. *It hasn't even been six months since his divorce! How could they get married in the Catholic Church so soon? And with such a publicized divorce, the former wife certainly didn't give him glowing comments on the Annulment papers!*

Gabriella bought the magazine.

It just so happened that Nick, who was also a Convention Meeting Planner, was in the process of organizing one of his largest conventions in San Francisco the following month, and Gabriella was going to accompany him there for two weeks.

Gabriella wasted no time in calling Pastor Peter, who had married the couple in the huge St. Cyprian Catholic Cathedral. When he answered the phone, she told him she was coming to San Francisco in a few weeks, and wanted to set a date to meet with him, regarding a huge donation. He happily agreed to meet.

Gabriella said nothing to Nick about her plans. The day of the meeting in San Francisco, Gabriella told Nick she was going to go shopping for the afternoon, while he was still busy planning the final details of the convention.

Pastor Peter an elderly man, in his early 70's, medium height, white hair, slowly entered the Rectory office where Gabriella was waiting.

> "Hello Gabriella. So nice to meet you." Smiled the Pastor, extending his hand.

> "Thank you for taking the time to meet with me Father." Replied Gabriella.

As he sat down, Gabriella took the magazine from her purse, opened it, and laid it in front of him on his desk. He looked down at it, a bit perplexed.

Said Gabriella,

> "Father, I see here that you married this divorced man, less than six months after his divorce. I would like you to do the same for my fiancé and me. I've been a good

Catholic all my life, and have never been married. My Nicholas, also a Catholic all his life, has been divorced for over 30 years. We want to marry in the Catholic Church, but our local Pastor told Nick that he has to get an Annulment first, which may take over a year, and may not even be approved."

"Now, in reading this article, Father, I can see that there are ways around this Annulment procedure, which quite frankly, I think it's asking too much from any human being. Will you do the same for me and my fiancé? Will you marry us?"

Pastor Peter started to shake his head.

"I can't, Gabriella. I'm sorry. There is more to the story than you know. Listen to your local Pastor, and have Nicholas get an Annulment."

"What could be more to the story, Father? Please explain."

"I prefer not to, Gabriella. Have Nicholas get an Annulment. I know you are disappointed—"

Instantly, Gabriella interrupted.

"No, Pastor Peter! I am not disappointed. *I AM COMPLETELY DEVASTATED!* My heart is shattered into a million pieces, and I'm hanging by a thread to try and justify a ruling by the Catholic Church—*my Church*!

Her voice started to rise.

"Why is it necessary for a man, who has been divorced for over 30 years, go back to his first wife and ask her *permission* to go on with his life and live in happiness? Has the Church never heard of a woman scorned? Is the Church's view so narrow that they think a person will wish someone happiness, when they have not found happiness for themselves? Please answer me, and help me understand, Father."

Searching to end this conversation, Pastor Peter concluded...

"Gabriella, we follow the rules laid down by the Pope. Until the Pope changes the Annulment policy, it remains. Perhaps you should take your questions to the Pope. I cannot help you."

"But you helped that billionaire. Why? Because he can donate large sums of money to this church? How much money did he donate, Father?"

"Gabriella, it's not about money."

"It's *always* about money, Father. If I told you that I would double the sum, would you marry us then?"

"Gabriella, you're making assumptions. You have to follow the rules of the religion," repeated the Pastor.

Gabriella responded quickly.

"I have to follow the rules, and you, Pastor Peter, can break them at your will! That doesn't sound fair, now does it? I'm serious. How much money will it take for you to marry us? I will double what he paid you! Give me a figure."

The Pastor sat there staring at this defiant young woman, who had come there specifically for justice. He really didn't know how he wanted to answer her. He needed time to think. Finally, after several long moments, he responded.

> "I have another commitment that I must attend to. Let me get back to you in a few days, and we'll continue this conversation then."

Gabriella continued to stare at him, with rage rushing through her veins. In shaking her head, she stood to leave.

> "That won't be necessary for us to speak again, Pastor Peter. You've given me your answer already. Oh...just so you know, I *have* asked *someone higher* than the Pope for guidance, and I will follow his advice, Pastor." As she snatched the newspaper article from his desk.

Pastor Peter smirked.

> "Someone *higher* than the Pope? I don't believe there is anyone higher, Gabriella."

With a smile on her face, Gabriella responded.

> "Yes, Father. There is. His name is Jesus Christ! I asked him what I should do, and he answered me. He always answers me! You see, Pastor Peter, I talk directly with Jesus anytime at will!"

Pastor Peter looked very puzzled.

> "What are you saying?" the Pastor asked.

> "Just what I said, Father. I have been blessed with the Gift of Channeling."

> "What is this... Channeling, Gabriella?"

"Channeling, Pastor Peter, is a Spiritual Gift given to me at birth, from Father God, enabling me to talk to Angels, Saints, Spirits, all deceased. And yes, I have constant conversations with Jesus and The Blessed Mother. I have gone beyond just talking to Spirits. But I won't keep you any longer. You have an appointment. Do have a nice day, Pastor."

Gabriella proceeded to walk out the door.

"Wait, Gabriella. I'd like to hear more. What do you and Jesus talk about?"

She turned holding on to the door,

"We talk about **everything!** Good day, Father. I hope someday the Church listens to Jesus, and what their true meaning and existence is meant to be."

Gabriella then started to walk away.

Pastor Peter quickly jumped up.

"Gabriella, wait. You said that Jesus gave you the answer to your question, about your desire to marry this divorced man, Nicholas. What was His answer?"

Stopping abruptly, she turned to him, smiled, and kindly replied...

"His answer was really quite simple, Pastor Peter. Jesus said, 'Follow your heart, Gabriella!' And that, Father, is exactly what I intend to do."

With that, Gabriella turned and continued to walk away.

Pastor Peter nodded and then shouted,

> "I'll call you in a few days, Gabriella. I want to hear more about this Channeling."

Gabriella just kept walking.

Standing there dazed, Pastor Peter watched her depart. He had been completely unprepared for God's messenger to visit him that day, and her words haunted him for many days thereafter. He murmured to himself,

> "I must remember to ask her what she meant: 'I hope someday the Church listens to Jesus, and what their true meaning and existence is meant to be.' Hhmm... I'll call her next week."

Gabriella returned to the hotel, still not feeling totally satisfied. Deep down inside, she was really hoping that Pastor Peter would have consented, to bend the rules for her and Nicholas, too.

However, prior to meeting with the Pastor, she had already decided to follow the advice of Jesus. But, she still wanted to meet with the Pastor, in hopes to find out exactly how the billionaire got around the Annulment proceedings, even though her common sense told her it revolved around money. After today's meeting, she knew that she had surmised correctly.

It would be 25 years before Gabriella would ever again return to the Catholic Church. For years, she always relished a time in the week, that was set aside primarily for her to talk to her Creator, in His House. For most, that would be Sunday Mass. But, she needed more healing time. At times, she visited the church alone, when there was no one there...in the afternoon hours.

There and then, she would enjoy some of the most spiritual chats with the Lord...just the two of them. Emotionally, she couldn't get beyond her devastation.

As time went on, the subject of marriage was mentioned less frequently, by Nicholas or Gabriella.

However, it was known, that anything or anyone who caused Gabriella pain or sadness, would be met vehemently by a loving Nicholas, who was ready to slay those dragons. However, this time the situation was totally out of his control, and he knew it.

During the years that followed, Gabriella suggested to Nick that they try other religions, and they did. Most were very warm and receptive, but none of them touched her heart like the Catholic religion. It had been embedded in her from birth, and could not be easily erased. The pain in her heart, just simply would not heal.

Gabriella especially missed receiving Holy Communion, as it was during Sunday Mass, that Jesus first appeared to her, talking with her at length, which continued for years. Although she no longer attended Mass, however, Jesus still would come to her, whenever and wherever she requested. His infinite loving nature, would always avail itself toward comforting her broken heart, and helping her dissolve any mental anguish.

Nicholas and Gabriella kept the Commandments, in trying to be a good Christians. They expressed their adoration to The Blessed Virgin Mary by saying the Rosary and Novenas. Additionally, Gabriella insisted that they both wear the brown wool Scapular of Our Lady of Mt. Carmel, which carries Our Lady's promise: "Whosoever dies wearing this Scapular, shall not suffer eternal fire."

For over 25 years, they each wore a Scapular every day, throughout the day and night, even while sleeping. They removed them only when taking a shower, and sometimes not even then.

Together, they would say the Rosary in the afternoon. In many ways, praying together in the quiet of their home, sometimes proved to be even more sacred than praying in a church, and strengthened their love to a deeper level.

Gabriella's spiritual bond with Father God, Jesus, the Holy Spirit, and The Blessed Mother never weakened. On the contrary, it miraculously intensified, becoming stronger and stronger over the years!

CHAPTER 20

FILING FOR BANKRUPTCY

Luigi had been Nick's best friend for many years. He was an Italian from Montreal, Canada, who worked in the Corporate Food and Beverage Department of the Senate chain. They shared numerous passions together, such as golf, cooking, frequenting Italian restaurants, traveling, and they both were in the Hospitality Field. One of their dreams, was to one day open their own restaurant/lounge together. It would be a natural, with Luigi overseeing the food and beverage, and Nick, the entertainment.

In perusing the Restaurant Magazine, Luigi called Nick excited to tell him about space he'd found for the restaurant of their dreams. Located in downtown Chicago, across from Union Station, the first-floor space was in a hundred-year-old bank building, that totaled over 6,000 square feet of space. The next day, they went to see it. As they entered, Nick became motivated by the many possibilities. Having studied engineering and architecture in college, he immediately began to design the ideal layout in his mind. However, it was going to take a lot of money to transform it into a restaurant/lounge.

Nick pledged a hefty sum of $250,000. Luigi said he could only come up with $15,000. Having a rough idea of the magnitude of this project, they also applied for a Small Business Association

(SBA) loan for the remainder. Developing this space into a restaurant/lounge was not going to be as easy as they had anticipated. For example, they had no idea that this hundred-year-old office building had granite floors three feet thick. So, to install plumbing and gas lines, the workers had to cut through granite. Everywhere they turned, each task just kept costing more and more money. The landlord had tenants renting office space twenty-seven stories above; and he insisted that they vent twenty-seven stories to the roof, so that the aromas of the cooking wouldn't filter into the offices. Finally, the renovations were completed, and they opened with grandeur, including TV coverage on the Chicago news.

They did well. After they were in operation for over three years, Nick noticed that Luigi started to be lax in his work schedule. He wasn't coming in on regular basis. He was missing a lot of days, and Nick was relying on him to be in the kitchen, ordering the food, and overseeing the staff. Nick met with Luigi to express his disappointment in his negligence. Luigi was definitely not holding up his part of the bargain.

It was at that meeting that Luigi shocked Nick with a confession:

> "I have Hodgkin's disease, and it's come out of remission!" confessed Luigi.

> "I didn't tell you when we were getting the loan 'cause I knew they wouldn't give it to us, and that would have ruined our plans. I felt I had to keep it a secret."

Nick sat there in horror and disbelief.

> "But, Luigi, you kept it a secret from *me,* your best friend, and you know I put a ton of my own money into this place. How could you do that to me?"

"I'm sorry Nick. I truly am. But, now I don't have the desire to be here anymore, and I just want to walk away. You can have my share."

"Your share! I put out over $250,000 and you put up a measly $15,000! Thanks for nothing!"

"You're going to leave me holding the bag to carry this whole place by myself? You know I have other business obligations on the books, in addition to this place."

"I just don't want to be here, Nick. I'm walking away from it," stated Luigi.

Nick was furious.

"Go!" Get the fuck out of my site!" yelled an enraged Nicholas.

At this point, the entire operation fell onto Nick. He ran newspaper ads, looking for a working chef, who wanted to make an investment toward a thriving business. His responses to the ads produced only people, who wanted a piece of the restaurant/lounge, without putting up any money. They wanted to be an owner without paying their share, like Luigi.

Nick was sick with worry and work. Gabriella was Director of Sales and Marketing for multiple suburban hotels, but would go to the restaurant after work, and sometimes stay till closing at ten o'clock. Needless to say, the situation was draining both of them, physically and mentally.

Nick relied on his staff heavily to keep the operation going, but not one member of the staff had managerial capabilities. Nick or Gabriella had to be there at all times. Nick was becoming more and more depressed, and Gabriella was very concerned.

"I don't know how much longer I can keep this going, Gabriella," Nick said one day. "My big concern is all the purveyors that I owe, and of course, the bank. As you know, the President of that bank and I go back about twenty-five years in friendship. I can't leave him in a lurch. I must repay that loan. This is going to drain me financially! I'm meeting with Carmen Tanco, my financial advisor, tomorrow."

The following day when Nick came home, he sat Gabriella down at the kitchen table.

"Baby, I have been a success in everything I've ever done in my life! But I'm not a success now. This is the first time I'm a failure, and I really don't even know how to handle it. I'm completely sick inside, and I don't have many options."

"Carmen advised me to walk away from the entire operation—lock the doors, and that would be the end of it. He said I don't even have to repay the bank or the purveyors. I could file Chapter 11 Bankruptcy."

Gabriella listened intently,

"Well, that's good news, isn't it, Nick?"

"Not really, Gabriella. I need to repay the bank and those purveyors, who were friends of mine from the hotel. They did everything for the restaurant, because they trusted *me*, not Luigi. As I said yesterday, this is going to drain me financially. In addition to that, I won't be able to have any credit cards. Filing Bankruptcy takes everything away from you! This is the eighties, and there are strict laws regarding Bankruptcy."

Gabriella just listened and then added,

> "Sweetheart, Luigi left you in a bad way. We both
> have tried to run the business along with our other
> commitments, and it can't be done that way. We're
> exhausted! Do what you have to do, Sweetheart. You
> should be **proud** of yourself. You have nothing to be
> ashamed of—nothing. You tried. You gave two-hundred-
> percent effort. Luigi left you holding the bag!"

Nick moved closer to her, took her hand, and looked into her
eyes.

> "Baby, listen, a Bankruptcy is not any easy thing. The
> government strips you of everything, although I can
> keep my car. I'm glad this Condo is yours, and under
> your name only. Gabriella, this Bankruptcy will last ten
> years! Did you hear me? Ten years! My God!" He covered
> his face with his hands. "That's a very long time!"

> "Gabriella, listen. I can understand completely if you
> want to leave me at this time. I wouldn't hold it against
> you. It's not going to be easy, and with most of my money
> gone, we'll have to make sacrifices. No wedding. Nothing
> for ten years! I have to pay out another $500,000 to
> cover the bank and the purveyors. You make up your
> mind. But I'm saying, with my whole heart, I wouldn't
> blame you if you decided to walk away from me."

Gabriella stood up and quickly wrapped her arms around Nick,
kissing him on the face. She knelt before him and looked at
him, with teary eyes.

> "Nicky, I am not going to leave you now or ever! How
> could I even think of that? You need me, and I'll be here

for you. We'll get through this, don't you worry. I have my credit cards, my car, and we'll live here. Don't worry. I love you so much."

"I'm so honestly and truthfully proud of what you accomplished at the restaurant, Nicky. You are *not* a failure! You fulfilled a dream that you had in your mind for many years! You took a chance, and not many people would have done what you did. And they certainly wouldn't pay off the bank and the purveyors with their own money! **I will always be proud of you!"**

"It doesn't matter to me that the doors must close. You hold your head up high, Nick Carcioni, and **be *proud* of yourself!** As far as our Wedding goes...again, I'm telling you, that I don't need a piece of paper to tell me that my heart is married to yours! I'm not leaving you! I love you so very much!"

Nick sat there in tears.

"Oh, Gabriella, the happiest day of my life, was the day you walked into it!"

Note: About eight years later, Gabriella and Nick happen to see Luigi at one of the gambling boat casinos. He looked very healthy. When he saw them, Luigi walked toward them smiling, wanting to shake hands. Nick stood there for a few seconds just staring at him, and then he turned to Gabriella, saying:

"Let's go, it's starting to stink in here!"

They both turned and walked away, repulsed.

**GABRIELLA, 40, FIRST CHRISTMAS
IN THEIR NEW HOME.**

CHAPTER 21

ARCHBISHOP CARDINAL JOSEPH BERNARDIN

Having a high-profile career, Nick met many people from all walks of life. Additionally, when he became General Manager of the Senate Hotel, his circle of friends expanded even more so.

One day, he received an invitation to attend a cocktail reception at Archbishop Cardinal Joseph Bernardin's residence in Chicago. At first, Gabriella declined to go, but Nick kept insisting that she attend with him. Still feeling an emptiness in her heart regarding the Catholic Church, Gabriella finally consented.

Nick had arranged for a harpist, who provided soft music, as the several guests chatted, and sampled from a lavish buffet table of raw oysters, shrimp cocktail, cheeses, meats, and desserts.

His Eminence, Cardinal Joseph Bernardin, was a very warm and charming host, greeting all the guests as they entered the foyer. Gabriella and Nick enjoyed conversation with His Eminence on and off throughout the night, and posed for pictures with him.

During the course of the event, after all the guests had arrived and everyone was mingling, Gabriella found herself wandering into an empty foyer. From there she noticed the cardinal's private chapel. It was a small, cozy chapel with stained glass windows, 10 pews, and kneelers covered in soft blue velvet material. The walls were painted a very soft blue and white, trimmed in a gold leaf border. On the altar was a large uncovered Golden Vessel. Gabriella stood there staring at the altar, and soon felt a presence stand behind her. He said,

"The Monstrance is called "The Gloria.""

Gabriella immediately recognized the voice as that of the Cardinal Bernardin himself. Turning, she answered,

"Really. I didn't know that, Your Eminence."

Cardinal Joseph Bernardin was a man, who was loved by all Catholics in Chicago. He had a gentle way about him that was sincere, amiable, and openhearted. Many said that he was in line to be the next Pope after Pope John Paul II.

"I'm thinking that I'm going to renovate this chapel, and decorate it as a duplicate to the one in the Sistine Chapel in Rome. Have you been there?" he asked Gabriella.

"Yes, we were there just a few years ago. It's done in rich reds and gold," she replied.

"Yes. That's right. Also, I found a huge crucifix in the attic, and I think I'll have it hung over this altar. What do you think?"

Gabriella replied quickly...

**GABRIELLA AND ARCHBISHOP
CARDINAL JOSEPH BERNARDIN**

"That will be extraordinary! I think ALL crucifixes in the church should be *huge* to make them more lifelike. I have noticed lately that some Catholic Churches have only a bare cross! That shouldn't be...the cross should always be shown with Jesus being crucified! That's what differentiates the Crucifix, from a wooden cross...The Crucifix is the Catholic way!"

Then lowering her voice, she added: "At least that's the way it used to be!...But, that's just my opinion, Your Eminence."

"I AGREE WITH YOU ONE HUNDRED PERCENT, GABRIELLA," said the Cardinal. **"EVERY CATHOLIC CHURCH SHOULD HAVE THE CRUCIFIED CHRIST ON THEIR ALTAR, OR HANGING OVER IT, PERMANENTLY!"**

"THAT'S OUR SYMBOL....AND ALWAYS HAS BEEN!" Stated the Archbishop firmly.

Gabriella added: "When I walk into a Catholic Church, I want to kneel down and look at Jesus...not a barren piece of wood made like a cross, or a piece of glass or crystal in the form of a cross. I want to look at Jesus and remember, **He died for Me!**"

"YES," whispered the Cardinal nodding. Then adding,

"I'm so very glad we had this conversation, Gabriella! You have given me much to think about, that needs to be addressed. Thank you!"

Upon turning and pointing to the sidewalls of the Chapel, the Archbishop expressed, "I'm thinking over here, I'll place the Stations of the Cross."

"Yes, that would be perfect, Your Eminence!" smiled Gabriella.

As he gazed at her, the astute Archbishop sensed sadness, behind her lovely smile.

"Gabriella, it seems that you have something on your mind. Would you like to talk about it?" asked the concerned Cardinal.

Gabriella half smiled.

"No, thank you, Your Eminence. I'm fine. All will work out."

"I have an idea," the Cardinal exclaimed. "Would you like a tour of the upstairs private residence? I'll show you where the Pope John Paul II slept when he was here."

Cardinal Bernardin had hit an excitable nerve in Gabriella, who quickly answered,

"Yes, I really would, and I'm sure Nick would too! When Pope John Paul was in town, my girlfriend and I came down here at 4 a.m., and we stood outside in the dark with candles. We were so thrilled when he came out onto the balcony! Later, he passed by us in his car. There were thousands here to see him, but we were first in line!"

The Cardinal listened with a smile on his face.

"You did! How very touching. He is so loved," replied the Cardinal.

"Yes, and so are you, Your Eminence," Gabriella responded smiling.

Just then Nick entered.

> "I was looking for you, Gabriella." He turned to the Cardinal. "Thank you for inviting us, Your Eminence."
>
> "You are welcome here anytime, Nick. I was just telling Gabriella that I am giving a tour of the upstairs private residence, if you would like to come too."
>
> "Yes, I'd love to see it," replied an excited Nick.

They all moved into the foyer. Cardinal Bernardin told his plans to his assistant, Father Clare, who extended the invitation to all those present.

Up the grand curved oak staircase, they all walked, with Gabriella and Nick first behind the Cardinal. He took them into a huge room filled with numerous extravagant gifts, that had been given to him over the years. Some were priceless. He pointed to several and explained their origin and donors. Needless to say, all of the guests were tremendously impressed. Then he walked them down the hall. He looked at Gabriella and smiled, saying,

> "And this is where Pope John Paul II slept when he visited us."

As the door opened, Gabriella stepped inside. The room was extremely modest—a twin bed covered with a white bedspread, and a small wooden crucifix hanging above. Off to the side was a small four-drawer dresser with a mirror. On one wall hung a picture of The Blessed Mother.

Gabriella couldn't help but remark,

"It's so barren. So humble. It should have at least a double bed, don't you think, Your Eminence?"

At that, the Cardinal and the other guests laughed. Nick laughed and shook his head. As everyone started to turn, and return down the hall to go back downstairs, Cardinal Bernardin said to Gabriella,

"Would you like to go out on the balcony, where the Pope waved to the crowd?"

Gabriella lit up.

"Wow...that would be wonderful!"

The Cardinal led the way to draped French doors, that opened onto the balcony. Gabriella stepped out and looked all around at the view. Filled with much emotion, tears filled her eyes, and she fought hard not to let them fall. Smiling, she lowered her eyes and stepped back inside.

"Thank you, Your Eminence. Little did I ever think that I would stand where he did. Thank you so much!" Nick stood smiling in the doorway.

"I'm glad that made you smile, Gabriella," responded the Cardinal as they walked to join the others.

Note: *When Cardinal Bernardin was showing all the priceless gifts given to him over the years, Nick asked if, upon his death, they would go to his family. The Cardinal replied,*

"No. They are the property of the Church and will remain here."

Gabriella quickly added...

"You'll have them to enjoy for several years, Your Eminence."

Cardinal Bernardin barely smiled and replied with a soft,

"Yes."

Two days later, it was announced in the Chicago news, that Archbishop Cardinal Bernardin was fighting pancreatic cancer. Gabriella and Nick visited the Cardinal's residence on several other occasions. He lived for just another two years, before God called him home on November 14, 1996. He had served as Archbishop from 1982 to 1996.

Archbishop Cardinal Francis Eugene George, was then appointed by Pope John Paul II to succeed Archbishop Cardinal Joseph Bernardin.

Nick and Gabriella were fortunate to make his acquaintance, also. Cardinal George knew that he had big shoes to fill, in following Cardinal Bernardin, and he did so with warmth, charm, and wit.

He became very visible throughout the Archdiocese, and many benefited from his spiritual guidance, and knowledge.

Cardinal George served from November 14, 1996 to April 17, 2015, when he died at the age of 78, after battling cancer for years. As he entered the final stages of illness, he appointed Archbishop Blasé J. Cupich from Spokane, Washington as his successor. Archbishop Cupich is serving now, at the time of this writing.

**GABRIELLA AND ARCHBISHOP
CARDINAL FRANCIS GEORGE**

CHAPTER 22

MORE QUESTIONS THAN ANSWERS

July 30, 2012

Gabriella was glad to see Monday come, at Asclepius Christian Medical Center. She anxiously waited to meet everyone on the Neurological team, to get their assessment of what they thought had happened to Nick, and how soon they expected him to awaken.

She wrote an email to all family and friends:

Dearest Family and Friends,

On Friday, Nick was given another CAT scan. The results show that there is no difference in the amount of blood on the brain, and some is even in his brain. The brain is swollen.

As I relayed previously, they inserted the feeding tube on Friday, and although he is in a Coma, they had to give him even more sedation, knowing that it was not going to help his situation. (My heart is breaking.)

Late Friday night, the liquid food arrived and began entering his body. We must wait about three days to see if the nourishment given will help him wake up. Dr. Edward is trying to cover all bases. Needless to say, I am extremely scared and worried, about what toll this entire ordeal has taken on Nick's mental ability.

Today is Monday, July 30. I have been playing all of Nick's CD's since Friday—every day, all day. Of course, I'm hoping that his singing and sax playing will arouse something inside of him, that will awaken him. I play his music so that everyone can hear it. The man in the next bed muted his TV because he likes Nick's music so much. When the Nurses and Doctors come in, they can't believe that it's Nick singing and playing. They all compliment him and find it so relaxing. Through my tears, I am very proud and delighted that everyone is enjoying his music.

Yesterday, Sunday, Nick developed an infection in his Bladder. He has had a fever for five days, and now they are giving him two antibiotics.

He has just returned from having a chest X-ray for Pneumonia. It turned out hazy, so they are taking another one tonight. His MD, Dr. Edward, is concerned.

Dr. Jeremy, an Infectious Disease Specialist, did not like what he was hearing in the chest, and thought the stomach was bloated. He immediately changed the antibiotic to a stronger medicine.

Nick was given an EEG. This is *the* test that I've been waiting for since last week. It indicates if he is having or has had any seizures recently. The neurologist team reviewed the test today.

Chief neurologist, Dr. Waters, said that it created more questions than answers for him. However, the test did show that he has *not* had any seizures. So, he is going to give Nick a special CAT scan, along with another test, to see if he can get a clearer picture of what is going on in the brain, and blood vessels that surround it. This test will occur late tonight. He mentioned that the infection could have already spread throughout his body, and this test will answer that question, hopefully.

Do you notice here, that *nothing* is a *definite*? It totally exasperates me!

Another veteran Nurse, Adele, who has 20 years' experience, confirmed to me that the sleeping pill should never have been given to Nick, because he had a hemorrhaged brain. This is taught and stressed in the first year of nurses' training!

I want to take this opportunity to Thank all of you who have sent get-well cards. I have them posted on the wall for him to see when he wakes up. It's an amazing site! Also, I want to thank you for all your prayers. I know your prayers are helping Nick to fight with all his might, and please know he is giving it a two-hundred-percent effort.

As Dr. Edward stated today,

"Nick is between a rock and a hard place presently!"

Nick and I love *all* of you, so very much!

Many of you ask me what we need. We need your prayers. That is all we need. Please pray for his complete recovery. Please pass this info on to others.

Thank you, and I will keep you posted.

Sorry—No visitors at this time.

Gabriella

CHAPTER 23

A SPINAL TAP COULD KILL HIM

Thursday, August 2, 2012, marked the twelfth day that Nick had been in Asclepius Christian Medical Center, and it was the seventh day of what they were now *finally* **calling a *severe* Coma.**

Gabriella was losing weight from not eating properly, and her sleep was constantly interrupted with nightmares.

Nick, having been in the Coma for seven days, was starting to frown when either a Doctor or a Nurse moved his head and neck. He responded with moans and groans. Although his body must have been tremendously stiff and painful, he still did not open his eyes or awaken.

The previous day, Dr. Kimba, neurologist, and his team had visited and persisted that they thought a spinal tap should be done, because Nick's infection and fever had continued for several days. They couldn't seem to locate the infection. The doctor had said that the latest CAT scan showed that most of the blood around the brain was gone; only some remained on the left side. However, Dr. Kimba warned that, if that blood was causing any pressure on the brain, then the Spinal Tap procedure would cause more pressure, flattening his brain like a pancake. This would **kill** Nick instantly.

Upon hearing this Gabriella shouted, "No! I will not give you my consent. *No!*"

Early that morning, as Gabriella was washing Nick's face and applying some of his favorite cologne, Dr. Yoko, Neurology, on the eighth floor, came to see Nick.

> "How's he doing today, Mrs. Carcioni?" he asked.

> "The same. What's your specialty, Doctor?" asked Gabriella.

> "I'm on the same team as Dr. Kimba. You know, Mrs. Carcioni, your husband is in a very critical state. We must find out where that infection is, because the infection could spread and hurt other organs. We must cure it."

> "I understand what you're saying, Doctor. But it sounds too risky. Surely there's another way?"

> "I wish there was, but no. This is the only way."

Gabriella stood there looking at Nick.

> "Okay. If I consent, then I *must* be allowed to be in the room, when you do the procedure."

> "No, Mrs. Carcioni. We don't allow that." Doctor Yoko responded.

> "Then forget it! If my husband is going to come that close to death, I need to be by his side to hold his hand, and

let him know I am there watching over him. The sound of my voice will calm him."

Dr. Yoko just stared at her.

"Okay. I'll tell Dr. Kimba."

"I'm still shaky about this, and wish there was someone else I could talk to about it. I will pray on this. When will it be done?"

"This afternoon."

"See me in a few hours. I will have my final answer then," Gabriella concluded.

Gabriella prayed the Rosary and asked the Blessed Mother for guidance. Although it seemed logical to follow the doctor's suggestion, something kept gnawing at her, forcing her to question it, and making her frightened to have this procedure done.

Later, at around 1 p.m., Dr. Yoko came in.

"Mrs. Carcioni, have you made up your mind?"

"Yes. Okay. We'll do it. What time?"

"At about 4:30 p.m. However, Dr. Kimba is off today, so Dr. Waters, the Head of Neurology will be doing the procedure," said Dr. Yoko.

"Is he an expert at this? Does he know what he's doing?" Gabriella asked sincerely.

"Oh, yes ma'am. He's the Head of the entire department! He's over Dr. Kimba."

"Why haven't I met him yet? I want to meet him."

"Yes, he will be in later to see your husband before the procedure. See you this afternoon."

It was nearly 3 p.m. and Dr. Waters had not yet come to the room. Only Dr. Bobbie Edward stopped by to examine Nick again, still perplexed as to why his patient was not awakening.

"I feel for this guy. Such a bloody shame," he said. "I hope you're eating and taking care of yourself, Mrs. Carcioni. You want to be healthy when he wakes up."

"Yes, I'm hangin' in there, Doctor."

Later, Gabriella stepped outside the room and saw seven white coats gathered by the Nurses' station. Then she recognized Dr. Yoko, so she approached him and pulled him aside. She asked when they were going to perform the Spinal Tap, and when was she going to meet Dr. Waters. Dr. Yoko assured her that he would be in to see Nick at around 4 p.m.

Gabriella returned to the room and began telling Nick all that was about to transpire, and how they must find that infection. Also, she told him not to worry, that she would be right there with him. All will be fine. Within a half hour, she started to doze off to sleep, as she held Nick's hand.

The sound of several voices entering he room, awakened her abruptly. It was Dr. Waters and his entourage of five interns along with Dr. Yoko.

Dr. Waters introduced himself. He was a nice-looking gentleman, about five eleven with brown hair and a soft voice. He complimented the music Gabriella had playing in the background, and she informed him that it was Nick singing and his Big Band Orchestra.

"I love that music. He sounds great. Very impressive!"

Gabriella reached for the CD Player.

"I'll turn it off, Doctor, so you can examine Nick without being distracted," said Gabriella moving toward the CD player.

Dr. Waters seemed very thorough in his examining. He asked Gabriella several questions: How had Nick ended up in this state? How long had he been like this? How had his health been prior? How often did he visit his Primary Care Doctor?

Gabriella replied that Nick was in good health, saw his Primary Care Doctor at least once a month, sometimes more, was very health conscious, and followed the Doctor's orders to the letter. Nick had had a heart stress test about a few months previously, and it had gone well. Dr. Waters listened as he kept examining Nick. He asked about Nick's rising temperature, along with several other questions. Dr. Yoko and the interns just stood there without answering, so Gabriella immediately answered all Dr. Waters questions, as she knew all Nick's stats by heart.

"You're really are on top of things, Mrs. Carcioni," he complimented.

"He's my husband … my entire world, Doctor."

Then Dr. Waters started to think out loud.

"I believe that your husband's blood vessels had a series of spasms, that put him in this state. Or... it could have been that an instant gush of blood exploded in his brain. However, the tests show no Aneurysms. I need more tests to find out the answer. I'll order a MRI and another CAT scan for later tonight. The results of these tests, will tell if an Angiogram should be done."

Just at that moment, Gabriella interjected forcibly,

"What about the Spinal Tap?"

Dr. Waters looked at her confused.

"What Spinal Tap?" he asked.

Dr. Yoko and the other interns stood there, saying nothing.

Gabriella responded quickly.

"Dr. Kimba and Dr. Yoko said that my husband needed a Spinal Tap, in order to find out where the infection is within his body. They said that it possibly could kill him on the operating table. At first, I said no, but they insisted it needs to be done!"

Dr. Waters became upset and looked at Dr. Yoko with a frown.

"There will be *no Spinal Tap*. Do you understand me?"

Then he turned to Gabriella.

"This would **not** be good for your husband, Mrs. Carcioni. I don't know why they would even suggest it."

Looking back over to Dr. Yoko, he repeated:

"No spinal tap. Understood?"

Dr. Yoko, answered a sheepish,

"Yes, Doctor."

Gabriella was so relieved! She thanked God as tears ran down her face. Gabriella stayed till 10 p.m., and was with Nick through that evening's CAT scan. The other tests were going to be done after midnight, so Gabriella left for home to get some rest.

Chapter 24

"LET HIM DIE"

The various tests that Dr. Waters had ordered, were done throughout the night. When Gabriella called the hospital at just before midnight on Thursday, August 2, 2012, she was glad to speak to a kind nurse, Deborah Ann, who apprised her of all the latest:

> "The CAT scan was done, but the MRI hasn't been done yet. It will be done later in the early morning hours. The special EEG test results are in, and they are now on the computer for the neurological team to read and assess. Dr. Jeremy, Head of Infectious Disease, took Nick off the antibiotic earlier tonight. He said he was noticing a slight increase in the liver readings, and did not want it to escalate. By tomorrow morning when you arrive, Mrs. Carcioni, they should have all the results in. Get your rest."

The next morning, Gabriella was at Nick's side at 8:30 a.m. again setting up the CD player and talking to him constantly with reassuring words.

At 11:00 a.m. the nurse's aides gave him a bed bath, afterward Gabriella applied his favorite Paco Rabanne cologne. It was his favorite, because Gabriella said she absolutely loved the scent.

As Nick's CDs played constantly, Gabriella reread all the cards and emails that had been sent. She did this every day, exclaiming that he had receive lots of mail, and everyone was praying for him to wake up.

Hearing footsteps and voices coming into the room, she looked up to see Dr. Waters and six interns, along with Dr. Yoko and Dr. Kimba. Happy to see them, Gabriella immediately asked about the special EEG test, in which they had to grease up Nick's hair and attach wires. But, to her dismay, they said it did not show anything worth discussing!

Dr. Waters added,

> "We have the results of the latest CAT and MRI. The CAT shows less blood than was there when he entered the hospital. This is good, or should I say this *should* be good news."

He motioned for Gabriella to walk outside of the room. He took her to a computer and showed her the difference in the pictures of Nick's brain—then and now. As he explained, she had to ask him several times to use layman's terms.

Dr. Waters, pointed to the pictures and said,

> "The MRI shows an enhanced version of the blood vessels on the outside. We *think* that the blood vessels started to have spasms. This *might* have caused him to go into the Coma. We're not totally sure. Although a lot of the blood is gone, some still remains."

> "However, with the amount that is gone, and has been gone for days, we still are faced with the question of why Mr. Carcioni hasn't awakened."

"Quite frankly, we're stymied! He really should have awakened days ago! And, unfortunately, the longer a person stays unconscious, the likelihood is there will be severe brain damage, if and when they do awaken!"

Dr. Waters turned and looked at the group of interns, who had followed them. He motioned and said,

"Let's take a walk inside."

Gabriella proceeded to join the group, and started to walk in with them, but Dr. Waters stopped her and said,

"You may want to wait out here. I'm going to have to hurt him a bit, and it may be hard for you to see."

Gabriella replied,

"I'm coming in."

When they were all in the room, Dr. Waters put a corner of the fabric from Nick's hospital gown into his eye. Nick didn't even flinch. He shined a bright light in Nick's eyes. Nick's pupils dilated somewhat, but very slowly.

Then—and this was *extremely* difficult for Gabriella to watch— Dr. Waters squeezed Nick's tender skin on his chest, just as hard as he could, and pulled on his hairs, squeezing with all his might, pinching harder and harder! Poor, sweet Nick frowned in pain and slowly made his left arm straight and stiff. His right arm finally started to move up very slowly, as it hasn't moved in ten days. Gabriella touched Dr. Water's arm, signaling for him to stop, as she started to cry. Dr. Waters stopped and remarked,

"What I did *really really* hurts, Mrs. Carcioni! A normal response would have been for both arms to come flying up fast, to push my hands away. He did not react fast enough. I'm sorry."

Gabriella stepped away to grab tissues, and then stepped back. Dr. Waters was leaning on the bed rails just thinking.

"I could do an Angiogram, and put a balloon in the blood vessels to try and open them up. It could cause some stir in him, but no guarantees."

Gabriella replied,

"With all due respect, Doctor Waters, I don't want you to use my husband as your guinea pig. At this moment, I'm saying, "NO" to the Angiogram. You aren't really sure what effect it will have, do you? It could open one eye. It could raise one arm. You don't know, do you?"

Dr. Waters answered honestly,

"No, I don't. I respect what you're saying, Mrs. Carcioni."

They all stood in silence for a few moments. Finally, Gabriella asked,

"What's the next step Doctor?"

"Mrs. Carcioni, you must consider what Mr. Carcioni would want."

Gabriella answered quickly.

"I know what he would want. He would want to get completely well, or he would want to go with dignity."

"Does he have a Living Will?"

"Yes." Replied Gabriella.

"Okay, then," added Dr. Waters, "Then let him go. Let him die."

A shocked Gabriella responded,

"What? What are you saying, Doctor?"

"What I'm saying, Mrs. Carcioni, is he has lived a good life—a great life from the sound of it—and now you should let him go."

Gabriella looked at him with intensity.

"Apparently, you have never loved anyone, Doctor!"

He responded,

"Yes, I have. But I knew when to let them go. You should really talk to Hospice, or look at Rehabilitation Centers that have availability. Or you should take him home, and get help to keep him comfortable at this stage. No one knows how long he will linger. His brain is gone!"

Gabriella stood there in shock.

"But, Doctor, he might come out of this coma! I must give him that chance! You don't know him like I do. He's a fighter!"

The Doctor responded confidently.

"That's highly unlikely at this point, Mrs. Carcioni. And if he does, he will have brain damage, and probably won't even know you. Are you ready to experience that? I don't think you want to."

A positively thinking, defiant Gabriella replied,

"I will not give up on him! I must give him every opportunity to come out of this. I know he's in there fighting. I must do all I can to help him!"

Dr. Waters just shook his head, and stated,

"We have done all that we can. There is no more that can be done to improve his condition. Therefore, there is only one way for us to go. We'll stop the antibiotic and the blood pressure medicine immediately. He will still receive insulin for his diabetes, liquid food in the feeding tube, oxygen through the nose tube to assist with his breathing, and he has a catheter. He looks comfortable."

Gabriella interjected,

"I noticed that his breathing has fluctuated the past four days. He has spikes of breathing fast and hard, and then moments of not breathing, like sleep apnea. I can tell when he's getting flustered or scared. I put my arms around him and give him kisses, and whisper that everything is all right, and that I am fine," she continued.

"I tell him he is getting better, and that seems to calm him. So, I know we are reaching him to some degree, Doctor."

Dr. Waters just shook his head and motioned for the team to depart. Being the last to leave, he stopped and turned to a disheartened tearful Gabriella, repeating,

"Let him go. Let him die!"

CHAPTER 25

EMAIL TO FAMILY MEMBERS AND FRIENDS

August 4, 2012

Dearest Family members and Friends...

Dr. Waters returned along with his team of interns and discussed with me the results of the tests they've done recently—EEG, MRI, and CAT scans of Nick's brain. Although the blood around his brain has receded, they are stymied as to why he doesn't wake up.

But me....I am not stymied! He does not wake up because of the 50 milligram Trezidone Sleeping Pill, prescribed by Dr. Hilda German! That was a very strong dose. But, with a hemorrhaged and swollen brain, he should *never have been given even a small dose of sleeping medication!*

They will *never* admit that the sleeping pill was a mistake, as they protect each other's butts, and of course, the hospital wants to avoid a lawsuit.

The bottom line? Dr. Waters had one final suggestion:

I should let Nick die!

Yes, in a matter of fact tone, his exact words were that "Nick has lived a good life—a great life from the sound of it—and now you should let him go. *Let him die!*"

I want all of you to know that I have no intention of doing that. As we all know, Nicholas Carcioni is a fighter. He is fighting now. He fought during World War II, and has fought all throughout his life. No one ever handed him anything. He got everything by working very hard, and many times more than just one job at a time. He's a winner.

I am doing all I can to bring him back. In addition to playing his CDs and talking to him constantly, reminiscing about our life together, I have brought in a vibrator and have started to massage his neck, arms, and legs. Yes, he moans when I gently move his head, as his neck must be excruciating painful, but I feel that, if I can get the blood moving in his body, then surely it will stimulate his brain. I have started to also exercise his arms and legs. I lift them gently and bend them slowly and gently. He is extremely stiff.

As I sit here all day and into the night, I am constantly thinking of what else I can do. If anyone has any other suggestions, please let me know.

Again, Thank You for your cards, emails, and voice mails. Les and Pamela, thank you for the brown bag of garden vegetables that you leave by my door each evening. When I get home at around 10:30 p.m. that is my dinner, along with a piece of cheese. You are most kind. I am so thankful for both of you!

Some of you are very upset with me, because I will not let you come and visit. Let me just say to you, that there is nothing here to see. Nick is sleeping. He would not want anyone here just staring at him, and feeling sorry for him. May I suggest to those of you who are having a hard time understanding my thinking, you write him a letter or email if you have something you want to say to him. Tell him how he has touched your life, and what he means to you. I promise you, I will read your messages to him.

The truth of the matter is, we cannot afford for me to be distracted with conversation at this time. The only conversation I want to have is with Nick. **HE IS MY NUMBER-ONE CONCERN, AND I WILL BRING HIM BACK TO ME. I SWEAR TO GOD, I WILL!**

Keep praying, dear ones.

We love you,

Gabriella and Nick

(Sorry...no Visitors)

CHAPTER 26

PRESSURE TO DISCHARGE

Later in the afternoon, after Dr. Waters' visit, Gabriella was visited by the hospital Social Worker.

> "Mrs. Carcioni, my name is Tracy. I'm a social worker here at Asclepius Christian Medical Center. You know, there is no more that we can do for Nicholas, and I believe that Dr. Waters has relayed that to you. Therefore, we're going to discharge him tomorrow."

A shocked Gabriella responded,

> "What? Where am I going to take him? You have to give me more time to find a place. I am just starting to make a list of the area Nursing Homes."

Tracy responded....

> "You must let me know by Monday. That's the most time I can give you," stating as she departed.

All of the staff had started to displayed an entirely different attitude since Dr. Water's earlier dramatic visit. They had all given up on Nicholas, and Gabriella could feel the isolation.

On the morning of Saturday, August 4, 2012, Gabriella got up early and went to visit three Nursing Homes. She found that two received a "Good Rating" in the area of cleanliness. She was not going to put him in just any place. She met with the Assistants at each, as most of the Administrators do not work on Saturday. When they heard that Nicholas was in a Coma, they immediately said they would not accept him. Medicare will pay only for patients, who show improvement.

Feeling disillusioned and dejected, Gabriella went to the hospital and sat by Nick's side. He still was not responding to all her efforts, but she continued her massaging routine. During that time, another staff member entered...

> "Mrs. Carcioni, I'm Patti, a Social Worker here at Asclepius. Have you found a place yet to move Mr. Carcioni?
>
> "No, I have not," answered an agitated Gabriella.
>
> "We're going to discharge him, Mrs. Carcioni. It could be tomorrow."
>
> "No, you're not!" responded Gabriella harshly! "I will not be badgered here. Do you understand me? I brought my husband to this hospital in decent condition, and it was *your* Dr. German who pushed him into a Coma. Do *not* come in here every day pestering me. I want to see your Supervisor right now!"

About fifteen minutes later, Supervisor Paula walked into the room.

> "Mrs. Carcioni. I'm Paula, the Floor Supervisor. I understand you wanted to see me."

"Yes. Your staff is badgering me every single day about discharging my husband, Nicholas. This is unacceptable! I'm trying to find a reputable place to take him, but I need more time. I went to three nursing homes this morning, and the Administrators don't even work on Saturdays. I plan to go to another three or four on Monday. When I find a place, I will let you people know. Meantime, *you wait!*"

"Mrs. Carcioni. I understand how you feel."

"No, you don't, Paula!" shouted Gabriella.

"You people here don't understand anything! When my husband came here, he could walk and talk, and had his senses. Now Dr. Hilda German has put him into a Coma by giving him a sleeping pill, which I, as his wife, KNEW HE DID NOT NEED, AND I TOLD HER SO! Now, you can't bring him back, and you want to just kick us out! Well, forget about it. When I find a decent place, then he'll be discharged, and not a minute sooner! Understand!"

"Okay, okay, Mrs. Carcioni. Take it easy. We'll give you a few more days. Don't get yourself all worked up. Please."

"I'm already worked up, Supervisor Paula! End of discussion! Good day!"

About a hour later, a kind and loving Father Artur from St. Francis Catholic Church stopped in, to see if she wanted Communion. Gabriella was glad to see him. He stayed and chatted with her for a while, as he could see the tension and stress building in her, since his last visit just a few days earlier.

"It will all work out, Gabriella. God will help you. Let us say a prayer together now. Don't worry. I can see you're tired and under a lot of stress," said a sympathetic Father Artur.

"Yes, Father I am. I must find a suitable place to take Nicholas. One that will help him to awaken! I'll be ok. My faith is strong that God will help me. You keep praying too, please!"

"You know I will," confirmed the Priest.

At about 6:30 p.m., Gabriella felt as if she was going to bust at the seams from holding in her tears of frustration, disappointment, and fear. She needed to get some air. She packed up the CDs, and kissed Nick a hundred times, telling him that everything was fine, and he was getting better, and she missed him so very much.

"Return to me, my darling. Please return to me," she repeated over and over.

Upon reaching the riotous parking garage, she could no longer hold in her torment. As she reached Nick's car, she dropped to her knees on the pavement, sobbing uncontrollably. Leaning against his door, she was able to release a volcano of emotions. In looking up to heaven, she screamed at the top of her lungs,

"Dear Jesus Christ, my Advocate, please don't desert me! I can't make it on my own! Nick, I need you....HELP ME!" she cried out in desperation.

The garage was a noisy place, with traffic moving at a steady pace, tires squealing, and the constant shrill of horns blowing.

It proved to be her perfect refuge. However, a few cars did slow down, and asked if she needed help, but Gabriella she just shook her head without looking up, and continued sobbing profusely.

About an hour had passed before Gabriella felt she could drive home safely. When she reached their home, she hesitated before proceeding up the driveway, thinking to herself,

Nick's not here. Nobody's home. I dread going inside.

When she walked through the front door, the silence in the empty house grabbed her, as it never had before. There was not a sound. No Nick. No music. Loneliness took hold.

Just then the phone rang. Gabriella let the answering machine take the message. It was Nick's friend, Cliff, from Las Vegas asking Nick to call him. Although she had informed many of their friends about Nick's condition, there were still several who had not heard the news yet. She walked over to the machine, and saw that there were five other calls. She hit play. Four of the calls were messages for Nick, regarding upcoming music gigs.

Numb and alone in their 4,500-square-foot home, she felt like a stranger as she walked into the vaulted ceiling living room. Shuddering with trepidation, she dreaded the thought that Nick might never step foot, in their beautiful home again.

Collapsing on the staircase, she cried out to him again, begging him to forgive her, and pleading for him to return.

CHAPTER 27

SHOPPING FOR A NURSING HOME

On Sunday, August 5, 2012, Gabriella visited two more nursing homes, bringing the total visited up to five. To her surprise, many of the Administrators did not work on Saturdays, and none of them worked on Sunday. She, however, took the opportunity to wander through the hallways, and look into various rooms, to get a feel of the place. Several times she was able to do this, without being stopped by personnel. A few other places were more attentive.

Unfortunately, the places that she visited were not up to her standards. There were strong odors, dirty floors, writing on the walls, residents lying on mattresses that were on the floor rather than a bed frame, and worse than that, she heard residents screaming for help or assistance. It actually reduced her to tears, as she departed quickly. She had used the list from the Internet as her base, but learned that their ratings, many times, were not in line with hers.

Sitting by Nick's bedside, she vowed that she would put him in a clean place with friendly helpful personnel, who would assist her in helping him get well.

Dr. Bobbie Edward visited around noon. Gabriella told him about all the badgering she was encountering from the staff, regarding Nick being Discharged, asking for his help.

> "I've gone to several nursing homes," she said, "and none of them are adequate. I just won't put him in a bad place. Help me gain some more time here, till I find a decent place, Doctor."

A sympathetic Dr. Edward responded,

> "Mrs. Carcioni, there is only so much I can do. Mr. Carcioni is not responding. Neurology can't decipher why, and now we have taken him off of most medicines. When it comes to a fork in the road like this, the hospital will discharge, so that his bed can be given to someone they can treat. You must find a place by Tuesday at the latest, but that will be it. I'll talk to them, and ask them to give you till then."

Gratefully Gabriella nodded her head.

> "Okay. Thank you. I have one appointment on Monday morning, but then I have exhausted the list of Medicare approved places listed on the Internet," Gabriella replied. "I pray they accept him."

On Monday, August 6, 2012, Gabriella rose early and drove to the last Nursing Home on the list. Upon entering, she was satisfied with what she saw. The Administrator, Kessy, was friendly. Everything was going well, until Gabriella told him that Nick was in a coma presently.

> "Oh, no! We can't take him if he's in a Coma!" responded Kessy sadly.

"But he will be coming out soon. I just know he will. Give him a chance, please," pleaded Gabriella.

"I'm sorry. We can accept only patients who have the ability to improve!"

Sobbing, Gabriella left with her heart once again broken in pieces. Feeling desperate, she felt she had exhausted all her options. But, something nudged her to look again, at the Internet list of Nursing Homes.

To her surprise, a *new listing*, that was not on the original list, was added, and it was even in the neighborhood: Lavender Gardens Nursing Home.

Quickly she drove there. When she walked in, it was clean, and she could tell it had been recently renovated. A friendly staff member, Jaime Mae, gave her a tour, and Gabriella was very impressed. Upon completion of the tour, tears formed in Gabriella's eyes.

"Mrs. Carcioni, what's wrong?" a concerned Jaime Mae asked.

"Oh, Jaime Mae, there's one detail that I've neglected to tell you. My husband, Nicholas, is presently in a Coma, because his Doctor made a mistake, and gave him a sleeping pill, when he had blood on his brain. Please believe me, I'm confident that he's going to wake up soon. I'm working with him every day, and I'm starting to see a change. Can you please take him in, and give him some time to wake up?"

"Asclepius Christian Medical Center wants to discharge him, and they're badgering me every day for us to leave. Please say you'll help us," pleaded Gabriella with tears streaming down her face.

"Wow ... Mrs. Carcioni, that's major! Normally we don't take any comatose patients. This is, of course, a decision our Head Administrator will have to make, and he'll be in later this morning. All I can say is...I'll tell him about your husband, and ask him to call you. Meanwhile, have the Social Worker there call me."

"Oh, thank you, Jaime Mae. Thank you for your consideration. I'll ask Patti to call you immediately. Thank you so much. God bless you!"

An overjoyed Gabriella left with at least some *hope*. She felt that her prayers were being answered, and the heavens had heard her plea.

When Gabriella reached Nick's room at the hospital, there were three people from Palliative Care waiting to meet with her. Passing by Patti, the social worker, Gabriella gave her Jaime Mae's card, and asked her to all her immediately.

"They're going to consider taking Nicholas. Please be positive in discussing the possibility of his recovery. I really like this place. Do all you can to help, please, Patti. They're my last hope."

"O.K. I'll do what I can," Patti replied.

Gabriella looked at the others waiting and asked, "Now, how can I help you?"

"I'm Rose Marie, this is Edmund, and this is Henry. We're from Palliative Care."

A confused Gabriella asked,

"What's that?"

"We outline the care, that your husband will receive while on Hospice care," responded Edmund.

"What? He's not going into Hospice care."

"But," explained Henry, "He may be soon, from what we understand, and we just want to outline what you can expect. Dr. Edward thought we should visit you."

"It's good for you to know all the services that will be available to you," added Rose Marie.

"Okay. Go ahead. Give me your information. I'm listening. But he's not going into Hospice care yet." responded a confident Gabriella.

Gabriella stayed with them for an hour, listening carefully, as she followed along while perusing their brochure. They were very thoughtful, and she learned a lot from the meeting. Afterward, she returned to the room, still thinking of Lavender Gardens Nursing Home.

She sat with Nick and explained to him, where she had been that morning, and how excited she was about this lovely place that she wanted to take him, to get well.

A knock came to the door. Hearing a voice at the doorway, she looked up at a stranger entering the room.

"Hello, I'm Lena Marie DiSalle, representative for Asclepius Christian Hospice."

Annoyed Gabriella responded…

"Everyone keeps talking about Hospice this morning. My husband is not going into Hospice care. He'll come out of this coma. I just have to find a place that will take him in. As a matter of fact, I found a very nice Nursing Home this morning, and they are considering him. I'm praying that they do!"

Lena motioned Gabriella to come with her.

"Perhaps we should talk outside, away from Mr. Carcioni."

"No. We'll talk right here. He likes to hear all that's going on. Really, it's okay. Sit down, Lena Marie."

"All right. Thank you. What happened to your husband, Mrs. Carcioni?" asked the sympathetic Rep.

Gabriella proceeded to tell her the whole story about Dr. Hilda German. After she was finished, Lena took a deep breath, shook her head, and said,

"I feel so sorry for you. You've been through a lot."

"No, Lena Marie," inserted Gabriella. "Actually, *he's* been through a lot! My heart aches for him. But I'm feeling so much better *this morning*, since visiting this one Nursing Home that I'm VERY interested in."

"What's the name of it?"

"Lavender Gardens—at 127 Richland Avenue."

"Oh Yes. I know a Doctor there," stated Lena Marie. "He's a Doctor here at Asclepius, and is also the Medical Doctor at Lavender Gardens. I can call him and ask him if he can do something, to move your husband over there. I'll try calling him now, OK?" as she grabbed her cell phone out of her purse.

Gabriella could barely control her excitement...

"Oh my God, Lena Marie. Please call him!" Gabriella implored.

Upon dialing, the doctor answered, and she apprised him of the Carcioni situation. He asked her to send all Nick's records over to him immediately, and he would have an answer within a few hours. She hung up, and explained the conversation to Gabriella.

"Done!" announced Lena Marie. "I'll tell Nurse Barbara Jo to Fax all Mr. Carcioni's records to the Doctor."

"Oh, Lena Marie, you're heaven sent! What's the Doctor's name?"

"Dr. Roland Yurkevich (*pronounced yur KEV ich*). We've been friends for years. He's very intelligent, and he'll do all he can to help."

"Lena Marie, I don't know what to say! You're an angel from heaven! Thank you so much for calling him. I'm so tremendously Happy and Grateful!" cried Gabriella, with tears rolling down her cheeks. "You say, we'll know in a few hours?"

"That's what he said. It won't take him long to assess the situation, and talk to the staff at Lavender Gardens. Meantime, why don't you go have some lunch in the cafeteria."

"I'm okay. I'll just sit here. Thank you. Thank you so very much!"

"I hope it all works out for you, Gabriella. I hope he awakens soon," she stated compassionately.

Gabriella hugged Lena Marie, thanking her repeatedly.

Gabriella immediately went to Nick's side, smiling from ear to ear,

"Sweetheart, did you hear that? This woman, Lena Marie just picked the phone up and called the Doctor, who is the Medical Director over at Lavender Gardens Nursing Home, where I want to take you. It's a beautiful place, and I know you'll be happy there. I'm so happy! Thank you, Dear God and Blessed Mother. Let's say our Rosary, sweetheart."

Tears of joy ran down her face, as she kissed Nick repeatedly.

About two hours later, Nurse Barbara Jo stepped in to say that Mr. Carcioni had been accepted at Lavender Gardens.

"We'll be transporting him there in a half hour. Please gather up all his belongings. Transport will be here shortly," smiling as she handed Gabriella several papers to sign.

A thankful and grateful Gabriella looked up to heaven with tears pouring down her cheeks.

"Thank you...Thank you... for answering my prayer! ...and Thank You for sending your special Angel, Lena Marie, to help me and my Nicholas!"

CHAPTER 28

WELCOME TO LAVENDER GARDENS

On August 6, 2012, at 4:30 p.m. the ambulance transported Nicholas to the Nursing Home. Gabriella followed behind in her car, filled with increasing jubilation, and thankfulness for this blessed place, named Lavender Gardens. Finally, she was going to be around positive thinking people, who wanted to help Nick get well.

Nicholas was placed in a room that had a huge window, looking onto an open grassy lawn with lots of trees and bushes. It was a serene setting. Within minutes, a friendly man, about five ten, in his late fifties, with gray hair entered the room.

"Hello. I'm John O'Reilly, Head Administrator here," he said with a friendly smile.

"Oh, hello Mr. O'Reilly. I'm Gabriella, and this is my husband, Nicholas Carcioni. It's so wonderful to be here! Thank you so much for accepting Nicholas. He's in a Coma now, but he'll be out of it soon. Believe me!"

A confident Gabriella spoke, while smiling at the Head Administrator.

"It's nice to meet both of you. You can call me John. I'm new here too—only been here a month, so we'll learn together," he said in a warm, congenial tone.

"Thank you, John."

"If you need anything, just ask at the desk. And if I can ever be of assistance, my door is always open, so please don't hesitate to see me."

Thank you, John. You're most kind," responded Gabriella.

John gently took Nick's hand before he left.

"So very nice to meet you, Mr. Carcioni." He turned again to Gabriella.

"I'll stop in from time to time to check on Mr. Carcioni. I do that with many of my residents on a regular basis. So, I'll see you tomorrow. Have a good evening."

"Thank you and good night, John."

"Goodnight Mrs. Carcioni."

"Please call me Gabriella...and my husband is Nicholas."

"Thank you and goodnight, Gabriella."

Gabriella almost could not contain her joyfulness! Her smile was beaming. Hugging and kissing Nicholas, she started to recap the day.

"Nicholas, my love, we found a very good place for you. John, the Administrator, is so nice, and I think he's going to take a special interest in you, which makes me so very happy. God has answered our prayers. Finally, we found a place, that will offer some support and help us."

"Let me massage your neck for you now, darling. It's been such a busy day. I'm running behind schedule. I feel what I'm doing here is very good for you, so I don't want to miss a day."

As Gabriella unpacked the massager and set up Nick's CDs to play, one of the Certified Nursing Assistants (CNA) walked in. Gabriella could tell he was gay, by his flamboyant walk and talk. Gabriella was not prejudiced, so it made no difference to her.

"Hi, I'm Lee. I'll be your CNA tonight."

"Hi, I'm Gabriella and this is my husband, Nicholas Carcioni. He's in a Coma, but he will be coming out of it soon. That's why I have his CD playing all the time."

"That's him singing?" Lee asked surprised.

"Yes, and that's his sax playing too. He has his own Big Band Orchestra."

"Wow. He's famous?"

"Yes, he's been known throughout the Chicago area for about sixty years, and has worked behind the biggest stars in the Entertainment Industry!"

"Oh, my God! He *is* famous."

"Yes. Now, be very gentle when moving him, Lee. His neck, arms, and legs ache so very badly, because he hasn't moved them in weeks.

"How long has he been in a Coma?"

"Fifteen days."

"Oh my! Wait till I tell the others that we have someone famous here. Let me get someone to help me turn him. I'll be back."

Around 5:00 p.m. that evening, staff members started to pass out dinner trays to all the rooms. Residents also had the choice of eating in the dining room area, where large tables were set up, suitable for dining and playing games.

Another CNA stopped into Nick's room with a tray, and when Gabriella told her that Nick was in a Coma, she offered the tray to her. Gabriella accepted. She hadn't eaten all day. She couldn't help but to think how little these CNAs were complimented, for all the good they did. They did all the grunt work as they tried to care for all the residents and patients, and yet they received very little appreciation, for their performance. CNAs are a godsend to all hospitals and nursing homes. Everyone should recognize their value, and show much gratitude.

Lee returned with his coworker, Jimmy, a husky guy who looked as if he could lift 200 pounds easily. Gabriella watched as Lee and Jimmy proceeded to change Nicholas and get him into a clean gown. When they turned Nicholas to his side, he started to moan, and Gabriella reminded them that his muscles were very sore.

"Please be as gentle as you can with him, guys," she reiterated, "and watch his feeding tube. We don't want that to come out."

"Yeah, we see it Mrs. Carcioni," said Lee.

"I play the sax too," said Jimmy.

"Tenor or alto?"

"Tenor."

"So, does Nicholas. When he awakens, you two will have to talk about music."

"Yes, ma'am. I'm looking forward to it."

At around 7:30 p.m. the Head Nurse on the floor, Virginia Margaret, came in to administer Nick's medicines. She was tall, thin, lovely green eyes, and long beautiful auburn hair. Gabriella could tell that she knew what she was doing, because she was very professional in every way.

"Hi, I'm Virginia Margaret. I'll be your husband's nurse this evening."

"Does he have different nurses every day?"

"Monday thru Friday it will be me. I don't work on weekends. I understand he's in a Coma. I'm so sorry to hear that! But, don't give up. He could wake up at any time. I've seen plenty of miracles in my 25 years on the job."

"Yes, thank you. I agree with you, Virginia Margaret," said Gabriella. "That's his CD playing. You'll probably hear this every day. I want him to hear himself singing again."

"Wow, that's great. He's a singer?"

"Yes, and he has a Big Band Orchestra too," proudly stated Gabriella.

"I love that music," Virginia Margaret added.

"That was a very classy era. When music was music. Not like today's crap."

She turned to dispose of some wrappings.

"All right, I'm all done. He's received all his meds for the night."

"Can you review with me what you're giving him?" asked Gabriella.

"Sure, I'll write a list for you too. Also, later tonight, at around ten, he'll be ready for another bag of liquid food. That should last him till the morning. Of course, he's getting blood pressure meds, diabetes meds, and he's still on Norco for the head pain. Hmmm. I'll mention that to the doctor. I wonder if that is really still necessary. Also, later, someone from an outside company we use will come by and take blood. That's all they do for us. So, expect them later. Dr. Yurkevich ordered blood samples, and he might stop in tonight or tomorrow to see Mr. Carcioni. His schedule fluctuates, and no one ever knows when he'll be here."

"Okay. Thanks for telling me. No way to find out if he's coming? I'm really anxious to meet him!"

"I'll try to find out for you."

About an hour later, Virginia Margaret returned to say that Dr. Yurkevich would *not* be in that night, but would possibly be in the next evening. Learning that the Doctor would not be in, and knowing Nicholas was changed and had his meds, she departed for home. This was the first day, she was heading home with a smile on her face, and some peace of mind.

Tomorrow a new exciting chapter would begin, as Gabriella continued to do everything possible to awaken Nicholas, and bring him back to her.

Yes, Gabriella was finally seeing light, at the end of a long, dark, tunnel.

CHAPTER 29

DR. YURKEVICH EXPECTED NICK TO DIE

Nick had been in Lavender Gardens Nursing Home for five days. Gabriella had met Dr. Yurkevich the previous evening for the first time. He was their Medical Director, and now was Nicholas' personal Physician.

Learning from the staff that Dr. Yurkevich was of Polish decent, Gabriella shared with him during their initial meeting, that her nationality was Polish and Italian. He was a soft-spoken devoted professional, and yet very direct in voicing what he was thinking. She smiled, as he reminded Gabriella of her father. The staff spoke very highly of him, and Gabriella was so glad he would be Nick's Doctor.

When Dr. Yurkevich entered the room, Gabriella had immediately thanked him for all that he had done for Nicholas, in getting him accepted at Lavender Gardens Nursing Home. He just smiled. He stood over Nicholas's bed, grabbed Nick's right hand, moved his fingers, and said he had a lot of arthritis. He noted that, if it is in the fingers, it's also throughout his body.

Gabriella told the doctor that, when she moved Nicholas' neck, he moaned.

"Yes, he undoubtedly has arthritis in his neck too."

Then Dr. Yurkevich moved to examining Nicholas' feet. He looked at Gabriella and remarked,

"Gabriella, you see how his toes are bent back toward his face?"

"Yes. I try to bend them back, but they are so stiff!"

"That's right." Dr. Yurkevich reinforced.

"Unfortunately, Gabriella this denotes massive brain damage."

"Nicholas' brain has had tremendous trauma. I don't know if he will be able to come out of this Coma, and I just want you to be prepared. Honestly, I accepted him here, because I didn't think he'd live past a week."

"Really, Dr. Yurkevich! I'm shocked to hear you say that! Well, all I can say is, I have more faith than you do, I suppose. My plan is for a full recovery. But thanks for your honesty. May I share a lengthy routine, with you, that I've devised to bring him out of that coma?"

"Yes...I'm listening."

Gabriella started to expound.

"It includes me placing my "healing hands" on him, and visualize a healing blue light surrounding his entire body. Physically, I lift his upper body, especially his head, and hold it for a minute or longer. Later, I run this massager (showing him the massager in her case), up and down his neck, shoulders, arms and legs. From now on, I'll add the feet."

"Additionally, I raise his arms slowly and gently trying to get them to reach his head. I raise his legs, and bend them. I do all repeatedly, every day. Yesterday, I added a heating pad for his neck, and it seems to relieve a lot of his neck pain. He didn't moan when the CNAs rolled him on his side.

"For speech, I play his CDs all night, so Nicholas can learn his words again. John, the Head Administrator, said that would be fine. The other residents nearby, say they enjoy the good music. So, everyone is happy. Additionally, I talk constantly to him, only using positive statements, reinforcing that he is healing and getting better every single day. I relive many of the memories that we shared. I read to him. And most importantly, I remind him to follow my voice, and return to me. I'm here waiting for him to awaken."

Dr. Yurkevich smiled and nodded in surprise, as he raised his bushy eyebrows.

"Very good! Keep me informed as to how that's working out, the next time I'm in. I'm here every few days. Meantime, no meds have to be altered. All we can do is wait till he is ready to open his eyes. He looks comfortable."

"You're a good wife!" commented Dr. Yurkevich, while staring at Gabriella.

"In fact, you were also a prime factor as to why I took him in. Your love, dedication, and defiance to be defeated, is remarkable and admirable, to say the least!"

"I'm just doing what *any* wife would do," Gabriella responded. "I believe with my whole heart that he'll awaken soon, Doctor."

With that, the good Doctor departed.

Gabriella sat by Nick's side every day from 9:00 in the morning until 10:30 at night. Some staff members asked her several times if she wanted to go out for lunch, but she would not leave Nick's side. When the staff members were too busy to change him (being comatose, he wore a diaper), Gabriella often took it upon herself to wash and change him. When she needed extra diapers, towels, and washcloths to accomplish this, she would go to the desk, and ask for a supply.

Eventually, the staff members at the desk told her to just go down the hall, and get what she needed in the closet, which she did. Everyone was very friendly toward her.

Gabriella got to know several of the residents, especially the ones across the hall and next door to Nick. One afternoon, suddenly there was loud screaming coming from next door. Gabriella ran into the hall. The screaming continued:

"Get out of here! Get out of here!" Wanda, a wheelchair-bound resident shrieked.

Gabriella ran into her room next door.

"Wanda, what's wrong?"

Hysterically, Wanda screamed.

"There's spiders all over my bed, and they're crawling on me!"

Gabriella grabbed Wanda, yanked her out of bed, and quickly placed her into her wheelchair, brushing the spiders off Wanda's clothes as Wanda continued to scream and cry. Then hurriedly wheeled the hysterical woman into the hallway, and told her to stay there while she ran to the desk. Gabriella informed the nurses of the emergency, and they came running immediately to get the other resident, Jodi, who was blind, out of her bed. The two women were moved to another room for the night, as maintenance sprayed their room, bedding and all.

What had happened?

Wanda had requested a nightstand of her own, because Jodi had taken over the only one in the room for her own use. Staff members had brought Wanda one that had been in storage, but they did not notice that, on the underneath surface, there was a huge spiders' nest. During the day, the nest had broken and the spiders had escaped.

Wanda was very thankful for Gabriella's help, and from that day on, she took a special liking to Gabriella and Nicholas. She watched over him, especially during the night and early morning hours, when Gabriella went home to sleep.

Gabriella started to notice that the CNAs were not checking on Nick in a timely fashion, so she started to keep track of when they attended to him.

Early in the evening, Gabriella had to go find Lee, the CNA, to inform him that Nicholas needed to be turned. When Lee came in, he did not bring anyone to help him, and so Gabriella had to pitch in. Nick also needed to be changed at that time. Lee had not brought any diapers or washcloths, and was glad that Gabriella had a supply in the drawer.

Said Gabriella...

> "That's my supply, Lee, for whenever I can't find you guys. When you come in, you should have a supply in your hands already, knowing that he probably will need to be changed."

> "Yeah, you're right. I just know that you are here, and so I get busy going to other rooms." replied Lee.

> "That's fine Lee. But taking care of Nicholas is *your* job too. Don't think that, because I'm here, I am here to do *your job* too. That's not right."

> "I know. I'm sorry. I'm having an off day." Lee replied apologetically.

> "What's wrong?" asked Gabriella.

> "Tomorrow I'm coming out!"

> "Coming out of what, Lee? I don't understand."

> "I'm transgender," he stated in a matter-of-fact tone to a clueless Gabriella.

> "I'm sorry, Lee. What are you talking about?"

Lee laughed.

> "Let me show you some pictures." He took some photos out of his pocket. "These are pictures of guys, who have had surgical operations to make them, into women."

"What? I've never heard of this. These can't be guys. They're gorgeous!"

"Yes, they were born men, but now they're women!" explained Lee. "And I'm saving money to have this done to me too. "Anyway, tomorrow I'm coming out, and I will *look* different on the outside, but I will look the way I *feel* on the inside. No more hiding!"

"My God, Lee. They have to do a lot of altering to change a man into a woman. It's unbelievable to think this can even be done. Are you sure?" asked a shocked Gabriella.

"Oh, I'm very sure, Gabriella. It's being done for years, especially in Europe," he replied with a chuckle, "and being done here now too,"

"Oh, okay, if you say so," replied Gabriella hesitantly as she thought,

What does he mean he'll look different?

Then adding....

"That's great. I'll look forward to seeing you tomorrow, Lee. But you take care of my baby all through the night. Hear me?"

"Yes, ma'am. Don't you worry."

CHAPTER 30

TRANSGENDER?

August 11, 2012.

The weekend schedule at Lavender Gardens Nursing Home was similar to that at the hospital, meaning that, when the weekend crew came on, the routine established during the week went awry.

Gabriella found herself meeting new staff members, reiterating Nicholas' condition, and evaluating their work habits. Some purposely hid during the day and night. Because they were nowhere to be found, the other CNAs had to pick up the slack, which many times did not happen. This was Gabriella's first weekend at Lavender Gardens, coming in at 8:30 a.m.

Now nearing 11:30 a.m. yet no one had come in to give Nicholas his bed bath for the day. This was usually done first thing in the morning, prior to 10:00 a.m. He would be washed, changed, new gown, and change of bed linens. For Gabriella, hygiene was crucial.

Gabriella went to the desk to inquire. "Who's the CNA for the morning shift today?"

'It's Vanessa," replied another CNA. "No, wait, Vanessa called in sick. Elaine is covering for her."

"Could you send her in as soon as possible? My husband has not been given a bed bath yet."

"Sure. We'll let her know. However, she's starting to take residents to the dining room for lunch, so it will probably be after lunch."

"Well, whenever. Ask her to come in, please." Gabriella was very unhappy that Nicholas could not expect a bed bath and change until around 2 p.m. *Not acceptable,* she thought. *I'll do it myself.* Luckily, she had a supply of clean towels and washcloths. For soap, she had brought a special scented body wash, Old Spice Denali, for the CNAs to use on Nicholas, as she loved the fresh scent it provided. Having very little in her backup drawer, she went to the linen closet to grab a few clean gowns, diapers, clean sheets, and pillowcases. As she bathed Nick, she vowed she would never let the procedure go past 10:00 a.m. again.

Afterwards as always, she sat by his side and said the Rosary out loud, asking Nick to pray along with her. Then she played his CD and proceeded to massage his body, now adding his feet to her routine, which took about an hour and half to complete.

When she finished, she proceeded to do something she had started to do that gave her much peace. She drew the curtain halfway around the bed, so that people walking down the hall could not see her or Nick. She lowered Nick's bed to her height, sat on a chair next to him, and positioned a pillow close to Nick's shoulder. She rested her head on the pillow and held his hand. This was the closest she could get to feeling, as if she was lying next to him in bed. Most of the time, because she was so comfortable, she would fall asleep. This afternoon's nap was a blessing, as she had been having so many sleepless nights.

While in a sound sleep, she was startled by the loud voice of someone entering the room:

"Nicholas and Gabriella, helllloooo!"

Gabriella opened her sleepy eyes to see a woman with long blond hair wearing lots of makeup—lipstick and bold eyelashes. She even had manicured painted fingernails. The woman sung her words as she talked, all the while batting her eyelashes.

"Helllooo! So, what do you think?" she said smiling.

Gabriella didn't recognize her, and asked,

"Do I know you? I don't think we've met."

The woman laughed.

"Gabriella, it's me, Lee! Except *now*, my name is Leesa! So, make sure from now on you call me, Leesa."

A stunned Gabriella spoke.

"Lee ... I mean Leesa, what have you done to yourself?"

"I told you. Today is my day for *coming out*," Leesa responded. "Remember I told you I'm transgender? Call me Leesa, please. From now on, I am no longer going to walk around like a guy. This is how I feel inside. I've always felt like a woman! So, I'm going to alter all that I can about myself, until I can save enough money, then get an appointment with a professional surgeon."

"Do you like my look? Do I look sexy? A couple of guys whistled at me today when I was walking through the parking lot at my apartment." She laughed.

Gabriella, still in shock, choked out,

> "Yeah ... you look great. You'll still be working here as a CNA, right?"

> "Oh, heavens yes," Leesa replied.

> "Great, cause you're my favorite, you know. I can always depend on you to take care of Nicholas. Today, no one came to bath him or change him. I did it myself!"

> "Oh my God! Nobody came in!?"

> "No."

> "Well, I'm here now, and I'll check on him after the dinner hour, probably around eight."

> "Great. I'll be here waiting, Leesa. Listen, I just want to say... that I wish you the best with what you're battling inside you. It must be awful! Does your mom know?"

> "Yes, and she is trying to be supportive, really. But I'm not to tell my grandmother. She'd have a heart attack, my mom says. So, I still have to hide it from her!"

> "Well, be careful. Some people are cruel. You know what I mean, Leesa?"

Leesa smiled. She liked hearing herself being called by that name, and she was so glad that Gabriella accepted her without judgment.

By 8:00p.m. Leesa still had not come in to see Nicholas. Gabriella went looking for her at the desk. "Where's Leesa?"

"You mean Lee?" Nurse Eleanor replied sternly.

"Lee ... Leesa ... whatever. Where is she?"

"*He* was sent home, and told not to come to work looking like a woman again!" she responded.

"I need someone to attend to my husband, Nicholas. Who's his CNA now?"

"I don't know. I'll find out and send someone in to see you. What do you need?" she asked.

"My husband needs to be changed. I've attended to him all day today, including giving him a bed bath. I even changed the bed linens. But I expect you people to do your job!" stated Gabriella firmly.

"Well, yes, but we're a little short staffed now," she responded.

"Yes, I keep hearing that! Please send someone as soon as possible. Thank you," Gabriella responded kindly. She did not want to get into an argument with Nurse Eleanor, as she wanted Nicholas taken care of, especially after she went home for the night.

The following days were peppered with care inconsistencies and staff shortages. Leesa argued with Charolette, Director of Nursing about her female appearance, and then was suspended. Turmoil was mounting.

Gabriella, being present there for approximately fifteen hours a day, seven days a week, noticed that the people hired to fill the vacancies were novices. They had just finished school, and completed their courses of study to receive their certificates as

CNAs. This would be their first job! She did not feel confident about their knowledge or dedication. However, she tried to be friendly with all of them, as her first concern, was for constant care and good treatment for Nicholas.

CHAPTER 31

NICHOLAS AWAKENS FROM THE COMA

Miracle #1

On Monday, August 13, 2012, Gabriella was happy to see the weekend over, and the regular staff back on duty, including administration employees and department heads. When she walked in, however, she noticed that Nick's liquid food was running very low, and now, at 10:00 a.m., no one had come in to replace it. She immediately went to the desk to inform the staff.

Immediately, Intern Jared, came in to replace it. He had been making his rounds, and Nick was next on the list. A very friendly and compassionate man, Jared asked...

> "How's Mr. Carcioni doing, ma'am? I said a prayer for him yesterday at his bedside."

Gabriella smiled.

> "Thank you, Jared! That's what he needs more than anything. Please keep praying."

'Yes ma'am."

###

Once again, a new CNA was assigned to Nicholas.

"Hi, I'm Diamond," the sweet young black girl stated as she entered.

"Hi, I'm Gabriella, and this gentleman is my husband, Nicholas. He's in a coma."

"Oh my! Do I have to do anything special in taking care of him?" she asked, seemingly frightened.

"No, Diamond. Just be as gentle as you can because he has arthritis all over his body. And be careful not to pull out the feeding tube too. I'm working on getting him to wake up, and I feel that will happen soon."

"Okay, I will be gentle, Ms. Gabriella," Diamond replied with a smile.

"Are you new as a CNA?"

"Yes, I just graduated."

"That's good. The medical field needs caring people like you."

"I think I will like it. I like to help people."

Gabriella stayed to watch Diamond give Nicholas a bed bath. At one point, she had to turn him to his side to wash his back. As she pushed him to the side, Gabriella was shocked to see

246

Nicholas open his eyes! She rushed to his side, but his eyes closed just as suddenly as they had opened.

"Did you see that, Diamond?" she asked excitingly.

"See what, Ms. Gabriella?"

"I'm sure I saw Nicholas open his eyes for a second!"

"No, I didn't see his face."

"When you're done with his back, let's push him to the other side. I want to see if he opens his eyes again."

Diamond did as Gabriella instructed, but Nicholas did not open his eyes again. Gabriella even started to question if he really had opened his eyes, or was this just wishful thinking on her part. Nevertheless, the possibility brought a slight smile to her face, and a glimmer of hope that she might, indeed, be reaching him on some level. It was a breakthrough that she had been praying for. This gave her even more reason to maintain a sunny disposition, and have high expectations of sanguinity.

On Wednesday, August 15, 2012, Feast of the Assumption of The Blessed Mother. Gabriella went to early Mass that morning, prior to coming to Lavender Gardens, so she was not there at 8:30 a.m. as usual.

Diamond was scheduled to be Nicholas's CNA. Gabriella had been training her over the past week, in the care that she expected for Nicholas. Diamond liked both Gabriella and Nicholas, so she was happy to please them, and was doing a good job. She was thorough and gentle. Gabriella felt comfortable leaving Nicholas in her care, while she went to Mass and attended to banking business, vowing she would not to be too long.

At 9:00 a.m. Diamond entered Nicholas's room as usual. She started to get herself set up for his bed bath. As she walked out of the bathroom carrying a small tub of warm soapy water, she glanced over at him. Nick was looking at her with his eyes wide open. Shocked, Diamond spilled most of the water onto the floor and almost dropped the pan! She went running out of the room, screaming:

"Mr. Carcioni's awake! Mr. Carcioni's awake!"

John, Head Administrator, came running out of another resident's room.

"What?" he yelled.

"Yeah, come and see!" Diamond pulled on his sport coat, with tears in her eyes. John ran to the room. He stopped suddenly, before entering, as he did not want to frighten Nick, who just sat there looking around the room, as if he was wondering where he was.

Taking a deep breath, John approached the bed slowly.

"Hi, Mr. Carcioni. I'm John. How are you today?"

Nick just stared at John for about five seconds, then finally responded,

"Okay."

He did not know who John was, and was probably trying to figure out *where* he was. The look on his face showed some fear.

"I'm glad you're okay, Mr. Carcioni. We've all been waiting for you to wake up. Your wife, Gabriella, is here every day, sitting by your side. She loves you very much," reinforced John.

Nicholas did not respond verbally or with any facial expression. He simply closed his eyes again, and did not reopen them.

Gabriella entered Lavender Gardens at about 10:30, an hour and a half after Nick opened his eyes. Immediately everyone started calling out,

"Gabriella, Mr. Carcioni woke up this morning!"

"*What!*" Gabriella exclaimed as she started running toward Nick's room.

Wanda, who was Nick's neighbor next door, was anxiously waiting in the hallway for Gabriella to arrive. Upon seeing her, she exclaimed,

"Nick woke up. He woke up, Gabriella! Just like you said he would!"

Gabriella smiled through her tears, saying,

"Yes ... yes!"

Nurse Gene followed Gabriella into the room and started to tell her the whole story about Diamond, while another aide called John on the phone to say that Mrs. Carcioni had arrived.

As happy as Gabriella was to hear the news, she felt heartbroken as she entered the room to find Nick asleep again. She kissed him and softly told him she was there, and that she would love for him to open his eyes and see her. But Nick did not respond.

John entered and recapped the entire story for Gabriella in an excited manner.

> "Nick not only opened his eyes, Gabriella, he spoke! When I asked him how he was, he responded, 'Okay'! Gabriella, you were right. Nick is coming out of his coma. All that you have done, has been very good for him. I put a call into Dr. Yurkevich to tell him the good news!"

Gabriella was understandably overtaken with emotion. She kissed Nick's hands and cried, leaning gently on his chest. She then took out her Rosary and started to pray, thanking The Blessed Mother for answering her prayers. She just kept repeating through her tears,

> "Thank you, Blessed Mother ... Thank You ... so very much!"

Every day after that, Gabriella patiently waited for Nick to open his eyes and speak again. But she would have to be patient, as it did not happen again soon.

CHAPTER 32

ONGOING EMAILS TO FAMILY MEMBERS AND FRIENDS

August 24, 2012

Dearest Family and Friends,

This is the latest update to a very fast-paced week.

In my last email to you, we were all celebrating Nicholas opening his eyes on August 15, and responding "Okay" when John, the Administrator, asked him how he was doing.

He then fell back asleep and has not awakened since. Of course, I'm disappointed that I was not at the nursing home to witness this, but it gives me a sign that he is coming out of the coma … slowly but surely.

Dr. Yurkevich stopped in last night. He was very surprised to hear that Nicholas had awakened, albeit for just a few minutes. I asked for his assessment.

He said,

'Nicholas is in limbo. He is stable ... not getting any better, and not getting any worse. I believe that he is trying to make up his mind which way to go—stay or go. When more blood leaves the brain area, the brain will then have more room, and we'll be able to see what kind of impact all this blood and pressure, has had on his mental state. Only time will tell. He will have to move from this point, sooner or later."

Dr. Yurkevich then recapped fees. "As you know, Medicare covers only 100 days here. Then, the individual is on their own, which costs about $500 per day, or $14,000 a month here at Lavender Gardens. You must start to think about what your next step is going to be in case he doesn't wake up again, Mrs. Carcioni."

Yes, dear friends, we're still walking on a tightrope!

Father Steve from Immaculate Conception Church, stopped in to give me Communion yesterday. He is such a friendly man, with a great sense of humor. He, of course, could not believe all that Nick has been through, and he blessed him with holy water.

He said,

"This should help him wake up. It's a fresh batch!" I needed that laugh. Believe me.

Please keep praying for Nicholas to awaken again. Thank you for all the prayers, cards, emails, and phone calls that you send on a consistent basis. I am here alone each day, but just knowing that you are not far away, gives me much comfort.

Pray for his complete recovery, or pray that Jesus, in his mercy, will hasten an end to his suffering.

Thank You. Will keep you informed.

(Sorry no visitors at this time.)

Gabriella

CHAPTER 33

GLIMPSE INTO NURSING HOME LIVING

On August 27, 2012, Gabriella had a meeting with John, Head Administrator at Lavender Gardens, and Charolette, Director of Nursing.

Gabriella had asked for this meeting, because procedures were starting to become very lax. During the course of the meeting, she advised them that, on several consecutive days, Nicholas had received his liquid food three hours late. When she had complained about this to the staff members at the nurses' desk, she was told,

> "That's okay. It doesn't hurt him. It's one of those details, that must have fallen through the cracks."

"I disagree," Gabriella told John and Charolette.

"I want him to be fed in a timely fashion so that he gets his nourishment. You'll have to implement a tighter schedule, *so his feeding doesn't fall through the cracks*, Charolette.

"Also, his teeth are not being cleaned properly, and they're stained. Unacceptable. I will perform his oral care and clean his teeth myself, if that's okay with both of you."

John and Charolette gave their permission.

"Lastly," Gabriella continued, "as we all know, turning Nicholas every two hours is extremely important to prevent bedsores. This, unfortunately, isn't happening. I must constantly go to the desk, and remind the nurses that he needs to be turned, and many times have done it myself. Therefore, I'm suggesting we implement this Daily Activity Form that I've designed."

She handed each a copy.

"The CNA will sign in, put the reason for being in the room, and add time in and time out. This will keep everyone on schedule, not only for turning, but for changing him, and for bed baths. I hope this meets with your approval, as I would like to implement it—*today*."

John replied enthusiastically.

"This is a great idea! I like it. How 'bout you, Charolette?

"Yeah, okay. We can start it today," Charolette replied sourly.

"Wonderful!" exclaimed Gabriella.

"I know this is a busy place, and with staff shortages, there are bound to be errors that occur. But, if we all put our heads together and work together to think of ways to improve, I'm sure there will be fewer omissions or problems. Agree?"

"Yes, absolutely, Gabriella," agreed John.

Charolette was silent, but nodded her head.

"I'll have the desk make copies," said Gabriella. "And I brought a clipboard. The clipboard will be located inside the closet, on the shelf. You'll inform all CNAs today, Charolette?"

"Yes. I have a meeting with them in one hour."

"Wonderful. Thank you both for your time," Gabriella said as she left John's office.

Lavender Gardens Nursing Home was listed on the Internet with an excellent five-star rating. It was an older facility, but was under new ownership and had been mostly renovated recently. It was, indeed, a beautiful place. Even still, apart from the face-lift, many aspects of fundamental care had been inconsistent or overlooked. This had become an unacceptable daily occurrence, that Gabriella was not going to accept. Many times, she had said to herself,

"Good thing I'm here to catch this!"

When Nicholas was admitted under Medicare, he was put in a room by himself, although each room had two beds. Luckily, he had been given the bed near the window with a nice view, and he was close to the air conditioner (maybe too close). It was also near the bathroom. One small closet for each resident was provided, and three dresser drawers. There were two wall-mounted remotely controlled televisions, and lines for two telephones. Not seeing one, she asked for a phone, and they provided one, that day.

Meals were served three times a day. Residents who preferred to eat in the dining room and could get there by wheelchair or walker were assisted by CNAs. When food service workers delivered trays to room-bound patients, they simply left the tray and did not offer assistance. If a patient or family member asked for help with meals, it was provided, based upon availability of CNAs.

After Nick had been at Lavender Gardens for about a month, a roommate named Zeke was assigned to that room. Zeke was a tall, well-built black man in his late forties, who had only one leg, and limited use of his one arm. He also had a speech impediment, and therefore did not converse often. When he did, he was a bit difficult to understand.

Gabriella felt sorry for Zeke, as he, along with many other residents, never had any visitors. He never even had any phone calls. Gabriella used to wonder where his family and friends were. So, she took it upon herself to watch out for Zeke, taking note of little things, like if Zeke needed help in eating his dinner. If so, she would inform the desk.

Additionally, she turned on his TV, and showed him options of shows to watch, such as the Bears' game. Zeke liked Gabriella. He noticed her attentiveness to Nicholas, and started to watch over Nicholas, during the night hours when Gabriella went home.

One morning, when Gabriella came in, Zeke told her that Nicholas had been calling her name all night long. He said,

> "I tried to tell him you were home sleeping, and you would be here in the morning, but he just kept calling your name— 'Gabriella! Gabriella!'

"I'm sorry, Zeke. You know he's in the process of coming out of a Coma, and I guess his brain just clicked, and he wanted me. I'm sorry if he disturbed your sleep. Thank you for telling me."

"Oh no. I wasn't sleeping. He doesn't bother me," replied Zeke sweetly.

"Does the CD playing all night, bother you?" Gabriella asked.

"No, I like hearing Nick sing," Zeke replied quickly.

MEET THE NEIGHBORS: Across the hall was an attractive, classy lady, Constance. She was 70 years old, and was at Lavender Gardens for therapy on her broken ankle. Gabriella and Constance immediately struck up a good friendship, after meeting one day at the Nurse's desk.

Constance invited Gabriella to visit her in her room later. When Gabriella entered, she noticed that Constance had her own flowered ruffled bedspread and matching sheets. Constance made it perfectly clear, that she was not a resident there. She was there only for therapy and would, hopefully, be leaving soon.

Gabriella was happy to have a friendly educated person to talk with occasionally, as they would compare happenings at Lavender Gardens. Some incidents were funny, and some were frightening. Constance also complimented Nick's music and singing and said she enjoyed it.

Gabriella noticed that Constance's daughter visited on Sundays only, and stayed for about two hours, bringing clean sheets and pillowcases and taking the dirty linens home to wash. She did not take Constance out for lunch or dinner, which Constance craved, and disliked being confined to Lavender Gardens. A few times, she asked Gabriella to take her out for lunch, but Gabriella told her she would not leave Nicholas. He was her #1 concern.

Being a night owl, Constance heard a lot throughout the night, and she shared her experiences with Gabriella.

> "Last night, Nick called your name all night long. At around two o'clock in the morning, Nurse Camille went into Nick's room, and I heard her say sternly,
>
> 'Shut Up! Either shut up, or I'll shut you up!'
>
> "Nick lay there very quietly for about fifteen minutes and then he started calling you again, only softer. It broke my heart. I was going to phone you, but it was after 2 a.m.!"

Gabriella was extremely upset to hear this. She told Constance,

> "I don't care what time it is! If you ever feel Nicholas is in danger, or really needs me, *please* call me! *Promise* me." Constance promised she would.

###

Next door to Constance, were two women who fought like cats and dogs. They were in their mid 80's. A very meek elderly Italian lady, Jelsamina, was starting to show signs of dementia.

Her roommate, Michele was a Jewish lady, possessing a loud laugh, and was more outspoken and strong willed.

Everyone liked Jelsamina, who had been a resident at Lavender Gardens for a few years. Although a sweet woman, she was starting to be very dependent on the staff, always needing some assistance. Michele had been Jelsamina's roommate for only a month, and slowly but surely sparks had started to fly.

Michele would say...

> "Jelsamina, why don't you push yourself in that wheelchair, instead of just sitting there calling out, 'Help me!' You're pathetic!" disciplined Michele.

> "I can't push myself. My arms aren't strong enough. I need help. That's what they're here for...they give you help when you need it," replied Jelsamina, as she continued calling,

> "Help me! Help me! Help me!"

> "Shut up! You're driving me crazy!" shouted Michele.

Gabriella could hear them from Nick's room. After about a half hour of this, she went over to their room, and stood in the doorway.

> "Ladies, what seems to be the problem? I can hear you all the way across the hall."

Of course, she already knew the problem.

Immediately, Michele started to answer, but Gabriella ignored her, and looked at Jelsamina, asking...

> "Can you at least push your wheelchair here to me, Jelsamina? I don't want to come into your room."

Jelsamina replied, "I'll try." And then she did it!

"That's wonderful, sweetie," said Gabriella. "Your arms must be getting stronger. Come on, I'll push you to the desk, and then someone can take you where you want to go."

Jelsamina smiled and replied,

"Okay, Gabriella. Thank you. I just needed a little help. How's Nick today? He and I had a real long conversation yesterday in the dining room."

Gabriella didn't correct her; she just let Jelsamina talk. Then she said,

"That's nice. He's sleeping."

Upon returning, Gabriella went directly to talk to Michele.

"Michele, you seem like a smart cookie. You know that Jelsamina doesn't like to argue, and she just wants a little attention. She can get out of bed and make it to her wheelchair, and you cannot. Is that what upsets you about her? Are you envious of her?"

Michele shook her head, then answering...

"Gabriella, I can't stand whiners. She always wants attention when, in fact, she really can do some of this stuff by herself."

"Does she get any company, Michele?" asked Gabriella.

"Not that I've seen."

"Phone calls?"

"No." replied Michele.

"Do you, Michele?" asked Gabriella.

"Yes, my son and daughter and their families come on Saturday or Sunday, to visit. Different ones come ... whoever is not too busy."

Gabriella nodded...

"Well, maybe that's why Jelsamina seeks attention. She's getting none from her friends and family. *WE* are all she has. The people in this place are her family. Cut her a little slack. I think you two could get along very well, if you both tried a little. Encourage her. Don't demean her. Just offering my opinion. Take it or leave it, sweetie."

Michele smiled slightly. With that Gabriella returned to Nick's room and whispered to him,

"Wake up, my darling. There's a whole Peyton Place going on here, and you're missing it!" she chuckled.

Later in the week, staff members told Zeke that they were moving him down the hall to room with another man. Zeke was devastated.

"I don't want to leave Nick and Gabriella. We're friends." He cried.

Gabriella just happened to be walking in.

"What's happening?" she asked.

"I have orders to move Zeke down the hall to room 410, but he's giving me a hard time," stated CNA Mimi.

"Why is he being moved?"

"I don't know. I was told to move him."

Gabriella went to the desk to inquire.

"Why is Zeke being moved? We're doing just fine in that room. Who ordered this?"

"Charolette said to move him. She didn't give a reason," replied Nurse Genevieve.

Just then Charolette approached the desk, so Gabriella asked,

"Charolette, why is Zeke being moved? We all get along so well. Let him stay."

"Gabriella, I have new male resident in 410, and I think he and Zeke will be good together."

"You know, he's in there crying like a baby. Charolette, please go help him understand the reason for the move."

"I don't have time for Zeke. Mimi will move him. He'll get over it. I'm not running a baby nursery here!" Charolette stated as she walked away.

Gabriella returned to Nick's room to find that things had gotten worse with Zeke. She handed him a box of tissue, bent down, and said to him,

"Zeke, sweetie, listen to me. Go with Mimi for now. Stop crying. I will come and visit you every day, I promise.

And I'll talk with Charolette, to see if we can get you moved back. But for now, just go with Mimi. It'll be okay. There's a nice man in that room, and you two will have great conversations! Go ahead. I'll see you later. Here take this candy bar."

"Okay, Gabriella. Come visit me later. Don't forget."

"I won't. I promise." Gabriella assured.

Gabriella knew she would *not* be able to persuade Charolette to change her mind, but she didn't want Zeke to get in trouble for putting up a fuss. She did not want Zeke to face any reprisal for being belligerent, which was a real possibility.

When Gabriella visited Zeke later, she was perturbed to learn that his roommate was lethargic and deaf. Zeke was happy to see her, and even happier when he saw that she brought him a few bags of potato chips.

Gabriella kept her promise and visited briefly every day, always bringing him a treat.

Across the hall from 410, was Baseball Billy. When Billy was younger, he had been a Major League third baseman for the Chicago White Sox. Now, at the age of 75, he was stricken with Alzheimer's. He thought he was still playing on the team, and he insisted on wearing his Sox cap. He always offered to sign autographs. Gabriella met him in the hall one evening, as he was returning from dinner.

"Hi, little lady," he greeted her. "I'm Baseball Billy from the Sox. Want my autograph?"

At first, Gabriella was taken aback because she had never met him, but the CNA nodded and responded yes for Gabriella. Then Gabriella got the point.

"Sure, Baseball Billy. Let me quickly get my pen."

Gabriella dashed into Nick's room and emerged with pen and journal. Baseball Billy quickly scribbled an illegible signature.

"Thank you, Baseball Billy!" Gabriella gushed.

"My pleasure. I love my fans!" he responded.

Next day, he happened to see Gabriella again, and once again, not remembering her, he asked if she wanted his autograph. Of course, she said yes. Anytime he saw anyone, he would ask the same thing—over and over.

Wanda and Jodi were in the room next to Nick's room. Wanda, very thin, about five feet tall and in her 70's, was almost completely bald. When Gabriella first met her, she thought Wanda was a man. She required a wheelchair to get around, because she had no power in her legs. Most of the day she would sit in her wheelchair near the nurses' desk. She would see a lot, hear a lot, and sometimes repeat a lot. She was very observant. Gabriella liked her.

Jodi, who was Wanda's roommate, was in her 80's, about five eight, blind, but used a walker, with assistance. Although blind, she let everyone know she was able to zero into a lot that was happening around there, and she had exceptional hearing.

One day, all of sudden, at around one in the afternoon, Jodi started screaming, from her bed.

"I need to be changed! I need to be changed! Somebody get in here and change me! My diaper needs to be changed! I need to be changed!"

Finally, after about a half hour, Gabriella couldn't take it anymore. She went to the nurses' desk.

"Do you hear Jodi screaming that she needs to be changed?"

"Yeah, we hear her!" said Jennifer, the shift supervisor.

"She can just wait. Next time we bring her lunch, she will think twice about calling it slop. She can just sit in her shit for a while. We're in no hurry."

Gabriella just looked at Wanda, sitting there in her wheelchair, and they both said nothing. Gabriella was learning fast, how the game was played in the nursing home. A person who never gets a visitor, or seldom gets one, is low man on the totem pole. Staff felt they could ignore or punish those residents, because the residents had no one to tell, and no recourse!

Gabriella went back to Nick's room and turned up the volume on the CD player to drown out Jodi's cries for help. She held Nick's hand and whispered to him,

"Wake up, my darling. Please wake up. I want to take you home, away from here.

I want you to be with me, so you're safe."

CHAPTER 34

"SCRATCH MY ASS"

Gabriella was most anxious when she awoke on the morning of August 29, 2012, at 5:00 a.m. She'd had a restless night's sleep, with reoccurring nightmares.

> "I might as well get up now, and get to my Nicky earlier than usual," she said to herself. "Please, dear God, help him wake up today!"

Since it was so early, she stopped at the small Catholic chapel that was in the neighborhood, which was open 24 hours a day.

She thought,

> *I love coming to this small chapel, and I'm so glad that they keep it open all day and night. All the churches used to be like this, until vandals started to ruin it for everyone. I light a real candle, and somehow, I feel that my prayers take flight. There's something special about lighting a real candle. Many churches are bringing them back...good thinking.*

At 8:00 a.m. As she walked into Lavender Gardens, she met Public Relations Supervisor, Diane a personable, friendly woman who made it a point to visit Nicholas early every morning.

"Hi, Gabriella! You're here earlier than usual."

"Good morning, Diane. I didn't sleep very well last night, and I was most anxious to get here today. How is he? Did you check on him yet?

"Yes, as a matter of fact I just came from there. He's still sleeping. But I feel, as you do, that God works in mysterious ways, and he will bring Nicholas back to you. Meanwhile you hang in there and keep the faith."

"You know my faith is strong, and I believe." Gabriella smiled.

She entered Nick's room and put her things on the chair. She turned off the CD player that had been playing all night, went to Nick's side, and leaned and kissed his forehead.

"Good morning, my love. I miss you. I can't wait for you to open your eyes, and tell me once again that you love me. I'm waiting. Please return to me, Nicky."

Within half an hour, a new CNA entered—a tall young man with a pleasant smile.

"Good morning. I'm Zachariah. Here to give Mr. Carcioni his bed bath."

"Wonderful! Zachariah. That's a very biblical name. I love it. Zachariah was a king, and wasn't John the Baptist's father named Zachariah, too?"

"Yes, ma'am. You are right. You know your Bible," he stated.

"No, not really. I read parts from time to time."

"This is Nicholas, my husband. He's been in a coma... today marks Day #34. I'm praying every day that he awakens soon. He woke up a week ago, for just a few minutes. But please pray along with me, Zachariah, that today he will awaken fully."

"Yes, ma'am I will."

Zachariah proceeded to get all his supplies ready, as Gabriella showed him where she kept the special Denali body wash, that she liked them to use. She put another CD in the player, mentioning to Zachariah that it was Nicholas singing. He was impressed and remarked that Nick had a beautiful voice.

While Zachariah washed Nick, Gabriella took out her journal and started to write a to-do list for herself. After Zachariah finished Nick's bath, he started to change the sheets. In doing so, he pushed Nicholas onto one side abruptly by gently.

Just then, Gabriella thought she heard Nick softly say,

"Scratch my ass!"

Gabriella looked up from her journaling, and she and Zachariah glanced at each other, but neither said anything. Not sure of what she heard, Gabriella said nothing, but slowly walked toward Nicholas's bedside. When Zachariah finished that side of the bedding, he came around to the other side of the bed, and pushed Nicholas to the other side.

Nicholas shouted—louder this time—

"Scratch my ass!"

Gabriella laughed, and could barely contain her enthusiasm.

"Oh my God! Nicholas, my darling. You're awake!" she exclaimed as she hugged and kissed him. "He's waking up, Zachariah!"

Nick's eyes were wide open, and he just kept staring at her.

"Darling, it's me, Gabriella." as she laughed and cried simultaneously.

"I'll be glad to scratch your ass!" she said, promptly doing so. She threw her arms around him, hugging and kissing him a hundred times, remarking....

"You know, Nicholas Carcioni, even in a Coma, you find a way to make me laugh! I love you so very much!!! kisses, kisses..."

Nick said nothing. He just stared at her. By the time she released her hug, Nick had already returned to sleep, which made Gabriella cry.

"Wake up, Nicky. I need you!"

But, Nick was asleep again. Turning to look out the window, she motioned for Zachariah to continue.

"Go ahead, Zachariah, continue with your work," wiping her tears. "You just witnessed a miracle. He's coming out of his coma—it's a slow process. But the point is, he's coming back!"

"Yes ma'am, he is! Don't you fret!" replied Zachariah.

When John, the Administrator, stopped by a few hours later, Gabriella told him about Nicholas's first words. He laughed— they both laughed.

"He's coming back, Gabriella. Slowly but surely," he confirmed. You have succeeded in bringing him back to you."

Gabriella was overjoyed.

The air conditioning unit located next to Nick's bed was going full blast, nonstop, as every day during July and August was around 100 degrees. Gabriella was concerned about the cold air blowing directly on Nicholas, so she made a cardboard deflector, and taped it securely onto the unit, so that the air blew up toward the ceiling. At around 2 p.m., Gabriella realized that she needed a bit more tape to hold her homemade deflector in place.

As she was applying the tape, she starting talking to herself out loud.

"I wish you would wake up, and say you loved me again, Nicholas. That's all I'm waiting for, sweetheart."

At that moment, she heard Nicholas mumble,

"Abbabbabba."

Gabreilla turned swiftly to see Nicholas awake and looking at her. Quickly she approached his bed, putting her face close to his.

"Darling, I wish you would say you love me again," she repeated.

Again, Nicholas mumbled,

"Abbabbabba." And then he continued to speak rapidly with garbled syllables.

"What? Sweetheart, I can't understand you. What are you saying?" she asked frantically.

Nicholas started to get upset, because Gabriella wasn't understanding him. He just kept rambling on and on, frowning.

She held his hand and thought to herself,

> *I'm going to just guess what you might be asking.*

"Are you asking me where you are, and what's happening?" Nicholas garbled a few more syllables.

"Okay, my darling. Let me fill in the blanks for you. You have not been well, and have been sleeping a lot. Now you really are getting better, and you will be home soon."

More garbled syllables from Nick.

"You're in Lavender Gardens Nursing Home to get well. It's a very nice place, and the people are extremely friendly. You're doing great. You're improving rapidly."

More garbled syllables.

"It's a little hard for me to understand you, Nicky, so please be patient with me. You are getting better," she said smiling, and then she kissed his face.

"I love you. I've missed you while you've been sleeping. You were exhausted, so I let you sleep. Everything will be fine now."

Nicholas just lay there staring at her, and finally fell back to sleep. Gabriella went looking for John, Head Administrator.

Unable to find him, she left word at the desk that she wanted him to come to Nick's room as soon as possible.

John arrived about an hour later, asking if anything was wrong. Gabriella apprised him of Nick's waking up.

> "John, his words are all garbled! I couldn't understand him."

> "Probably a result of the brain damage. We still don't know how much damage has been done, Gabriella. It's got be frustrating for him, when he sees that you don't understand, what he's saying."

> "John," Gabriella interjected, "would it be possible for a speech therapist come see him, and work with him a few times a week…maybe starting tomorrow?"

> "Sure. Let me look into it with the Rehab supervisor. I'll get back to you. Meantime, you just keep telling him that he is getting better. I'm sure his number-one question is… 'What am I doing here?' I know it would be mine!"

> "Yes. You are so right!"

While Gabriella waited for John to return, she lowered Nick's bed to her chair height, took his hand, and rested her head on a pillow near his shoulder. She fell asleep. Suddenly, she heard the sound of a familiar voice.

> "Helllooooo! Gabriella!" the voice sang out.

She opened her eyes, and there stood Leesa … Lee … whoever.

"Lee … Leesa …where have you been?" she said, laughing. "I see you're still wearing your long locks, so it must still be Leesa?"

"Yes, it is, my dear," she replied.

"Charolette suspended me, but John had her call me back, because they are so short staffed. Also, many of my residents were asking about me, and told John that they really liked me, and they missed me 'cause I always gave them good care. Did John ask you about me?"

"No, but if he had, I would have told him that you're a pain in the butt!" Gabriella replied laughing.

"Thanks, girlfriend." replied Leesa smiling, and batting her eyelashes.

"Sincerely, I am so glad you're back," stated Gabriella.

"Today Nicholas woke up and tried to talk. His words are all garbled. I couldn't understand what he was saying, so I asked John if the Speech Therapist could come in and help him. He'll let me know."

Leeza's eyes widened....

"WOW, That's such wonderful news! I'll let you know if he keeps talking throughout the night. I'll be here till midnight," assured Leesa. "This is a miracle!"

"Yes, definitely," replied Gabriella... "and remember"...

"If he does try to speak, just go along with him, as if you can understand him. He started to get frightened, when I couldn't understand what he was saying. Tell him where he is, and what day it is, and that he's getting better."

Leesa nodded.

"Got it! I'll see you after dinner to change him."

"Great."

Nicholas remained asleep for the rest of the night while Gabriella was there.

Leesa did come in at around 8:00 p.m. and changed Nicholas, but even when she moved him, he did not wake up again. Gabriella went home at 10:30 p.m.

CHAPTER 35

DO YOU KNOW HER?

The following three weeks presented a severe challenge. Nicholas tried hard to communicate, but many times his brain would not give him words that were understandable. His speech continued to improve very slowly, but many times it remained garbled, yet Gabriella constantly tried to interpret his mumbling.

John did provide a speech therapist, Mary Karolyn, who came three days a week, for half hour and worked with Nicholas. This was very strenuous work for Nicholas. He grew tired easily, and kept wanting to go back to sleep, but she insisted and persisted, until she finally got him to the point of saying his name, his birthday, and where he lived. On the other days, Gabriella would teach him to say simple words, numbers, and colors, using children's books.

One day, as Gabriella stood listening to Mary Karolyn's session with Nicholas, she voiced how delighted she was with their progress. Then Mary Karolyn pointed to Gabriella, and asked Nicholas the ultimate question:

"Do you know her?" motioning for him to look at Gabriella.

Feeling confident, Gabriella stood smiling at Nick, who just stared at her, and he then responded,

>"No, I don't!" shaking his head and frowning, he asked, "Do I know you?"

Immediately, Gabreilla's eyes welled with tears, but she did not want to cry in front of him. She forced a smile, and replied,

>"My name is Gabriella. I'm here all the time. You'll get to know me."

That was all she could muster. Swallowing hard, she quickly left the room. Stepping into the hall, she leaned against the wall, and slowly slid down, till she reached the floor, all the while crying like a baby.

Constance and Wanda came over to her. Constance asked softly,

>"What's wrong?"

Without looking up, Gabriella simply replied,

>"He doesn't know me."

Stunned. They both looked at each other, shook their heads in regret, and walked away leaving Gabriella to have her privacy.

Mary Karolyn soon joined Gabriella in the hallway. Knowing that it was devastating, for Gabriella to hear that Nick didn't know her, she took Gabriella's hand and said,

>"We're in the *beginning stages* of Nick coming out from a long coma. Every day will produce more and more results. Give him time. His brain needs *time* to recover."

Gabriella, a woman who never dwelled long on the negative, smiled and replied,

"Yes, thank you. You're right. He's been through something so horrific! Mary Karolyn, I'm thinking, on the days you're not here, I'll work with him too, to help him speak and remind him that I am his wife."

"Good. Do it!" she replied smiling. "That will be a big help!"

When Gabriella returned to Nicholas's room, he was already asleep. She approached his bed, kissed his face, and whispered,

"Nicholas, my darling, this is your wife, Gabriella. I'm so proud of you! Rest because, as you rest, you will heal. Always remember, Gabriella loves Nicholas—*and* Nicholas loves Gabriella!"

The next morning, Gabriella came in with four colorful poster-board signs she had made at home. Each read "Gabriella loves Nicholas, and Nicholas loves Gabriella!" She taped one to the TV that hung on the wall. She pinned another to the curtain that separated him from the next bed. She taped one on the bathroom door that was closed most of the time, and she taped one so that it hung from his tray stand.

She decided that selective TV programs could be a learning tool also, and tuned in any talk shows that weren't excessively loud or vulgar, so that Nick could hear words—lots of good words. She played the weather station, old time comedy movies, shows about nature, travel, and the like, but definitely nothing that would frighten him. Those avoided were: hospital shows, gunshots, reports of crimes and killings, rapes, or vandals, which, of course, eliminated the evening news.

She played his CDs intermediately, and before she left for the night, she put on a Theta Brain CD, which she purchased at Barnes and Noble, designed with tones and sounds that activate certain brain waves. She bought children books—kindergarten level or earlier.

One book, in particular, makes her smile to this day. It was a book of learning to associate the ABCs, with an illustration of an animal, whose name began with that letter. Next to the letter A, was a picture of an Alligator. In the afternoon, she decided to show Nicholas the book.

> "Nicholas, look at these lovely pictures of animals. I just bought this book, because I know you love animals," she stated in bringing the book to his bedside.

> "Okay, the first animal starts with an A. What is it?"

Nick looked at the picture and said,

> "Alligator."

> "Right! Very good!"

> "The second animal starts with the letter B."

> "Bird—that's a bluebird." he replied.

> "Yes, yes! That is a bird, and it *is* blue! Oh my God, you're doing great! You're so smart! Now the next letter is an animal that begins with a C. It's a little bit different, so take a look and really think hard."

Nicholas looked and said quickly,

> "Alligator."

> "No, honey. It looks like an alligator, but it's name begins with a C."

She thought,

> *Mercy, why didn't they show a cat?*

> "Alligator," Nick replied again. "That's an alligator."

> "No, babe. Think. It begins with the letter C sounds like Cra Cra Cra"

> "Alligator," Nick replied again more strongly.

Sighing, Gabriella confessed,

> "Actually my love, it's a Crocodile. See? It begins with the letter C."

Nick grew tired, and he seemed upset that he had not known the answer.

> "Yeah, okay. I don't want to play this anymore. I'm tired," he replied as he closed his eyes quickly.

> "Oh, okay. You did real good, sweetheart. You really know your animals."

Gabriella covered him with a sheet and in kissing his face, she whispered...

> "Yes, my intelligent baby. ...C is for Alligator," smiling at the man she adored.

> "I'll always remember that! I love you so much! Thank you for telling me... C is definitely for Alligator."

Nick kept his eyes shut, but gave a little smile, as Gabriella showered him with kisses.

CHAPTER 36

JOHN O'REILLY FIRED

Without warning, on October 1, John O'Reilly, Head Administrator, was fired. They did it quietly.

He exited the building, without saying a word to anyone. Gabriella found out three days later, in mentioning to a staff member that she hadn't seen John in a few days. She was particularly shocked and saddened, as John had become a friend to her and Nicholas, supporting her efforts to help awaken Nicholas from his coma. John had always been optimistic to her ideas, and provided the resources she needed.

All the residents really liked John, as he would visit as many as he could every day, spending time at their bedsides. Many staff members and residents joined Gabriella in being disheartened to see him go.

With no new administrator hired to take the helm, everyone feared that things would get progressively worse, and they were spot on! Gabriella took a walk to John's office one morning, hoping to learn more about why he had been terminated, and more importantly, to find out who was hired as the new administrator.

She found Jacob, the owner's grandson, a nice guy in his 20's, sitting at John's desk.

"Where's John?" Gabriella asked innocently.

"John is no longer with us. I'm acting Administrator. Do you need help with something?"

"Yes, Jacob. There seems to be a shortage of towels and washcloths every day. The shelves used to be replenished constantly, when washed. Now there are no linens on the shelves."

"I'll look into it. Meantime, they have a small supply at the desk," replied Jacob.

"Okay. Thanks. So, who's the new administrator, Jacob?

"We haven't hired anyone yet. We're still interviewing candidates. Meanwhile, come to me if you need anything, Gabriella."

Gabriella departed, thinking, this guy is not licensed by the state to be an Administrator, and he doesn't have the experience. Oh well, not my problem. I'm sure they'll hire someone soon. This is a big facility, and a hands-on knowledgeable person like John, is needed to run it.

In the following weeks, a drastic decline in the overall operation at Lavender Gardens took effect. Clean supplies of towels, washcloths, sheets, pillowcases, and hospital gowns were suddenly sparse. Basic standards of cleanliness and resident hygiene, deteriorated quickly.

Needless to say, those in power didn't seem to be in a hurry to hire a new Administrator. Drastic cutbacks were obvious. As a matter of fact, word from the CNAs was that Jacob, Charolette, and Supervisor Skyla were all vying for the position. Each one was trying to make a favorable impression on the owner, in hopes to get the job. It was a fight for power, and the employees were stuck in the middle. One would bark orders, and then the other would contradict those orders. It was becoming a frustrating and ugly situation, for employees as well as residents. Tension was mounting.

Gabriella just kept focusing on Nicholas all day, every day, so that he would continue to get the best of care. Luckily, Nick was assigned attentive CNA'S: Kerista, Shyann, Tyler and Lisa, who would come in daily to attend to Nicholas, and while there, would vent their frustrations over the management. Gabriella was fast becoming housemother, psychiatrist, and sounding board. She didn't mind listening to them, as she maneuvered them into doing tasks to benefit Nicholas,—turning him, changing him, giving him bed baths, changing bed linens, while they vented. In liking her, they even snuck her a few extra diapers.

Needless to say, she was very sympathetic to their grievances. Most of them were in their early 20's, and she looked upon them as kids, who needed guidance and direction, and most of all, loving words of encouragement.

However, the CNA Daily Activity Form that Gabriella had instituted was soon removed.

One morning, Charolette entered Nick's room, opened the closet, removed all the sign-in sheets from the clipboard, and turned to Gabriella, saying...

> "We're *not* doing this anymore. The CNAs do not have to sign in, effective immediately."

"Really, Charolette? Why's that? They seem to enjoy keeping track of their tasks on the sheet, and time spent. It was invaluable for me, as I monitored Nicholas's care."

"Not necessary. I will keep track of their duties and time," replied Charolette abruptly as she departed quickly, with sheets in hand.

It was obvious to Gabriella that she was not one of Charolette's favorites. Ever since Gabriella had that meeting with Charolette and John, it was evident that Charolette had it in for Gabriella, because John had sided with Gabriella.

It didn't matter to Charolette, that what Gabriella had brought to their attention in the meeting was of utmost importance to Nicholas's care. All Charolette focused on was the fact that "weaknesses" in her managerial capabilities, were being exposed. This gave Charolette cause to dislike Gabriella from that day forward. Without proof, Gabriella was quite certain that Charolette, had been very instrumental in John's firing.

The following day, Gabriella went to get more diapers, so she could change Nicholas herself, and she found no diapers on the shelf. When she went to the nurses' desk to complain, Nurse MaryBeth handed her one diaper. MaryBeth told Gabriella that she would no longer be permitted to go into the hall closet for supplies.

"That's fine with me," stated Gabriella firmly.

"Just make sure that you have a CNA in my husband's room, in a timely fashion to do their job every day! Understand? For right now, I need a couple towels and washcloths to use when I change him. Do you want to send in a CNA right now to change him, or do you want me to do it?"

Nurse MaryBeth smirked, and handed Gabriella two towels and two washcloths.

"Thanks," responded Gabriella, holding her tongue from further comment.

Since Zeke was no longer sharing Nicholas's room, staff members removed the bed frame and the nightstand and leaned the mattress up against the wall. Zeke's phone sat on the unwashed floor. Gabriella passed Jacob, acting Administrator, in the hall and asked if the room was going to stay that way—like a pigpen, with a dirty floor and an uncovered, soiled mattress. Jacob said he would have the mattress removed and the floor moped the next morning, which he did. Gabriella was pleased to see that at least Jacob was listening to her.

Gabriella wasn't interested in management's inner battles and squabbles; she just wanted high standards to be maintained, regarding the care and cleanliness for Nicholas.

A week later, upon arriving one morning, Gabriella noticed several people outside of Michele and Jelsamina's room. The door was closed. About an hour later, she emerged into the hall to see Michele's family of six still standing in the hall. Just then, she noticed Jelsamina sitting in her wheel chair at the desk. She walked up to her, and asked what was happening in her room. Jelsamina started crying.

"Michele is dying. She was having trouble breathing early this morning. Her doctor came, and then they called the family. You know, Gabriella, I'm gonna miss her. We used to fight, but lately we've been getting along really good."

"Yeah, I know," replied Gabriella.

"Michele was a good person. I loved her blunt honesty. Let's say a prayer for her, Jelsamina." *"Hail Mary full of grace, the Lord is with thee ..."*

Gabriella returned to Nicholas's room and lowered the sound of Nick's CD out of respect for Michele. As she sat there, she recalled passing Michele's room on that prior Sunday when her family was visiting. She had heard Michele pleading with her family members,

"Please let me come home. I'll be good. I won't ask for anything. Honest. I just want to come home, and be with you guys."

Shockingly, she heard no response from anyone in the family, who was sitting there.

Thought Gabriella...

Why is it, when you're older, you're tossed aside by your own family members and friends? All the good things you've done for them throughout your life are forgotten! Why do you no longer serve any importance, just because you need help in taking care of yourself as you reach old age? Why have we become so callus and dehumanizing? This thought nauseated Gabriella to tears.

About four hours later, Michele's body was removed from the premises.

"May you now rest in peace, Michele." Gabriella whispered.

CHAPTER 37

MEDICARE OMBUDSMAN

As mandated by the Federal Older American Act and the Illinois Act on Aging, the Ombudsman Program protects and promises the rights and quality of life, for those who reside in nursing homes or long-term care facilities. In short, they're the "defensive line advocate" for the elderly. They offer assistance with complaints, grievances, and information requests, with a goal to resolve complaints expeditiously in an impartial, confidential manner. Every state is required to have an Ombudsman Program. The Ombudsman addresses concerns such as abuse, neglect, mistreatment, poor care, insufficient staff, unsafe and unsanitary conditions, and dietary problems.

On October 2, 2012, immediately after John O'Reilly was terminated, procedures, supplies, and overall management at Lavender Gardens plummeted. Additionally, management had not hired An Illinois licensed Administrator, which was in violation of Illinois law, Department of Public Health.

Because Gabriella's CNA Daily Activity Form had been abolished by Charolette, the Nursing Director, the frequency of CNA visits to Nick's room was sporadic. Once again, no schedule was being followed. Gabriella would go numerous times to the nurses' desk to request required assistance.

"My husband needs to be turned. It has been over four hours, and I don't want him to develop bedsores."

Or she might say,

"My husband's liquid feeding has been empty for almost an hour, and it needs to be replaced, ensuring he gets his proper nourishment in a timely fashion."

Or...

"My husband's bed linens are soiled and need to be replaced."

"It's 11 a.m. and my husband hasn't had his bed bath yet."

Upon arriving one morning, Gabriella was watching Diamond give Nicholas his bed bath, and was shocked when they both noticed a bedsore at the base of Nicholas's spine.

When Virginia Margaret, Nursing Supervisor, came on duty later that afternoon, Gabriella called her to see the sore. Virginia Margaret said that she would contact Dr. Yurkevich immediately, to get the needed cream to administer, until it was healed.

Gabriella was livid that Nicholas now had a bedsore, which she had been trying to avoid in the first place. Now, when he was positioned on his back, Nicholas complained of pain.

There was no question, that lack of turning him and the poor cleanliness standards, were at the root of this new situation. There were many times that Gabriella turned Nicholas herself, but her hands were now tied, to provide him with clean linens and hospital gowns; she'd been banned from the linen closet, and many times laundry did not provide enough newly washed ones.

Becoming disillusioned with the deplorable descent of standards at Lavender Gardens, Gabriella was forced to place a call for the help of an Ombudsman. She received a response from a congenial person named Rosalie. Rosalie listened to the list of deficiencies Gabriella outlined. When Rosalie called Lavender Gardens, she spoke with Jacob, acting Administrator, who suggested she come there in person for a meeting. Jacob was too young and inexperienced to want to answer Rosalie on his own, so he needed the backup of someone experienced such as, Charolette.

Jacob told Rosalie that he would inform Gabriella of the meeting, because Rosalie wanted Gabriella present too. However, Jacob never told Gabriella about the meeting!

Two days later, they had their meeting at 10:30 a.m. Gabriella was not informed about the meeting. When Rosalie asked for Gabriella, Jacob simply said she was not at the Nursing Home yet that morning! In reality, Gabriella had been sitting in Nicholas's room since 8:30 a.m. that morning, unaware.

At the conclusion of the meeting, Rosalie had another appointment, so she left quickly and had no time to visit Nicholas's room; otherwise, she would have met Gabriella.

When she called Gabriella the following day, she asked why Gabriella hadn't made time to attend the meeting. After Gabriella explained that she had not been informed of the meeting, Rosalie was shocked, not only to learn that Jacob had never invited Gabriella, but that he had lied to her, a government Ombudsman!

Gabriella pointed out to Rosalie, that this was exactly the kind of behavior everyone had been subjected to, since John left on October 1. Rosalie was astounded and angered!

Immediately, Rosalie took steps to make sure that all allegations, presented by Gabriella, were put in writing. She sent this list to Jacob and Charolette, and a copy to Gabriella.

In this document, Rosalie listed her findings and her suggested solutions. She stated that she would make a follow-up visit, to ensure that Lavender Gardens had been brought up to appropriate standards, in meeting with federal regulations and certification rules. She advised them, that it would be in their best interest, to implement corrective procedures immediately!

In the days to follow, Gabriella noticed some improvements. For Nick's bedsore, Dr. Yurkevich prescribed a thick healing ointment that was administered by Virginia Margaret. When she finished the first application, she handed Gabriella the tube and asked her to apply it every morning after his bed bath.

> "Gabriella, keep this tube with you. Don't leave it here in the drawer. Every night they're going through your drawers. I'm sure you noticed items missing lately."

> "Yes, I have, Virginia Margaret. Someone has taken deodorant, body wash, and cologne! I had to replace these items for Nicholas. This is absurd. This is Nick's room. His possessions should not be touched."

> "It doesn't work that way, Gabriella. Take important things home with you each night. That is the only way they won't be stolen!"

CHAPTER 38

"F*** THIS!"

Miracle #2

Nick's brain never did completely heal. He never came back to being the man he once had been. However, his brain did heal enough for him to learn to speak clearly again. Sometimes he was lethargic, living again in the past, thinking it was the present. No less, he was indeed a medical miracle!

On October 2, 2012, he asked Gabriella...

> "What is this place?" Nicholas asked upon awakening from his sleep.

> "I'm not well. What's happening?" then adding quickly,

> "Are you well, Gabriella?"

Nick had always worried about Gabriella, and to hear him ask about her well-being, now, was even more touching to her.

Gabriella could tell by the look in his eyes, when he couldn't remember her name, or even who she was. When she saw this, she would say her name, and repeat who she was, while working it into a sentence, as a way to enlighten him. She always encouraged him, never made him feel deficient.

Wanda and Jelsamina told Gabriella that, in the middle of the night, Nicholas called Gabriella's name constantly.

There were moments when he would be spot on, and then there were many moments when he would revert to the past, thinking it was the present. On one particular evening, he asked Gabriella.

> "Where's my brother, Anthony? He said he was going to come by, but I haven't seen him. Have you?"

Anthony was Nick's older brother, who had passed away about 20 years earlier.

> "No, I haven't seen him lately, babe."

> "Call him up. I want to talk to him," demanded Nick.

Gabriella didn't want to disappoint Nick, and was curious about what he would say to Anthony. So, she called her brother in Pennsylvania, and asked him to call her phone and pretend to be Anthony. He agreed. Within minutes her phone rang, and she announced that it was Anthony. She handed the phone to Nick.

> "Anthony, where *are* you? You said you were going to come by and visit," demanded Nick.

> "Hi, Nick! How are you feeling today?" Gabriella's brother asked.

> "I'm doing okay, but I thought we could go to lunch."

"Oh, I'd love to Nick, but right now I am very busy at my music studio. I have so many students. Maybe in a few weeks, okay?"

"Yeah sure, Anthony. You still play?"

"Oh yeah, man. Love the accordion. How about you? You still play the sax?"

"Yeah, but not as much as I used to," Nick replied sadly. "I miss you, Anthony. I wish you would stop by again soon."

"I really miss you too, Nick. I promise I will stop by just as soon as I can. I want you to know that I'm thinking of you every day," Gabriella's brother concluded. "You keep getting stronger, and I'll see you soon. We'll have that lunch, okay?"

"That's sounds great! Thanks for calling, Anthony." A delighted Nicholas smiled.

As she hung up, Gabriella remarked that it had been so good of Anthony to call.

"Yeah," replied Nick. "But his voice sounded different. I don't know why. It just did."

"Really? Maybe it was the telephone line. Sometimes reception in here is not the greatest," suggested Gabriella.

"Oh, I didn't think of that. That must have been the reason," Nick concluded.

"Yes, sweetheart."

###

The following morning when Gabriella arrived, she was met by a sweet, soft-spoken CNA named Norma. For the past few days, Nick had been very quiet. He had hardly said a word and had slept most of the day. Gabriella was starting to become concerned. On this particular morning, Norma said that, when she turned Nick abruptly during his bed bath, he had shouted,

"What the fuck is happening?"

She told Gabriella that she was shocked, and hoped she didn't have to be subjected to that language all the time.

Gabriella, quite frankly, was happy that Nick had started to speak again, but she told Norma that sort of language was very unusual for Nick.

"This must be *Coma Talk,* Norma, because he never used language like that before. Don't be too hard on him. He doesn't know what he's saying."

(Coma Talk—yeah right! He's Italian! Come on, Gabriella! haha)

Well, folks, one "F" word led to another, and before Gabriella knew what was happening, Nick was "fucking" everything that was happening in his little world. Virginia Margaret, who had been a Nurse for over 25 years, said that a separate part of the brain was being enlightened. It was the part of the brain, where he stored all those pent-up feelings, and it was really good news that he was using that part of his brain again.

Gabriella agreed, and was glad to hear him talking, clinical reason or not. However, that being said, when Gabriella was alone with Nick that afternoon, as he lay there with his eyes shut, she whispered in his ear...

"Darling, these people here are very nice. They're helping you to get well. They don't want to hear you swearing at them, and I don't want to hear it either. So, knock it off!"

"They don't deserve it. They like you so much. I want you to *thank* them for their help every time they do something for you. Please keep that in mind, okay? Thank you, darling. I love you!"

Well, the following day when Gabriella walked in, Norma approached Gabriella happily announcing,

"Guess what Mr. Carcioni told me today?"

"What?" an apprehensive Gabriella asked.

"When I came in to give him his bed bath, *he told me he loved me*, and before I left he said, Thank you!"

A relieved Gabriella sighed.

"That's wonderful, Norma. See? It was just his brain continuing to heal. I think you're one of his favorites."

Norma smiled.

Later that afternoon, when Virginia Margaret came in to administer his medicines, Nicholas looked at her and exclaimed,

"Hello, sweetheart!"

"Wow, what's gotten in to you today, Nicholas Carcioni? I like it!" said Virginia Margaret with a smile.

Gabriella sat there smiling and thought to herself,

> *Okay, Nicky, you're laying it on pretty thick now, but I'm not saying a word! Hahaha! God, I love this guy!*

Gabriella continued on a daily basis to massage Nick's neck, arms, hands, legs, and feet. She lifted his arms more and more each day, and finally got them to reach his head. She put a hairbrush in his hand, and asked him to brush his hair. Slowly but surely, he was finally able to brush it in front. His curled-up toes were starting to relax as Gabriella really worked on them, knowing they had some relationship to the brain.

Mary Karolyn, the speech therapist, had noticed a remarkable difference, as Gabriella continued her own therapy program with Nicholas. Gabriella asked the Director of Rehab if it would be possible for physical and occupational therapists to work with Nick at least once a week, and she agreed to provide one half hour a week. That was all the energy Nicholas could offer.

CHAPTER 39

GALLBLADDER OPERATION NEEDED

Miracle #3

On Wednesday, October 4, 2012, while watching Nicholas's bed bath, Gabriella noticed that his stomach was swollen. She mentioned it to Virginia Margaret, who then mentioned it to Charolette, Nursing Director.

Charolette came in early the next morning to examine Nicholas. She measured his stomach with a tape, and then called in her supervisor, Micki, for a second opinion. Their first thought was that it was a bowel blockage, so they gave Nicholas a suppository.

The next day, Nicholas's stomach was twice the size, and Nick was not moving his bowels. The nurses consulted with Dr. Yurkevich immediately. He had Nick transported back to Asclepius Christian Medical Center for tests.

Nicholas would sleep on and off all day, and when awakened by ambulance attendants, it frightened him, as they lifted him out of his bed and placed him on a stretcher. His damaged brain could not comprehend what was happening. Gabriella was with him every second, assuring him that everything was ok, and he was just being taken for more tests, in order to get better.

"Just relax my love. I'm here. They're going to take some tests at the hospital, and then you'll be back here at Lavender Gardens again. Everything is going to be okay. You're getting better!"

"Gabriella, I want to go home," Nicholas replied in a childlike fashion.

"I know, baby. And I'm going to get you home just as soon as possible. But for right now, there are some more tests needed. When you come home, I want to you to be as well as you can be. Don't you want that?" She spoke to him with a broken heart.

"Yes, I want to get well," Nicholas replied.

"Okay, just relax. I am here with you. I won't leave you. I'm trying my best to take good care of you, Nicky. I swear I am! I love you so much!"

Dr. Yurkevich ran some blood tests, ordered an X-Ray, and a special test that required running a tube with a camera down his throat, so they could get a better view. If it showed that Nicholas's Gallbladder was "hot," the surgeon would wait for about five days for it to cool down; otherwise, if it was touched during surgery, it could explode into several pieces, and the infection would spread all over.

Tests showed that Nick's gallbladder was indeed hot and infected; it was surrounded by fluid. The surgeon wanted the name of Nick's heart doctor, which Gabriella provided, so he could find out if Nick's heart could withstand the surgery.

The doctors wanted to do a Laparoscopy, but because of the infection, they said they might have to open him up. As a matter of fact, the surgical team of the Gastroenterological Department wanted to do the surgery, that very next morning!

Gabriella questioned their quick judgment, sighting Nicholas's age. Several questions were still unanswered, and she thought they were rushing a decision. Her Intuition had kicked in again.

> "I understand there is no such thing as a simple operation. Before anyone even thinks of operating on my husband, I want to hear that he or she knows exactly what is wrong. We wait for all the tests to come back, and we wait for Dr. Yurkevich to evaluate. Is that clear?"

They complied, as they had no other choice.

After getting him settled and answering the various questions about allergies and other pre-op concerns, Gabriella left exhausted to go home at 10:30 p.m.

> "I'll see you first thing tomorrow morning, Nicholas my love. You sleep well. Everything is going fine. You have nothing to worry about."

> "I love you, Gabriella. Don't forget to come tomorrow," replied a sleepy Nicholas.

> "I won't sweetheart. Go to sleep." She hugged and kissed him a hundred times.

On Saturday morn, October 6, more blood tests were taken. As it usually is on the weekends in all hospitals, it was very quiet, and very few doctors were present. In the afternoon, however, Dr. Yurkevich did stop by. Gabriella was very happy to see him.

"We're scheduling the Gallbladder operation for Monday morning," he said, shaking his head. "Honestly, I would never have guessed that he would have ended up with an infected Gallbladder. I feel so sorry for this guy! I really do."

Gabriella nodded.

"I know, Doctor. So do I! He's so precious, and he's such a trooper, fighting fiercely to get well. I love him so much, and this just breaks my heart. Look how far he's come, and now this!" stating as she wiped her tears.

"We'll keep taking more tests even tomorrow, and see where we're at," Dr. Yurkevich concluded before leaving.

Sunday, October 7, was another quiet day with no doctor visits. Gabriella arrived early, at 9:00 a.m. As she unpacked her CD player and Nick's CDs, she gazed around the room, checking it out for cleanliness. On the tray table was a paper. As she started to read it, she became horrified. It was about a particular medicine, stating *not to be given to anyone with Tinnitus* (ringing in the ears), a condition that Nicholas had suffered with for years since the war.

She hurried around the table to look at the bag of fluid going into his arm. It was, indeed, that medicine. Gabriella went running out of the room to the Nurses' desk. No one was there. Instantly, she ran back into the room, and pulled the tube out of Nick's arm. An alarm sounded, and Nurse Fern came running in.

"What are you doing?" Nurse Fern asked angrily.

"I pulled this out because **my husband has Tinnitus, and should *not* have been given this**

medicine. Here, read this paper! Call the doctor—whoever prescribed this. Ask him to call me, but mark on his chart, that this medicine must *never* be given to Nicholas Carcioni again!"

Nurse Fern left and returned shortly, saying she had talked to the doctor, and not to worry. They hadn't given him very much, so it couldn't have hurt him.

"Really?" replied Gabriella. "The bag said 1,000 milligrams. I think that's a lot! Did you mark his chart, Fern?"

"Yes, ma'am, I did. He won't get any more of it. I'm sorry."

"Yeah, right!" Gabriella shook her head in disgust mumbling.

Around 1:00 p.m. Catholic Priest Father Artur passed Nick's room. He was surprised to see Gabriella there.

"I thought Nicholas was at Lavender Gardens?" he questioned.

"Yes, Father, but the last few days he has developed an infection in his Gallbladder, or so they think. They want to remove it tomorrow, even though they are still testing to make sure. Oh, my God, my poor Darling has been through so much! Honestly, Father, it's something new every single day!" expressed a bewildered Gabriella with tears in her eyes.

Father Artur blessed Nicholas, and said prayers for the anointing of the sick. He suggested that he and Gabriella pray together.

"Pray with me, Gabriella. We are asking God our Father to heal Nicholas completely and restore him to perfect health. In Jesus's name, we pray. *Our Father, who art in heaven, hallowed by Thy name, Thy kingdom come, Thy Will be done -----Amen.*

"Let us also ask our Blessed Mother to watch over him, ease his pain and discomfort, and bless him with peace. Amen."

Gabriella was so glad that Father Artur had come, and while there, gave her communion.

"Thank you, Father, for stopping by."

"Please take care of yourself, Gabriella. Get your rest." he stated as he grabbed her hand.

Sunday evening about 6:00 p.m. blood was drawn for more tests.

Monday morning, October 8, Gabriella arrived early at 8:00 a.m. She didn't know what time they would operate, so she got there early.

At 8:30 a.m. Dr. Yurkevich arrived, shaking his head as he entered.

Gabriella looking at him grim-faced, asking ...

"What's wrong? What is it?"

Dr. Yurkevich replied with a big smile,

"Gabriella all his infection is gone!"

"His Gallbladder is back to normal! I don't know what caused it to become infected in the first place, and now all the infection is gone! There will be no operation!"

He continued…

> "You know, I must tell you… the surgeon confided in me yesterday, that he really didn't want to do the operation. He was scared that Mr. Carcioni would not survive. We're sending him back to Lavender Gardens within the next hour."

Gabriella smiled as her eyes welled with tears.

> "Oh my God…this is a miracle. Praise God! You know, it was Prayer that healed him Doctor Yurkevich…Prayer! "Thank you, dear God. Thank you!" replied Gabriella in tears.

Doctor Yurkevich nodded in agreement…staring admiringly at this woman, with a stronger faith, than he had ever witnessed before.

CHAPTER 40

PNEUMONIA

Glad to be back at Lavender Gardens, on Monday, October 8, with a healthy Gallbladder, Nicholas's previous routine of scheduled liquid feeding, daily bed baths, regular turnings, light bedside physical therapy, and speech therapy commenced. Gabriella continued to massage his limbs and kept trying to stimulate his brain through reading to him, showing him pictures, and asking him many questions.

However, upon arriving on Wednesday morning, October 10, Gabriella noticed that water was backing up into Nick's nose from his oxygen machine. When she reported this to Charolette, a Nurse came in to put a new tube onto the machine.

The next day, Thursday afternoon, Gabriella noticed the same thing was still happening, and aggressively reported it again to Charolette, who had another tube put on the machine. Surprisingly, no Nurse or CNA who visited the room to administer to Nicholas, had taken note of this happening, even though some of the backup, was causing his hospital gown on his chest, to be soaked!

On Friday, October 12, Gabriella found that the oxygen machine was still backing up into Nick's nose. Enraged, she burst into Charolette's office.

> "Charolette, there is something *definitely* wrong with Nick's oxygen machine, and don't tell me you're going to put another tube on it. It's not the tube! The machine is malfunctioning, and having water back up into his nose is *totally unacceptable*. He's going to get *pneumonia* from that!" she fumed.

Continuing...

> "I want a new machine *today*! If he gets pneumonia, I will sue! I'm *serious*. I'm tired of bringing a major problem to your attention, and not having it corrected! Now, get this remedied today!"

She stormed out, not even waiting for Charolette to respond.

That afternoon, a repairman, Gavin, from Sammy's Equipment Rental, came to service the machine. When he was finished, he said to Gabriella,

> "There's nothing wrong with the machine. I checked it out."

Gabriella stood in front of him and blocked his exit.

> "There **is** something **wrong** with that machine! It's not making oxygen. It's sending water through the lines, and that water is going into my husband's nose and into his lungs. He's still recovering from a Coma. He does not get out of bed. He does not get any exercise. And his lungs are weak. This moisture is going to cause him to get Pneumonia. Now **change** it!"

"I'm not asking you, I'm *telling* you! If you don't, I will sue your ass, Gavin!" stated a fiery Gabriella.

"Gee, lady, I have to see Charolette. She has to give me the okay," he replied sheepishly.

"Then *see* her and *get it*, Gavin! And *do it* **today!**" demanded Gabriella.

About two hours later, Gavin returned with a larger *new* oxygen machine, which worked perfectly.

Although the new machine was operating correctly, Gabriella could already hear that Nicholas's breathing sounded congested, even though no one else took notice. When Virginia Margaret came in that day (returning from vacation), Gabriella apprised her of the situation immediately.

"I'll listen to his lungs shortly," said Virginia Margaret. "I have to distribute these meds first. I'll see Nicholas's last, so I can spend more time with him."

Around 6:00 p.m. Virginia Margaret came into Nicholas's room. She listened to his lungs and agreed that they sounded congested. Immediately she called Dr. Yurkevich, and he ordered X-rays to be taken that night.

The next day, Saturday, October 13, when Gabriella arrived at the nursing home, she could hear that Nicholas's breathing was even more stressed. At 4:00 p.m. Dr. Yurkevich visited the room, and stated that Nicholas *did,* indeed have vascular congestion in both lungs—**pneumonia!** He started him on an antibiotic immediately.

Gabriella couldn't contain her outrage.

"You know, Dr. Yurkevich, this could have been avoided *if* Charolette had changed that machine, the **first** day that I asked her. Don't get me started about the lack of management around here. Nothing is done until you threaten a lawsuit. It's sickening! When do they intend to get a licensed Administrator here, Doctor? One who knows how to run a nursing home properly!"

Dr. Yurkevich looked at his papers and replied softly, as he continued to check Nicholas all over,

"They're interviewing."

Gabriella responded quickly,

"Yeah, well they need to step it up a notch, Doctor!"

Hearing that, Dr. Yurkevich briefly looked up from his papers. Saying nothing, he gave her a half smile. He knew not to tangle with this red-headed ball of fire!

CHAPTER 41

JESUS VISITS NICK

Diane, the Guest Services Director, was one of the friendliest employees at Lavender Gardens Nursing Home. Her main duty was to register new residents, making sure that all the necessary paperwork for Medicare, as well as other insurances, were processed correctly. Diane wore several hats, and was always smiling. Everyone could tell that she was a spiritual person, because of her kindness, and the small gold crucifix that she wore around her neck.

Every morning, Diane made it a habit to check on Nicholas. She would converse with him for several minutes, offering words of encouragement, about how well he was progressing. Later in the afternoon, she would tell Gabriella about their short talks, as she arranged water and snacks for visitors at the coffee bar.

On one particular morning in the middle of October, Diane visited Nick at around 8:00 a.m. When she asked Nicholas how he was, he replied, "I'm doing good."

But Diane could tell that there was more on Nick's mind.

"Did you sleep well last night?" she asked.

To which Nick replied,

"Jesus was just here. He wanted me to go with Him! I told Him I couldn't go...Gabriella needs me! Then I repeated, 'I'm staying. You owe me. I'm not leaving, now!'"

"Wow!" replied an astonished Diane.

"What did Jesus say to that?"

"Nothing. He just left," replied Nicholas.

Diane was then on the lookout for Gabriella. As soon as she entered Lavender Gardens that morning, Diane called her into her office, relaying her conversation with Nicholas.

"What did he mean telling Jesus, 'You owe me'? What's that mean?" asked Gabriella.

"I don't know, Nicholas didn't offer an explanation. Maybe he'll tell you."

"Yeah... maybe....interesting." replied a perplexed Gabriella.

As she entered Nicholas's room, Gabriella gave her usual cheerful greeting...

"Good morning, my darling" kissing his face. Then asking...

"Anything new happen this morning?"

Nicholas looking down, replied softly,

"No."

"Any visitors? Doctors? Anyone?"

Nicholas just kept staring at his hands.

"No," he replied softly.

"Good. Well, maybe Dr. Yurkevich will stop in today," said Gabriella, adding,

"You know, I love you so very much, Nicholas Carcioni.

"I love how you have always watched over me, and I know that, no matter where you are, you will always be watching over me. And I, my Darling, will always watch over you."

As she spoke, she took his face gently in her hands, and made eye contact with him. Smiling, she kissed him, saying...

"I love you."

He just looked at her. She figured that he didn't want to tell her about Jesus visiting, because he didn't want her to worry that he might be leaving her. He was truly thoughtful that way, and now, even with the brain damage, his caring and concern did not waiver.

"Did you hear me? I said, I love you. What do you say?"

"I love you more," Nicholas slowly replied his usual reply...with a smile.

"No, I wuv *you* more." She giggled.

"No, I love *you* more," Nicholas repeated, smiling.

"Yes, my darling. I do believe you do!" She gazed into his eyes and added,"

"And I really do love you for that, Nicholas!"

She stared at him for several minutes, looking into his eyes.

Then cheerfully added...

> "Just for that you get more kisses" .....kissing him multiple times, till they both start laughing.

CHAPTER 42

NICK FALLS OUT OF BED

By Tuesday, October 16, 2012, Nick was responding slowly to the antibiotic for the pneumonia; and so it continued to linger. He didn't have the strength to cough up the phlegm; consequently, much of it just sat in his lungs.

> Lavender Gardens provided a bed for Nick that did not have any sidebars. Gabriella had complained about this, as she thought that, now that he was starting to move around more in bed, he might fall out. So, she voiced her concern to Jacob and Charolette. They informed her that Illinois had a law stating he has the, "right to fall."

> "He's sleeping on an air mattress bed, that's about three feet off the floor," explained Gabriella passionately. "I'm very concerned that he might fall out! Can you put some bars when he's sleeping at night? During the day, I can watch him, but it is the nighttime that concerns me."

Jacob answered quickly,

> "Illinois law states that *he has the right to fall*, Gabriella. We cannot add anything other than extra pillows on the edges."

"This doesn't make sense to me, Jacob. I'm trying to avoid a problem, *before* it happens."

"I know you are, but there is only so much we can do according to the law."

"What Jacob is saying is correct, Gabriella," added Charolette. "Bed rails cannot be used for restraint, as they are sometimes a problem with seniors getting caught in them and risk of suffocation."

Charolette added....

"We'll just put extra pillows on each side. I'll instruct the CNAs to do so, after his bed bath and during the night.

"Okay, but I was hoping for more of a bar or barrier," concluded Gabriella.

At 9:00 a.m. on Thursday, October 18, just 2 days later, Gabriella's phone rang as she was pulling into the Lavender Gardens parking lot. It was a nurse, Carla, informing her that Nicholas had fallen out of bed that morning.

Leaping out of the car, Gabriella ran into the building and arrived breathless in Nick's room. CNAs and Charolette had just helped him back into bed. Rushing to Nick's side, she asked frantically,

"What happened here? Look at his face. His cheek is red and swollen. His forehead is cut! He hit something when he fell. I knew something like this was bound to happen! Tell me, what happened?"

Charolette started to explain,

"The CNA—"

"*What* CNA?" interrupted Gabriella.

"Frankie, the new CNA, gave Mr. Carcioni his bed bath. He said that he put pillows on each side of the bed, and put Mr. Carcioni on his side before he left. He moved the oxygen machine a little closer, so that the tube would not pull out of his nose. He said that everything looked as it should, before he left."

"What time was that?" asked Gabriella

"About 7:15 this morning. Then at 8:15 a.m. Jurlisa, the Nurse, came in to redress the skin tear at the base of his spine, and then she repositioned him. It is possible that she positioned him too close to the side of the bed. As he slept, his head slipped over the side, and that pulled the rest of his body over. It's the only possible scenario I can surmise," recapped Charolette honestly.

"This happened before with another resident, that Jurlisa took care of recently. I'll be speaking to her more in depth about her work, later today!" added Charolette as she continued recapping the events.

"At 8:45 a.m. Roberta, another Nurse, was passing the door and didn't see Mr. Carcioni in his bed. Came running in and found him on the floor—"

Nicholas then interrupted in pain,

"Ohhh! My face...my back and my shoulder hurts, Gabriella," he moaned.

Gabriella was furious!

"I want CAT scans—his shoulder, back, and his brain, Charolette."

"Well, Dr. Yurkevich already okayed the CAT for his shoulder only, but not his brain and back. He said that, as long as he was talking okay, it wasn't necessary," replied Charolette.

"You call Dr. Yurkevich back, and tell him I said that **it is necessary**! This man has brain damage already, and now he has hit his head during this hard fall. I want a CAT on his brain today too, and on his back! He might have broken bones! He might even be bleeding in his brain! Oh, my God! I feared that this might happen!"

Charolette nodded and looked concerned. She departed quickly to make the call. Meanwhile, the ambulance was on its way to transport Nicholas to Asclepius Christian Medical Center—again. Within minutes, Charolette returned to say that Dr. Yurkevich had given the okay, for a scan of the brain and back, also.

Nicholas and Gabriella were transported to the Emergency Room at Asclepius Christian Medical Center. They were there all day, and slowly but surely, CAT scans were done on Nicholas's brain, back, and shoulder. Nick was not connected to liquid feeding, and Gabriella, although very hungry, would not leave him, not even to get a candy bar.

Finally, at 8:00 p.m., almost eleven hours later, the hospital staff reviewed the test results with Gabriella. There were no broken bones. The brain scan showed no new blood on the brain, but blood from the July fall remained.

However, the doctor at the hospital warned that sometimes, *a few days after a fall, blood could start to trickle* from the brain. It could be seen days later in another CAT scan. He warned to watch for signs of change from Nicholas—speech, severe headaches, or other symptoms. If anything seemed abnormal, he warned, have another CAT scan done immediately.

Nicholas and Gabriella returned to Lavender Gardens at 9:30 p.m., completely exhausted. Nick had slept during most of the day, but when he was awake, he had complained of pain all over. She was thankful that he was sleeping when they returned, and hoped he could get through the night, without waking in pain.

Having plenty of time to rethink Nicholas's fall, Gabriella concluded that he must have hit the oxygen machine, as he fell hard onto the floor. She was already thinking of what to do, to prevent it from happening again. She planned on meeting with Charolette the next day, to present ideas to keep Nicholas safe.

CHAPTER 43

MATS PLACED TO SOFTEN A FALL

Gabriella's angst mounted as she looked at the cuts and bruises on Nick's face, sustained from the fall on the previous day.

Kissing him gently, Gabriella whispered...

> My precious darling. My heart breaks for your suffering. I'm trying to protect you the best way I can. I don't ever want you to fall again. Dear Archangel Michael, protect my baby from future harm!" she prayed.

Leesa, visited that day, and informed Gabriella that Jurlisa had been fired. Leesa said they were all happy to see her go, as she had a caustic personality, and really thought she knew it all!

When Charlotte stepped in that day to check on Nicholas, Gabriella asked her about Jurlisa. Charolette concurred that Jurlisa had been terminated. When Gabriella asked if it was due to Nicholas's fall, Charolette replied,

> "Oh no, Mrs. Carcioni. She wasn't working out. We have high standards here, and she just wasn't making the grade," replied a savvy Charolette.

"Yes, I can see that, Charolette," responded Gabriella, knowing she was getting typical "BS."

Gabriella stepped closer to Charolette, speaking sincerely....

"It's extremely important to me that Nicholas never encounters a fall like that again—or a fall period, Charolette!"

"Yes, well the CNAs have been instructed to be extra careful, from now on, when they are positioning Mr. Carcioni," responded Charolette.

"That's good to hear. However, Charolette, *not good enough, unfortunately*! I've been giving this a lot of thought. Here's what I want you to do. I would like you to place thick rubber mats on the floor every night on both sides of the bed—the thick ones like you see at a wrestling match. I'm sure you have them, or know where to get them."

"I'll have to look into it," replied Charolette, wanting to stall.

Gabriella responded more firmly....

"No Charolette, I'd like you to look into it **today** so we can put them down **tonight**! I'm very serious about this! Nick could be bleeding from his brain as we speak. It certainly wasn't good, by any means, for him to experience a fall and hit his head again. I want those mats *today*, and before I leave every night, I'll personally put them down on the floor, where they must remain all night till morning. Please instruct everyone on the night shift not to move them."

Charolette knew what Gabriella was saying was true. The fall did not do any good for Nicholas, and probably did him great harm. She also knew by now not to play around with Gabriella, when it came to her Nicholas.

She nodded.

By 4:00 pm, two thick blue mats were placed in Nicholas' room, and Gabriella positioned them before she left that evening. When the CNAs came in that evening to turn and change Nicholas, she explained to them about the mats. She said they would be down on the floor *every* night. The CNAs liked Nick and Gabriella, and agreed that he needed some extra protection, now that he was awake more frequently.

CHAPTER 44

DR. GERMAN CHANGED THE RECORD!

Gabriella was nobody's fool. She knew that Dr. Hilda German at Asclepius Christian Medical Center Hospital should not have prescribed a sleeping pill to Nicholas, considering that he had a hemorrhaged brain, and then ignoring Gabriella's own wishes. As Nick's wife, she had clearly expressed her objection as soon as Dr. German mentioned the sleeping medication.

Several friends and relatives mentioned to Gabriella, that she should talk to an Attorney, about what had happened at Asclepius Christian Medical Center Hospital. She decided to do so, and paid for copies of all of Nick's records. On October 16, 2012, she contacted the office of an Attorney, who had been recommended by a friend.

When she called Vincenzo Attorneys at Law in Chicago, she reached Vinnie Vincenzo. He was very interested in the case, but upon hearing the name of the Hospital, Gabriella could tell that his tone changed. Nevertheless, he asked Gabriella to send him the records, and he would get back to her. Gabriella sent them FedEx. A few days later, Attorney Vincenzo's secretary called to say that this was not a case they wanted to pursue. They returned the records to Gabriella.

The following week, Gabriella saw a TV infomercial promoting the prestigious law firm, Sarlo Brothers, Attorneys at Law in Chicago. The firm specialized in malpractice suits. It showed the partners to have several years of success, especially with high profile cases. Gabriella contacted them.

The next day, Dick Sarlo, Senior Partner, returned her call. He asked for a brief synopsis of what had happened, and then asked her to send him all the records.

Upon receiving them, he called her, and requested several additional records, including daily notes, and comments, that the hospital had neglected to include. Gabriella then secured remaining records, and spent nearly $1,000 total to do so, as she asked the Records Department to include every piece of paper regarding Nicholas's stay.

Upon receiving everything, Attorney Sarlo called Gabriella and asked,

> "What day did you say your husband went into a Coma?"

Gabriella answered quickly,

> "July 27, 2012."

> "Did you read the records that you sent me?"

> "No," responded Gabriella, "The box is about two feet high."

> "Well, let me read it to you."

"July 27—Patient alert and anxious to go home."

"July 28—Patient alert and anxious to go home."

"July 29—Patient alert and anxious to go home. July—"

Gabriella interrupted, with a shout.

"**No, stop**! That's not true! He was in a coma for 34 days!"

Attorney Sarlo intervened.

"My dear, they changed the Record on you!" he sadly informed her.

"They saw how upset you were, and knew you were going to seek legal action, and so the Doctor, along with the Nurse, changed the Record! You don't have a leg to stand on. You see, in court, the Doctor is God! The judge will believe the Doctor, not you! I'm sorry. I'll ship all this back to you. There is nothing you can do!"

"But, Attorney Sarlo, I sent constant emails to family and friends, and they can verify the days, he was in a Coma! That's written documentation. I have the name of the Doctor who was Dr. Hilda German's replacement. He took care of Nicholas—Dr. Bobbie Edward. He will testify. I know the name of the Nurse who gave him the sleeping pill—Destini—and the Director of Rehabilitation, Dr. Cristina, and his Nurse that morning, Ann. All of them can be put on the stand, and they'll be forced to tell the truth—or commit perjury!"

Attorney Sarlo responded,

> "They will say, 'It's been so long. I can't remember. I see so many people.' "Again, I'm sorry. You have no case, Gabriella!"

With tears running down her face, she replied,

> "I'm a writer, Attorney Sarlo, and I promise you, I **will** have the *last word!*"

> "Good luck, Gabriella! And I mean that sincerely. I wish you *much* good luck! Sadly, I've seen this happen a hundred times!" he stated emphatically.

CHAPTER 45

NATURE'S HEALING EFFECTS

Nick's pneumonia lingered. He was receiving two antibiotics a day, as a result of the water from the oxygen tank leaking into his lungs, and wasn't getting any better, according to the X-rays, taken every few days.

By October 16, 2012, the weather had finally cooled down from the hundred-degree temperatures, that had been the norm, during that hot summer. Being in the comfortable seventies, Gabriella asked that a Geriatric chair with wheels be ordered for Nick, so that he could be taken outside on the patio. It was standard practice that everyone had to have his or her own personal chair, so that disease would not spread from one patient to the other.

Charolette ordered his chair, and on October 18, it arrived. Gabriella planned to take him outside every day, weather permitting. Today was a beautiful autumn day, so Gabriella contacted the desk, to say she wanted to take Nicholas outside.

In order to accomplish this, two CNAs had to be present. One directed a huge motorized hoist, and the other put large straps under Nick's body. He was locked in among the straps and could not fall out. Then the machine operator pressed a button that caused the machine to raise Nick up out of his bed a few feet, and then lower him into his Geriatric chair.

Every time Nick was raised out of the bed, he got very excited and waved his arms and legs violently, thinking he was going to fall. Gabriella would put her hand on him, and tell him that he was okay, and would not fall. However, that did not calm him, and he would remain fearful. Within several minutes, he was lowered into his chair.

Surprisingly, this flapping-around activity in the hoist, helped to loosen the mucus in his chest. Amazingly, after a few days, he coughed up so much phlegm, that he began recovering faster from the pneumonia!

Prior to heading for the patio outside, Gabriella placed Nick's dark sunglasses on his face, making him look like a movie star, as she wrapped him in a blanket so he wouldn't get chilled, even though the weather was warm. Down the hall and out the door, she pushed him in his huge reclining chair.

He loved being outside in the sunshine, and usually fell asleep for a while. Many times, they both did. The fresh air provided tremendous healing effects for Nick. Gabriella usually designated at least two hours for them, in the warm fresh air.

When he was awake, Gabriella would talk to him. At times his words were still "mumble jumble," but more frequently he started to say sentences clearly. His brain was healing slowly. Sleep, a little exercise, and fresh air was exactly what he needed, at that time.

One day, as Gabriella was wheeling him back to his room after much time being outside, she heard him mumble something.

She stopped, put her ear closer to his mouth, and asked him what he had said. He repeated loudly,

"When am I going to get off this damn train?"

Gabriella laughed, hugged him, and replied,

"You'll be off this train in about ten minutes, my love. Hang in there."

The only train story Gabriella recalled him telling her, was his recollection of the time when he enlisted in the Marines, during World War II. The recruits boarded a train that took them from Chicago to San Diego, California. He had told her that they had spent many days on a hot train, before arriving. Perhaps he was reliving his time enlisting in the Marines.

CHAPTER 46

SWALLOW TEST

By October 19, 2012, Gabriella had been noticing that Nick could swallow, when she put an excessive amount of water on his mouth sponge. Ever since July, when Nick went into a coma, he had not had any solid food. He had been nourished by liquid food, going through a feeding tube, that was inserted into his stomach.

Likewise, he was not permitted to drink anything, and even when Gabriella or a CNA was brushing his teeth, they had to have a suction machine going simultaneously, to suck all toothpaste and water from his mouth. They had to keep reminding him *not* to swallow, because swallowing is a reflexive reaction, however, any liquid at this time would go directly into his lungs.

Gabriella watched him when he was sleeping, and many times, she would see his mouth moving, as though he was chewing something. She believed that he was dreaming, that he was eating some of his favorite foods.

Awaking from his sleep, several evenings before, he said to her,

"Let's go out to dinner. Where would you like to go?"

Gabriella's heart broke knowing that he wanted to leave there, and didn't realize that he actually was not physically able to, but his brain resorted back to being his ol' self, who was always ready to suggest going someplace where they could have fun, and eat good food.

> "Oh, darling," she replied, "I'm not hungry at this time. Let's just stay here and talk."

> "I'd really like to take you out, Honey," he insisted.

> "Maybe tomorrow, my love."

> "Okay. Tomorrow we're going to dinner. Pick a nice place," he added.

> "I will." Gabriella whispered.

Gabriella asked Mary Karolyn, speech therapist, to order a swallow rest. If he passed, he could start to eat real food. She was trying whatever it would take, to bring him happiness. Charolette and Mary Karolyn discussed it, but they both thought it was too early, and that Gabriella was pushing Nick too fast. They recommended that they wait at least two more weeks. Gabriella reminded them that Nick's last day at Lavender Gardens would be November 16.

> "Let's schedule it for October 31, recommended Mary Karolyn. We don't want him to fail."

> "Okay. That's fine," agreed Gabriella.

On October 31, a specially equipped truck parked outside in the Lavender Gardens parking lot. Mary Karolyn transported Nick to the truck in his Geriatric chair, as Gabriella walked along side, holding his hand. Upon arriving at the vehicle, they were met by Leonard, who would administer the dynamic swallowing test.

Several factors play into swallowing difficulties. One is, most certainly, age because years of wear and tear on the esophagus, can decrease the ability to swallow. In Nick's case, there were additional risk concerns because of the neurological issues caused by 34 days in a Coma.

> "Hello, Mr. Carcioni. My name's Leonard, and I'll be with you as we go through the testing. Are you comfortable?"

Nick responded,

> "Yes"

> "I'm going to be giving you various foods of different consistencies, and all you have to do is swallow what I put in your mouth. It's very simple. Okay?"

> "Okay," replied Nick.

Leonard arranged Nick's chair so that he would be sitting up straight. He was very respectful, and explained everything to Nick, as he proceeded with the test.

Leonard could monitor Nick's swallowing mechanism on an X-ray machine. Each of the various food items was barium coated, and provided a clear image as they traveled through Nick's mouth and down his throat. The X-ray video images would show any problems in the coordination of his mouth and throat muscles. Leonard checked carefully for aspiration—food going into his lungs as Nick breathed. He also checked to see how much was still left in Nick's mouth. He made notations all through the test.

Gabriella and Mary Karolyn sat behind Nick, and watched his swallowing test on another TV monitor.

The following day, Mary Karolyn came to Nick's room, with the results. Nick did *not* pass the Swallow Test. Another Swallow Test would be arranged at a later date.

CHAPTER 47

REALITY BURSTS

By November 1, 2012, it had been almost three months since Nick awakened from his Coma. Gabriella sat with him many days in awe of her Nicholas, marveling at how far he had come. She recalled Dr. Waters at Asclepius Christian Medical Center Hospital suggesting that she *'let him die'* back in July, and was so grateful and thankful to Jesus, for giving her the fortitude to have *faith* and *believe,* that Nick would come back to her. Gabriella referred to this time as "Bonus Months!"

During this time, Nicholas had given her moments of unforgettable laughter, pride, and, yes, he had even said, "I love you," which were words she had prayed to hear again. There had been moments—not entire days, but moments—during which his brain "kicked in" and he was up to speed with reality. He would be alert and spot on. She called these moments "Reality Bursts." Though many of these bursts were happy moments, some also proved to frighten him.

Over the past month, he had had several of these frightening moments. Earlier in October, he awakened one afternoon from a nap. He looked at Gabriella and asked,

"What's going on? What is wrong with me, Gabriella?"

She thought carefully, how she could answer this honestly and delicately. He kept staring at her. Finally, she tried to explain.

> "Recently, Nicky, you fell and hit your head, very hard. You then went into a deep sleep. But now you're awake, and you're getting better every day. You're almost totally recovered, and soon you'll be coming home."

> "How long was I asleep?" he asked.

> "Not too long. Three or four weeks, darling."

> "Oh, my God, Gabriella! Oh, my God!" he had responded in a frightened excitable tone.

Rushing to his side...

> "Nicky, that's all behind us! Right now, you're getting better! You're doing great, and you'll be home soon. Don't worry. Everything is fine now!"

> "Honestly, Gabriella? You wouldn't lie to me, would you?" Nicholas asked.

> "No, my angel. I would not. Give me kisses." Then, to change the subject and lighten the mood, she added,

> "You know you have the softest lips of anyone in the world." She smiled at him.

That made Nick smile too.

> "Thanks, Honey. Your lips are nice too." he laughed.

> "I can't wait to go home," speaking seriously.

"I know," Gabriella replied. "And I will take you home just as soon as possible."

He fell back to sleep shortly thereafter, and Gabriella could see him frowning and mumbling in his sleep. She was hoping that he wasn't having nightmares about his condition. She just kept kissing his forehead, and whispering that he was getting better, and that everything was okay, and not to worry.

During this entire ordeal, she prayed that he would have a full recovery. She asked others to pray for the same outcome. She did not want his brain to recover, only for him to learn that he would forever be an invalid confined to a bed. This would be the ultimate nightmare for him, and she prayed to God not to let that happen! It would be better for God, in his mercy, to call Nicholas home instead.

One Sunday, Gabriella suggested that they watch the Bears football game together. This would be the first time they had watched any sport on TV. As he watched for a short while, he finally said,

"Please call the coach and tell him, I'm too tired to play anymore. I want to go to sleep!"

Gabriella was shocked to learn that Nick thought he was truly playing the game. So, she pretended to call the coach, as he had requested.

In picking up the phone, she pretended to dial.

"Okay. I'll call him now. Hello, Coach? Nicholas is too tired to play anymore. He's going to sleep now. Get someone else to take his place. Okay. Thank you, Coach."

She turned to Nicholas who was looking at her, waiting to hear what the Coach had said.

> "Okay, Sweetie. The coach has taken you out of the game. He said you are to rest. He also said that you did a great job playing today. He's proud of you. You can go to sleep now, Darling."

> "Oh, Thank you," Nick replied. He was obviously relieved, and he dozed off quickly. Gabriella turned off the TV and never turned it on again.

###

Gabriella's daily schedule was to arrive at Lavender Gardens at around 9:00 a.m. and leave at around 10:00 p.m. Normally, visiting hours ended for most at 9:00 p.m.

The daily routine was usually as follows:

Nick would sleep on and off all day long, sometimes sleeping for four or five solid hours at a time. Virginia Margaret usually came in and gave him his nightly medicines between 5:00 and 7:00 p.m. At that time, Gabriella would apprise her of any alarming situations.

For example, one night Nick had become extremely itchy, all over this entire body, from one of the medications. In learning this, Dr. Yurkevich ordered Benadryl. A daily injection was added to Nick's chart, and he received it without fail, which immediately helped.

Also, Nick started to complain of severe, sharp pains shooting in his temple, causing him to grab his head instantly. Virginia Margaret called Dr. Yurkevich immediately, and he prescribed Prednisone.

When visiting the next day, Dr. Yurkevich, said that he thought Nick was developing temporal arteritis (not to be confused with arthritis). Temporal arteritis is a condition in which the arteries in the temple area that supply blood to the head and brain, become inflamed or damaged. It can lead to strokes, blindness, or aneurisms.

The CNA usually came in at around 8:00 p.m. to change Nicholas and his bedding, if necessary. At 9:00 p.m. Gabriella would start to dim the lights in the room and even close the door three-quarters of the way to block the hall lighting and noise, which often kept Nick awake. As it got closer to 10:00 p.m. she would depart quietly.

One evening near 10:00 p.m., Nick was sleeping. An exhausted Gabriella, started to quietly pack up personal items prior to leaving, but Nick woke up instantly.

"You aren't leaving, are you?" he asked.

"Yes, Darling. It's 10:00 p.m., and I want to go home, shower, and get some sleep. I'll be back tomorrow morning bright and early. Give me kisses, and go back to sleep."

"No, Gabriella. Don't leave me. Please."

"Nicky, I've been here all day, and it's late. It's ten o'clock. You go back to sleep. Soon it will be morning, and I'll be here again."

"No! No! Gabriella, *don't go!"* Nick was shouting at the top of his voice.

Gabriella had never seen him act this way. Usually, he would eventually say okay, and then she would leave.

"Nick, honey, what's wrong? Calm down."

"I don't want you to leave me, Gabriella. I'm scared!"

"Scared. Scared of *what*, Nicky?" He grabbed Gabriella's arm, and held it tight.

"Nick, what are you scared of? Does anyone hurt you when I'm not around?"

"Gabriella, if you go, *I'll kill myself!*" Nick replied in a serious tone.

A shocked Gabriella froze.

"Nick ... my God, why would you say such a thing? Relax, I won't go. I'll stay here with you. I don't ever want you to be afraid. I'm here. Let me hold you."

She hugged him, with her one free arm. Gabriella sat back down by Nick's bedside, as he continued to hold her arm tightly. She had never seen him act this way before, and couldn't help but wonder, if someone on the night shift had scared him, or even hurt him. This gave her tremendous cause for alarm!

She sat there in the semi dark, and even if she made the least little movement, Nick would awaken suddenly, and say again,

"Don't leave me. Stay here, okay?"

"Yes, my love. I'm here. Go to sleep! Relax! I won't leave you!"

At midnight the night nurse Supervisor, Cynthia, came in the room.

"Mrs. Carcioni, Charolette just called, and I told her you were still here. She said to tell you, that you must leave."

"Cynthia, for some reason Nick is very frightened tonight," Gabriella answered in a whispered voice. He's very anxious. I'm going to stay with him to keep him calm, until I know he's fine. Relay that to Charolette, will you, please?"

About fifteen minutes later, Cynthia came back into Nick's room and told Gabriella that Charolette was on the phone at the desk, and wanted to speak to her. Gabriella told Nick that she had to go to the desk to get something.

"Okay. But hurry back, okay?" he insisted.

"Yes, darling."

Gabriella picked up the desk phone.

"Hi, Charolette. Did Cynthia tell you that I have an unusual situation here tonight with Nicholas? He's really frightened about something."

"Yes, she did," replied Charolette. "But I must insist. You have to leave, Mrs. Carcioni. Visiting hours are over."

"Charolette. Did you hear me? Nick is very frightened tonight. Scared like I've never seen him! I don't know if he had a bad dream or what his brain is reliving for him, but I am *not* going to leave him in this terrorized state. Do you understand me?"

"Mrs. Carcioni. We have designated hours for visitors, and you have exceeded those hours. You must leave. Mr. Carcioni will be fine."

Becoming furious over Charolette's lack of concern, Gabriella countered,

> "Charolette, stick your designated hours up your ass. I'm not leaving my husband in the state of panic that he's in tonight. Good-bye!"

With that, Gabriella hung up the phone, as other nurses sat there staring.

Upon returning to Nick's room, she immediately texted Dr. Yurkevich, and then put a call into his emergency number. She apprised him of Nicholas' panic-stricken state, and told him that he had even threatened to kill himself, if she left.

Within minutes, Dr. Yurkevich responded:

> "Stay as long as you have to!"

Gabriella was not bothered any more that evening by Cynthia nor Charolette. She stayed till 2:30 a.m. Nick fell into a deep sleep, and she was able to move her arm from the bed, without waking him.

As she drove home, she still could not shake several unnerving thoughts.

> *What had frightened him? Who had frightened him? Was there someone on the night shift who scared him purposely? Had they punished him for any animosity they felt toward her? Had they scared him, and told him that I had left, and was never coming back? Do they ignore him, and not give him any care during the night?*

When she arrived home at 3:30 a.m., Gabriella's mind could not find rest. One of the main issues that plagued her was

Charolette's lack of concern for Nick's state of mind. It didn't seem to bother her one bit that he was terrorized! Gabriella realized immediately, that she had to make sudden drastic changes, to her proposed timetable.

She set her alarm for 7:00 a.m. to awaken that morning. When entering Lavender Gardens at 9:00 a.m., she could hear Wanda's boisterous voice, down the corridor, telling Nick that Gabriella would be there soon.

As Gabriella turned the corner, Wanda happy to see Gabriella, called out to Nick, joyfully...

"Here comes Gabriella now!" she turned to Gabriella.

"Gabriella, he's been crying, and calling you all morning.

He just kept saying,

'Oh, Gabriella, why did you leave me? Come back.'

"I would have called you at home, if I had your number."

Gabriella looked at her in shock, and then entered the room. Nicholas was in tears. His face and eyes were all red from crying. As soon as he saw her, he was so happy, and cried out,

"Oh, Gabriella, I thought you left me. I thought you were never coming back!"

Gabriella grabbed several tissues and wiped his face.

"Oh, my darling Nicholas! I will *never* leave you! Don't ever think that I would leave you! Never! Ever! Do you hear me? I'm here. I just go home at night to sleep. But when I wake up, you're the first person I think of, and

I come running over here as fast as I can, to be with you all day long! I love you so very much. You're my everything in this world. Don't ever forget that, okay?"

"Now, stop crying and give me hugs and kisses." She threw her arms around him, and hugged him tight. Give me more kisses. That's my baby. Calm down now. You're okay now? You know I would never go away from you."

An overjoyed Nicholas was now smiling....

"Yeah, I'm so glad you're here. I love you so much!" responding while holding her tight.

Just then, Glenn the CNA came in to give Nick his morning bed bath.

"Look who's here, Nicky. It's Glenn Miller, your favorite CNA!

"Good morning, Glenn Miller!" responded Nicholas.

"Good morning Mr. and Mrs. Carcioni. It's such a beautiful day!"

"I brought some new cologne for you to put on Nick after his bath." Replied Gabriella as she waved the bottle under Nick's nose.

"Here smell, Nicky. It's one of your favorites from home. Smells good, yes?"

Nick smiled and nodded his head in agreement.

"That does smell good!"

"Paco Rabanne One Million," she said.

"Only the best for you, my love!"

Nick was now calm and happy.

She handed the bottle to Glenn Miller, and then stepped out of the room.

CHAPTER 48

WE'RE LEAVING!

While Nicholas was preoccupied with having his morning bed bath, Gabriella went across the hall to see Constance. They always talked daily, and each was a sounding board for the other.

That morning, Constance told Gabriella how she was trying to get hold of her doctor, as she wanted to be discharged from Lavender Gardens that weekend, or the next at the latest. She had gone to look at Retirement homes with her daughter, and had selected a very nice place in the suburbs called, Fountain Ponds. Gabriella was not familiar with the place.

"You look tired, Gabriella," observed Constance.

"Yeah, I am. You know, last night Nick was so frightened. He told me, if I left to go home, he was going to *kill himself.*"

"Oh, my God. Why didn't you come and get me? I could have kept him company."

"No, I would never impose on you, unless it was an emergency. I left here at 2:30 this morning! Charolette tried to kick me out at midnight, but I called Dr.

Yurkevich, and he said to stay as long as was necessary. Honestly, that woman!"

"Oh, she's the queen here. I don't like her one bit. She's such a smart-ass bitch!" replied Constance.

Gabriella nodded....

"Constance, I'm very upset! I couldn't help thinking as I drove home ... Remember, weeks ago, you told me about a conversation you overheard one night, when Nick kept calling my name, and one of the nurses told him to shut up or she would shut him up! I'm wondering if there have been more instances when she, or someone is scaring him! It makes me sick and fearful with anger to even think of it, but something scared the hell out of him last night, and I don't think it was a dream, even though it could have been."

"Yeah, who was that nurse? I forget," asked Constance.

"I think you said, Nurse Camille," Gabriella replied.

"Oh yeah, that's right. She's a bitch too!" assessed Constance. "However, I can't really say that I've heard another conversation like that, but I've been taking sleeping pills lately, cause I was having trouble sleeping."

"I thought so," said Gabriella with a giggle.

"I came in quickly last night, after I talked to Charolette on the phone, and you were sawing logs." They both laughed.

"Nick's one hundred days ends on November 16, but in giving this *a lot* of thought, I'm going to tell Diane, that I want to take him home tomorrow, November third!"

"Tomorrow! Oh, why not finish out the hundred days, Gabriella? I'd hate to see you go, and leave me here with these idiots," expressed a saddened Constance.

"No, Constance. My intuition is telling me to take him home as soon as possible! Last night was a real eye opener! I can care for him nicely in the comfort of our home. In his bedridden state, he probably would qualify for Hospice. Don't you think? I have two cards from Hospice representatives. One is through Asclepius Christian Medical Center. Although I despise that hospital for what they did, Dr. Yurkevich is connected to it, and if I ever need him, I'm sure he'd help me. So, I'm leaning toward them. I'm going to call both. I'll see you later."

"Keep me informed. Let me know what they say," Constance called out.

Gabriella immediately called both Hospice reps, and both made appointments for them to come the next day to evaluate Nicholas. They were quite certain, after hearing Gabriella's synopsis of Nick's condition over the phone, that he was a Hospice candidate.

The next day, Saturday, both reps came at different times. Although they were both congenial, Gabriella really preferred the rep from Golden Stallion Hospice, especially since the rep's Mother was a resident of Lavender Gardens.

Gabriella had met the mother, one day when she and Nick were outside on the patio. The woman asked about his progress. She was an extremely kindhearted woman, and she passed along her daughter's card to Gabriella. Also, the benefits of this particular Hospice provider included four levels of care—24-hour care if needed, veterans' care, and music therapy. Gabriella had been advised by several people to look closely at all the Benefits, when choosing a Hospice provider.

However, when she talked to Dr. Yurkevich, he pushed Asclepius Christian Medical Center Hospice, and Gabriella thought that, because he was familiar with Nicholas' case, he could end up being her ace in the hole, should she need him.

Also, truthfully, Dr. Yurkevich had been a real supporter of Gabriella, and had given Nicholas excellent medical attention, in her opinion. He never refused her calls, and he visited Nicholas regularly. In short, she had become quite fond of him. Yes, after careful consideration, it made good sense to go with Asclepius Christian Medical Center Hospice, primarily because of Dr. Yurkevich.

When she discussed an early Discharge with Dr. Yurkevich, he confirmed that he would have to examine Nicholas one last time. The earliest he could do this, would be Monday, November 5, at 1:00 p.m. as Charolette, Nursing Director, needed to be present along with two CNAs. He would inform Charolette.

In the meantime, Gabriella informed Diane, Public Relations Supervisor, of her plans to take Nicholas home early, and Diane contacted the most economical ambulance transport service, which they used often. Gabriella paid $400 in advance with her credit card, as Medicare did not cover that expenditure.

Actually, Monday worked out well for Gabriella regarding Nicholas' discharge; there was much for her to coordinate. This gave Hospice time to deliver the hospice bed and all equipment necessary: hoist, Geriatric chair, feeding machine, over-the-bed table, inhaler machine, electric toothbrush, and suction machine. In addition, she wanted to make their home festive by putting up their Christmas tree, and some other decorations, as they had done for 33 years.

Hospice had been notified, and now Gabriella had to make room for all that Nick needed. The sofa and two end tables with lamps remained in the room, as did a small round table. And, of course, the TV was in the corner by the fireplace. In using all space, she wanted the Hospice bed to be positioned where Nick's favorite reclining chair had been located. This way it would face the TV, in case he wanted to watch.

Although it broke her heart, she knew she had to get rid of his recliner chair. She was very fearful that, if he saw it, he would want to sit in it, and of course, he was unable.

So, late Friday night, she dragged Nick's chair through the foyer, out the front door, and down the driveway for pickup by the Salvation Army the next morning. It just so happened that, when the truck pulled up the next morning, Gabriella was looking out the upstairs window. Two men loaded Nick's comfortable recliner onto the truck. Tears rolled down Gabriella's face as she watched, but she knew she'd had no choice.

On Saturday morning at 9:00 a.m., Hospice delivered the bed and other equipment; however, Gabriella was not pleased, because they brought a bed that was not motorized. It had to be physically cranked, which she was unable to handle. She stopped the deliverymen and immediately called her Hospice rep, saying she couldn't manage with a manual bed, and needed a motorized one, with a thick pressure-reducing mattress.

Later that evening, the motorized bed and mattress were delivered as specified. In between these deliveries, Gabriella went to Lavender Gardens and spent hours with Nicholas. She kept telling him that he was going home in two days, and he was so ecstatic! She then returned home, when the second bed was delivered.

Early Sunday morning, Gabriella went to the mall and purchased seven sets of the softest 3,000-thread-count Egyptian cotton "double bed" sheets in various colors. Double bed sheets fit a Hospice bed, which is somewhere between a twin and a double bed in size. Also, since winter was approaching, she purchased flannel sheets, as they would keep him much warmer. While shopping, she was reminded about a baby monitor she had seen on TV. It had a small TV screen and a speaker. With it, one could observe and listen to the baby from another room. Thinking she was going to be sleeping in the Master bedroom upstairs, and Nicholas would be downstairs in the Family room, she purchased the monitor, so she could hear and watch him at will.

With everything in place, Gabriella was able to comfortably spend the remainder of Sunday with her loving Nicholas. She was tremendously excited to have Nicholas come home with her, so she could personally care for him and know he was safe.

In Gabriella's mind, she truly believed that she could help him get stronger and return to a semi normal life, weaning him off of some of the more potent drugs, to which he was presently addicted.

In Gabriella's mind, she truly believed that she would have him home with her, for at least one year.

Yes, Gabriella had very high expectations.

CHAPTER 49

NURSING HOME PLEADS

Excited about this being Nick's last day at Lavender Gardens, Gabriella arose earlier than usual on Monday, November 5, 2012, filled with much exuberance and joy.

At 1:00 p.m., Dr. Yurkevich, Charolette, and two CNAs entered Nick's room. Dr. Yurkevich started to examine Nick, but then noticed that he had not been changed, so he ordered the CNAs to do that immediately. He looked harshly at Charolette, as it was obvious that he felt Nicholas should have been attended to, prior to their coming.

He motioned for Gabriella to follow him to the other side of the room, and there he proceeded to give Gabriella a sales pitch regarding the Benefits of having Nicholas stay at Lavender Gardens.

> "You should leave him here where he can get proper care," he emphasized.

> "I can give him proper care in our home, where he'll be more comfortable, Doctor," replied Gabriella.

> "Look at what needs to be done," he said, pointing to the CNAs changing Nick's diaper.

"Do you want to be doing that?" he asked.

"Hahaha! Who do you think's been changing him here almost every day? Me! Many times. That's no strain!" replied Gabriella shaking her head. "No, he's going home, *today.*"

The Doctor continued.

"Think about it, Gabriella. In being here, he has speech therapy, and he's already started with some physical therapy. He really should stay here for his own welfare," coaxed Dr. Yurkevich.

"His own welfare? Don't you think I can help him with both those functions? I implemented both, even before the staff here got involved. I taught him words when he was babbling, and I taught him how to brush his hair when his arms were stiff. Because I massaged his arms, legs, and feet, he became more agile—"

Dr. Yurkevich interrupted,

"Gabriella, we could offer you a discount if you let him stay. Instead of $14,000 a month, we could probably lower that to $10,000 a month," suggested Dr. Yurkevich.

"Thank you. That's very generous of you, Doctor, and I appreciate it. But, with that kind of money, I can get a lot of personalized attention for him, in the comfort of his own home. The main reason that I'm taking him home, is that he is happiest when he's with me. And I'm happiest when I'm with him! This way, I'll be with him 24 hours a day. I need to feel that he is safe! Hospice will come and assist a few days a week. We'll be just fine!"

Continuing...

> "The best thing for Nicholas is for me to take him home.
> That's what he wants most of all—to be home with me,
> and that will happen today. I'm extremely excited. You're
> welcome to stop over any time, Doctor."

Dr. Yurkevich just smiled. He could see there was no way he
was going to change Gabriella's mind. As he stood looking at
this woman, he marveled at how happy she was, to be taking
her husband home, an invalid with brain damage, with a slim
chance of complete recovery.

Yes, Gabriella was happy, even in knowing, he would require
her undivided attention seven days a week, 24 hours a day.

When Dr. Yurkevich finished Nicholas' physical examination,
he completed a chart that outlined all Nick's medications and
procedures, that needed to be done on a daily basis, and handed
it to Gabriella:

> "Here you are, Gabriella. Good luck to you both," he
> added with a smile.

Medications:

- NovoLog insulin twice a day
- Bisac-Evac once a day
- Coreg twice a day
- Ferrous sulfate once a day
- Keppra every 12 hours
- Omeprazole every 12 hours
- Triamcinolone topical twice a day
- Benadryl every 4 hours
- Milk of magnesia at bedtime

- Prednisone once a day
- Norco every 8 hours

Procedures:

- Cleanse G tube site with saline once a day
- Cleanse and apply ointment to bedsore at base of spine once a day
- Suspend heels off bed 4 times a day
- Turn and reposition Nicholas every 2 hours
- Flush external feeding flush 3 times a day
- Administer Glucerna liquid food 3 times a day
- Water flush 3 times a day
- DuoNeb inhaler every 6 hours
- In addition, the hospice nurse will provide other drugs to be given, including morphine.

Word got out, and soon employees started to enter Nicholas's room to say their Goodbyes.

Mary Karolyn, Speech Therapist, stopped by to give Gabriella instructions for occasionally giving Nicholas morsels of real food. She reminded her that Nicholas had coughed during his Swallow Test each time he swallowed, because his throat muscles were not working properly. To prevent aspiration, food would have to be extremely thick like paste, she emphasized. His main nourishment would still come through the feeding tube—3 cans a day.

CNA Leesa entered with open arms and gave hugs to both Gabriella and Nicholas. She also gave Gabriella her phone number, in case Gabriella needed extra help. Other CNAs did the same, as they all were looking for part-time work. All the CNAs really liked Gabriella and Nicholas, especially as Gabriella often offered them advice about their problems, and listened to them vent. And, best of all, Gabriella always had candy and snacks, and bought pizza for all of them, on several occasions.

Wanda came to the doorway in her wheelchair, crying.

> "I hate to see you go, Gabriella. You were always so nice to me. Nicholas, I'm gonna miss your singing. Will you come and visit me sometime?"

> "If we can, Wanda. You know Nicholas needs to heal more."

Then, giving Wanda a huge hug, Gabriella added,

> "Thank you for always watching over him, when I was not here. You're an angel!"

Constance entered giving Gabriella a long hug. She also had tears in her eyes.

> "I'm going to miss you. Do you think you can ever come and visit me at Fountain Ponds, Gabriella?"

> "Not immediately, Constance. I just can't leave him. You understand."

> "Yeah. Well, I hope everything works out for you," added Constance.

> "Thank you, Constance. It's been a joy knowing you. So, when are *you* leaving?" Gabriella asked.

> "Doctor says he'll discharge me this Friday. Thank God!" she replied with a smile.

"That's wonderful. I wish you much happiness in your new home! I'm sure you'll be happy there."

"Thank you, Gabriella. Come visit when you can."

Gabriella nodded.

Another knock at the door came as Diane, Guest Services Director, called out to Nicholas.

"Nicholas, I'm going to miss our morning chats. You take care, okay?"

"Yeah," replied Nicholas as he lay there, patiently observing.

Leaning over him, Diane gave Nicholas a hug, and then turning, she approached Gabriella to hug her.

"You take good care of *you!* Make sure you eat and get some rest. You are one in a million. He's lucky to have you."

"And I'm lucky to have him, Diane," said Gabriella, smiling.

"God has given him a second chance, and answered your prayers, Gabriella."

"Yes, he most certainly has Diane, and I'm tremendously grateful!"

Another knock at the door, interrupted them….with a cheery Hello…

"Hello, anybody home?"

It was House Chaplain, Julie.

"Just heard you're leaving today. Wow! So soon?"

"Yes Chaplain, it's time to take my baby home."

She started to hand Gabriella a book....

"Here, I want you to have this book of Daily Inspirations... they will give you a lift. I've had this for years, and it's always been my favorite. I want you to have it." said Chaplain Julie with tears.

"Oh, thank you so much. I will think of you each morning when I read them." replied a thankful Gabriella.

Chaplain Julie smiled and hugged her. Then she walked over to Nicholas and gave him a hug and kiss on his cheek.

"God bless you Nicholas. You are definitely one of God's favorites!"

Nicholas smiled and replied, "Thank You!"

So, you're leaving us today? Called out Virginia Margaret, as she entered.

"Here I brought you a going away present," she laughed, handing Gabriella a tube of ointment for Nicholas, as they both chuckled.

Then, Virginia Margaret became very serious, stating...

"You know *I have to say this*, Gabriella.....A lot of people here had their opinions about how you cared for Nicholas. But, all I can say is, if I was in that bed, **I would want _you_ to be _my_ Advocate!"**

This glowing compliment reduced Gabriella to tears! Virginia Margaret was truly a professional, who Gabriella admired greatly, and was emotionally touched by her words.

> "Thank you, Virginia Margaret. Thank you so much for all the special care you showed toward Nicholas and me. We will never forget your kindness!"

> "You're welcome, Gabriella. It was truly my pleasure!"

> "Nicholas, give your sweetheart here a big hug," she said as she hugged him.

> "Okay, sweetheart. You're the greatest!" replied Nicholas smiling.

> "Golly, I'm going to miss being called sweetheart! Take care." Departing quickly wiping her tears.

Yes, everyone became very emotional that morning, because they finally realized the miracle that they had all witnessed, while they, too, became an integral part of it. No one expected Nicholas to awaken, nor did they expect him to live. Only his Gabriella! Yes, they played along with her, all in the name of being virtuous and mannerly. But, God stepped in, and taught them all a *lesson* they will never forget!

A final knock at the door signaled, that the ambulance service was there to take Nicholas home. Gabriella looked around the room, one last time. A kaleidoscope of memories flashed through her mind, confirming that this had been one unforgettable experience for both Nicholas and her.

All in all, she decided, Lavender Gardens was filled with several goodhearted people, trying to do their best, with what they had! She would miss several of them.

But now, it was time to start yet another exciting chapter in Nicholas's journey toward recovery.

Gabriella remained even more optimistic!

CHAPTER 50

HOSPICE

November 5, 2012

The day had finally come. The day Gabriella had prayed for! The day she was bringing her Nicholas home for good.

As she drove her car, the ambulance followed closely behind. It was a glorious sunny autumn day, and Gabriella felt just as sunny inside her heart. She teared up thinking about how far Nicholas had progressed, and thanked God numerous times, for giving him back to her.

When they reached their multi-level home, Gabriella quickly put her car in the garage, went inside to open the front door. On her way through the Family room, she paused to plug in the hundreds of blinking lights, that decorated their Christmas tree.

The ambulatory men were very attentive, as they gently placed Nicholas in his Hospice bed, located in the spacious Family room. They departed promptly.

Just then the phone rang. It was the Hospice CNA, who would be caring for Nicholas. She said she would stop over in about fifteen minutes. As Gabriella hung up, the woman who would be Nicholas's Nurse, called to say that she would be there in an hour.

The doorbell rang.

Gabriella greeted a short Mexican woman with black hair and a soft voice, who announced that her name was, Jane. Gabriella took her to meet Nicholas, who was sleeping. Tapping him, so he would awaken, she introduced Jane. Jane informed Gabriella that she normally would come around 8:30 a.m. every Monday and Friday.

"Oh, just two days?" asked Gabriella.

"If you would like, I think, because of his condition, they would agree for me to come 3 days a week—Monday, Wednesday, and Friday."

"Oh, that would be wonderful."

"I'll ask," Jane responded.

"Great, Jane! Would it be possible, that today you could give Nicholas a bed bath? I'd like to get the Nursing Home off of him, and put a clean T-shirt and pajama top, as well as clean sheets on the bed. Would that be possible?"

"Sure. Where do I get the water? Do you have special soap you want me to use?"

"Yes, let me show you." Gabriella walked Jane to the first-floor powder room and gave her the Old Spice Denali gel to use.

"I love this scent, so let's use this each time. Here is a wash pan, washcloth, and clean towel, and powder. Throw the dirty gown and linens down the basement steps along with the sheets. I'll wash them later."

"Yes, ma'am."

"Meanwhile, let me put the thermostat up. It feels a little chilly in here," stated Gabriella.

The doorbell rang once more. In opening the door, Gabriella greeted a black woman, about five-seven in her mid 50's.

"Hi, I'm Bernie, Mr. Carcioni's Nurse."

"Yes, come in. The CNA, is here giving Nick a bed bath. Can I offer either of you ladies a soda?"

"No, thank you. I'm fine," said Bernie. Jane just shook her head.

Bernie seemed to know Jane. Immediately Jane asked Bernie about coming there three days a week instead of two. Bernie replied that would be fine, but that Jane had to run it by Sally, Office Manager, first.

Bernie was not a warm, friendly person. She was a no-nonsense sort of person, who didn't smile easily, and had little to offer in conversation. Bernie was not what Gabriella had been hoping for, in a Nurse for Nicholas.

As she opened her bag and proceeded to unpack several papers, she also emptied a separate bag of drugs and syringes without needles. She placed them on the round table, where Gabriella sat. As she pulled each drug out, she explained its use. Each drug had a purpose, and was to be used at Gabriella's discretion, and all of them must be kept refrigerated.

Gabriella took lots of notes on a legal tablet.

Bernie pointed to several syringes full of medicine.

"This is morphine. It's for severe pain. Give it to him orally if he coughs continually. It will slow down the coughing. Are you a nurse?" she asked.

"No, I'm not," replied Gabriella.

"You *will be* when this is all over!" Bernie replied seriously.

"I'm going to check him over," she said as she rose from the table.

Jane was in the middle of the bed bath, but let Bernie have her way with Nicholas. Gabriella, seeing that Nicholas was beginning to shiver, so she put a blanket over him, but left room for Bernie's stethoscope.

"I don't want him to be chilled," Gabriella said. "You okay, sweetheart?" she asked.

"I'm cold," Nicholas responded.

"I know. That's why I put the blanket on you. That feels better, doesn't it?"

"Yes," said Nicholas softly.

"Keep him covered as much as you can, Jane. And please get the T-shirt and flannel pajama top on him as soon as possible," instructed Gabriella.

"Okay," Jane replied.

Bernie started to pack up. Obviously, she wasn't going to spend any extra time getting to know Gabriella or Nicholas.

"Okay. He's fine."

"How's his lungs? Does he still have Pneumonia?" asked Gabriella.

"His lungs sound fine to me," Bernie responded.

"Well, let's keep an eye on it, because he just recently had Pneumonia at Lavender Gardens. You check his lungs each time you come, don't you?" asked Gabriella, adding,

"Incidentally, how often do you come?"

"Once a week, on Friday. Yes, I'll check him all over," replied Bernie.

"Oh, you come only once a week?" asked Gabriella.

"Yes. Unless there's an emergency. If you ever have any questions, just call my cell. Here's my number on this form. Okay. Any other questions? If not, I'll see you on Friday, and then each Friday after that. Put those in the refrigerator," Bernie said, pointing to the bag of drugs.

"Yes, I'll do that now." Gabriella ran up the three steps into the kitchen, put the drugs into the fridge, and then walked Bernie to the door.

Jane finished Nick's bed bath, threw the dirty linens down the basement stairs, and started to put her sweater on.

"Jane, when you come, I'll have clean sheets, towels, washcloth, T-shirt, and pajama top here so you have everything at your fingertips when you arrive," Gabriella stated, referring to the round table in the family room.

"Diapers will always be stacked here in their package, against the wall."

"That'll be great, missis," responded Jane as she put her coat on and departed.

At last Nicholas and Gabriella were alone. It was getting dark out, and the twinkling tree lights created a lovely atmosphere.

"Hi, sweetheart," she said as she kissed his face.

Nicholas opened his eyes and smiled.

"You're home now. Look at the beautiful Christmas tree. I know how you love all the blinking lights. Isn't it pretty?"

"Yeah, I like my lights."

"You and I, Mr. Carcioni, are going to have a most spectacular Thanksgiving, Christmas, and New Year's Eve together. God has blessed us with this extra time together, and we're going to cherish each moment that we have. Right, Darling?"

Nicholas nodded and smiled. Then he surprisingly said,

"I love how you take care of me!"

Gabriella was really touched when he said that. She needed support from him. She needed to know that what she was doing was pleasing him.

"You look so comfortable all snuggled up in your bed," Gabriella said with a smile, and so glad to have him bathed, clean and at home with her.

Nicholas just kept smiling. Little did Gabriella realize, at that time, but his smiling was just as miraculous as his speech. One day soon, she would realize that.

> "You relax. I'm going to take a shower, and I'll be down just as fast as I can." Gabriella stated, and then started to go upstairs, but Nicholas immediately started calling her name.

She came back downstairs and explained that she was only going upstairs to shower. She was not leaving. They were home now, and she would never have to leave him again in the night.

> "I'll shower and be back downstairs soon," Gabriella informed him.

> "Okay," replied Nick.

When she was halfway up the stairs, she heard,

> "Gabriella ... Gabriella ... Gabriella ... where are you? Gabriella?"

She came back down.

> "Sweetheart, I'm right here. It's getting late, and I'm going to get washed, and then come back down here and be with you."

> "Hurry," replied Nicholas.

> "I will, sweetheart. Meantime, you listen to the Christmas carols I have playing for you." After inserting the CD, she started up the stairs.

> "Gabriella ... Gabriella," he called.

Back down she came.

> "Nicky, darling, are you listening to this beautiful music? It's Nat King Cole, your favorite. Just relax, and I'll be back soon."

Up the stairs she went. Nick continued to call her name, but she proceeded to shower, and then returned as quickly as possible. When she came down, Nick looked so surprised.

> "Oh, there you are. I thought you left me."

> "No, darling. I would never leave you. Never!" she said shaking her head, as she approached him to give him kisses.

It was now completely dark outside, and the blinking tree lights looked heavenly.

> "Don't turn out my tree lights. I like them," said Nick suddenly.

Gabriella smiled.

> "I won't, my darling. You just keep enjoying them. Those are *your* tree lights."

He dozed on and off, and Gabriella went to the kitchen to look at the medication list, as it was time for a few meds.

After giving him the meds, she started to go back upstairs to go to bed. She had the baby monitor set up in the Master bedroom. Immediately, Nick started to call her name. She stayed upstairs, and got into bed, watching him on the monitor, and thinking he would stop shortly and go to sleep. He continued calling her. After about ten minutes, she went back downstairs, and decided she was going to sleep on the sofa located next to his bed. Once again, he was surprised to see her.

"Oh hi. I'm so glad you're here!" he exclaimed.

"Yes, darling. You're home now, and it's just you and me. I will never leave you again in the night. Try to remember that, okay?"

"Okay."

"I'll just sleep here on the sofa tonight. I'm right here, so don't you worry."

"Can you get in bed with me?" he asked.

"That bed isn't big enough for two of us."

"Oh, please. I want you to hold me."

"Really, Nicky, the bed is too small."

"Gabriella, please."

"Okay, let me see what I can do here. She lowered the bed and put half of herself next to him with her arm around him.

"Oh, that's nice. I like this," he said.

"Okay, but I can't stay like this for long. I'm not a contortionist, you know," she said, laughing. "I don't want to fall, because who would take care of you if I got hurt?"

"Don't get hurt, Gabriella, please!" Nick sounded very alarmed.

"I'm okay. Close your eyes. Are you comfortable?"

"Yes, I love when you hug me," Nick repeated.

"Thank you, sweetheart. I plan to give you hundreds of hugs. I love you so much."

As Nick went to sleep, Gabriella slowly climbed off the bed, and slept on the sofa. The sofa became her bed every night thereafter, while Nick was home.

Gabriella woke up at around 3:00 a.m. Since she was up, she turned one lamp on dimly and checked Nicholas' diaper. He needed to be changed. She washed and changed him, which of course meant that she awakened him too. This became the routine every night. Then she turned the lamp out and returned to the sofa. Sometimes Nick would feel like talking, as they sat there in the semi dark. She kept the light on over the stove in the adjoining kitchen, just so it would not be completely dark in the family room. One night, he asked her,

"What are all those motorcycles doing?"

Of course, she had no idea what he was seeing, so she just went along with whatever he thought was happening.

"I think they're getting ready to race," replied Gabriella.

"Oh, where are they racing to?" he asked.

"They're going to see who can get to downtown Chicago first."

"Oh. There are so many of them."

"Yeah. Looks like a hundred," replied Gabriella.

"Maybe more than that, Gabriella." Nick corrected.

"How many would you say Nicky?"

"Yeah, about a hundred."

"Do you like the music I have playing?"

"Yeah. But it seems like it's the same songs over and over."

Gabriella laughed.

"That's because I have it set on Repeat. I'll turn it off."

"Okay. Thanks. I'm tired of listening to those songs," replied an honest Nicholas.

Gabriella laughed.

"What song would you like to hear?"

Nick just looked at her without answering.

"Okay. Let's just go back to sleep. It's 4:30 in the morning!"

"I'll try," he said.

"I love you, and I'm so glad you're home. Are you glad you're home, Nicky?" she asked.

"Yes. I'm so glad to be home."

"Watch the blinking lights, and see if you can get some more sleep," she suggested.

"Okay."

Gabriella awakened every morning at 7:00 a.m., so she could give Nick his liquid food and medicines. She would then get herself dressed upstairs. When she returned she would change him, give him a bed bath, dress him in a clean T-shirt and pajama top, change the bed sheets. Additionally, she would shave him, brush his teeth, comb his hair, clean the bedsore and apply ointment, clean the stomach area around the feeding tube, give him a nebulizer treatment, flush the feeding tube, elevate his feet off the mattress, turn him every two hours, and massage him.

This was the daily routine on the days when Jane did not come. Three days a week, Jane gave him his bed bath, changed him and the bed sheets. Gabriella preferred to personally do all the rest of his personal hygiene, on *all* days.

On Wednesday morning, Gabriella put the radio on to hear the news while she was feeding Nicholas. She heard the reporter talk about a bad flu that had hit the Chicago area. Being concerned, when Jane arrived, Gabriella asked her to wash her hands immediately in the Powder Room, before she entered the family room and touched Nick.

Jane questioned this.

"Why?" she asked.

"Because there is a bad flu going around, and I don't know where you just came from. I want your hands to be as germ free as possible."

"But I always put sanitizing gel on my hands, before I come to your door," commented Jane.

"Jane, don't argue with me. Please just wash your hands in the Powder Room, every time you come."

Jane finally consented, but Gabriella didn't like her defiance. Shortly after, Bernie arrived, and Gabriella told her the same thing. Bernie just looked at Jane.

"She's wants us to do it every time we come in the house," said Jane.

"Why?" responded Bernie.

"Because there's a flu going around, and I don't want Nicholas to get it," explained Gabriella.

Then, firmly added...

"What's the big deal, ladies? Wash your hands. Dry them with the paper towels that are in the Powder Room. Please, do it! My God, let's not make it a federal case!"

On that note, Bernie proceeded to the Powder Room. They both saw that Gabriella was not going to tolerate anyone questioning her care for Nicholas.

As usual, Bernie was not in a pleasant mood, and now there was some tension in the room.

"You two ladies want a soda?"

They both shook their heads, meaning No.

Gabrielle looked at Bernie as she examined Nicholas.

"He started to cough last night, but I gave him some cough medicine, and he fell asleep," Gabriella reported.

"I did not have to give him morphine. How's his chest sound?"

"It seems to be okay," replied a semi-unconcerned Bernie.

When Bernie finished, Gabriella sat with her and discussed the supplies she needed. Gabriella always asked for extra, especially diapers. She reviewed her list of meds too. Their pharmacy would deliver the meds at any hour—sometimes that very day.

One night, Gabriella was surprised to hear a knock on the door at 10:30 p.m. Being alone, Gabriella never opened the door during the night. She ignored the knock and the doorbell, but was very alarmed.

Who would be at my door, at this hour? She thought.

All of a sudden, she looked at the three small windows at the top of the front door. She could see the face of a black man, who was looking in. Gabriella quickly moved out of sight to the living room. Her heart was pounding. She was very frightened. Just then the phone rang. It was the pharmacy, saying that they were delivering Nick's meds that night. Gabriella scolded the caller for not notifying her in advance, and told him that she thought the delivery person was already at their home. She instructed the caller from the pharmacy, to *always* call her in advance.

Then she called through the door,

"Who's there?"

"Jeffreys Pharmacy," he replied.

She opened the door and turned the porch light on.

"Who's that medicine for?" Gabriella asked, still frightened, speaking through the locked screen door.

"Nicholas Carcioni," he replied.

She opened the door and scolded...

"Please, *always* call me *before* you come, especially if it's going to be at such a late hour. Put that on my record, so this doesn't ever happen again!"

"Yes, ma'am," he replied. "I'm sorry we frightened you. We know your situation, and wanted you to get your husband's medicine, as soon as possible. From now on, we'll always call first."

As the week progressed, Gabriella noticed that Nicholas was coughing on and off. She gave him some chocolate pudding, mixed with a product called Thick-It, a thickening powder for people who have trouble swallowing. Nicholas really seemed to enjoy it, but later that night he started coughing constantly. Gabriella had a stethoscope—a professional one, she had "borrowed" from Asclepius Christian Medical Center. She listened to his chest and his heart on a regular basis.

It was now Thanksgiving Day, and Gabriella had decided she would cook the full Thanksgiving dinner with all the trimmings, just as she had done for the past 33 years, so that Nicholas could smell the heavenly aroma of the turkey in the oven. He had always loved waking up smelling the turkey cooking.

Nicholas used to beg her to go out to an upscale restaurant for Thanksgiving and Holidays, but she refused.

She would tell him...

"Holiday meals are to be eaten in your own home, at your own table, surrounded by family members, and friends, too."

Gabriella was adamant about this rule, probably because that was the way she had been raised.

Today would be no different...

"Good morning, Nicholas my love. Happy Thanksgiving! Smell the turkey?"

In a soft voice, Nicholas replied,

"Yes."

"Smells so good, doesn't it?"

"Yes." He smiled.

"Later, I'm going to give you some of your favorite— sweet potato pie (mashed up sweet potatoes with butter and brown sugar). I know how you love that. You should be able to eat that with no problem. Of course, I'll still add the Thick-It."

With the turkey cooking in the oven, Gabriella went upstairs to get dressed. When she returned, she washed Nicholas, changed his clothes, sheets, shaved him, brushed his teeth, combed his hair, and put some Paco Rabanne on his face, and a little on his chest.

"You look so handsome, as always, my love. And you smell *so* good, I could just eat you up."

She laughed as she kissed him all over his face and neck. Nick started laughing too, as she tickled him.

Pulling out a Sinatra album from Nick's collection, she put it on the turntable.

> "Here's some Sinatra you haven't heard in a long time," she said.

Nick smiled upon hearing him sing. Then he fell asleep.

At around 2:00 p.m., Gabriella took the turkey, stuffing, and sweet potatoes from the oven. She even added Thick-It to the cranberries. She mixed some Thick-It into the stuffing, and also into the sweet potatoes. She wasn't sure if he was going to be able to eat the stuffing. She would have to play that by ear.

> "Nicky, it's time for Thanksgiving dinner. Hope you're hungry!" She positioned the head of the bed in an upright straight position.

> *Thank God for this motorized hospital bed*, she thought. Nick opened his eyes, not saying a word.

> "Okay, open wide. Here it comes. Let me know if I'm still a good cook," she remarked.

She put a bit of sweet potato onto a very small spoon and placed it in his mouth. He maneuvered it around, and she kept repeating,

> "Swallow, sweetheart ... swallow."

And finally he did. She did the same with the stuffing—an extremely small portion—and then cranberries.

It was a very slow process for him to eat only three small morsels of each. He took a sip of thickened water, that she had prepared. That was all he wanted, and she knew he had probably only eaten that small amount, so he wouldn't disappoint her. He closed his eyes and went back to sleep.

Later, though, she noticed, he was coughing for a prolonged period. To provide him relief, she went to the refrigerator, pulled out a syringe of morphine, and gave him his first dose.

> "Open your mouth, sweetheart. I'm going to squirt this in, and you swallow. Go ahead, Nicky, swallow. That's good."

He did as she instructed, and it did start to ease his coughing quickly.

> "Thank you," he whispered.

Gabriella thought,

> *Although Nicholas really enjoyed finally, having some food in his mouth, I don't want him to be constantly coughing. That's not good for him. To spare him from aspirating, I'm going to just stay with the tube feeding for now, until he gets stronger.*

While he slept, Gabriella returned to the kitchen to fix herself a plate of this luscious Thanksgiving feast. She sat in his chair at the kitchen table, which faced the Family room.

As she looked at Nicholas in his Hospice bed, she couldn't even bring herself to eat more than one forkful of her meal. Placing the fork onto her plate, she cried inconsolably, fearful that the end was going to come sooner then she desired.

Memories of holidays gone by, flooded her mind, which only made her sob more. Alone and depressed, with tears streaming down her face, she saw a glimpse of the desolate life she was about to face, without her beloved Nicholas.

Her knight in shining armor was charging forward to fight his final battle.

> *Nothing will ever be the same again*, she thought as she cried.

> "Dear God, give me strength to face this!" She prayed aloud.

The weeks progressed. By the beginning of December, Gabriella could see that Nicholas could not eat anything by mouth.

###

Not being confident in Bernie's assessment of Nick's lungs, she asked to speak to the Doctor who was in charge of Asclepius Christian Hospice. Not only did she not have faith in Bernie, but she did not like her demeanor at all.

> "Bernie," Gabriella asked, "Who is the Hospice Physician that you report to?

> "Dr. Vivek Greyson. Why?"

> "Could you give me his number? I want him to come here and check Nicholas. I would feel better having a Doctor check him, at least once a month."

> "Just call the office and leave word for him to call you. This isn't normally done, so I don't know if he'll come here or not," Bernie replied indifferently.

When Jane and Bernie left that day, Gabriella called Asclepius Christian Hospice, and asked for Dr. Greyson. A woman identifying herself as Sally, asked Gabriella what her reason was for wanting to speak to Dr. Greyson. Gabriella repeated what she told Bernie.

> "I want my husband to be checked by a doctor, at least once a month. I don't think that's asking too much. May I speak to him please?"

> "He's not in at the moment, but I will have him call you," answered Sally.

About an hour later, Dr. Greyson called. He said he would come and see Nicholas Friday morning at 10:00 a.m. Gabriella was glad he was coming, and she hoped to speak to him alone, when he was there. He was going to arrive at 10:00 a.m. Jane would be leaving then, and Bernie would not be there yet, as she usually arrived between 11:00 a.m. and noon.

But, on Friday, Jane came at 9:00 a.m. rather than her usual 8:30, and when the doorbell rang at 10:00 a.m. there stood Bernie alongside of Dr. Greyson, a very tall handsome East Indian man with a wide smile and a friendly attitude.

> "Thank you for coming, Dr. Greyson." They stepped into the foyer. "I ask everyone who comes in, to wash their hands in the Powder Room first. So, would you, please?"

> "Yes, of course." He cheerfully went in and washed his hands. Then, Bernie followed afterward.

Entering the Family room, Dr. Greyson remarked...

> "You have a lovely home, Mrs. Carcioni."

"Thank you, Doctor. "This is Nicholas. Nicholas, Darling, wake up. This is Dr. Greyson. He's come to check on you."

She turned to the doctor.

"He seems to be coughing more, Doctor, and sleeping more. I'm worried that he might have Pneumonia again, but Bernie says, he does not. Please check for Pneumonia."

Nicholas did not open his eyes. He just lay there quietly.

Jane moved aside, as she had just finished Nicholas's bed bath. She put a sheet over him, as she could see he was chilled. Gabriella was glad to see that she had noticed that.

After Dr. Greyson checked Nicholas thoroughly, he said that he was hearing some congestion, and just to be safe, would start him on an antibiotic. He also suggested that, if he was coughing more, then instead of giving him three cans of liquid food a day, Gabriella should reduce it to two cans. Perhaps that would help.

Gabriella felt so much better having Dr. Greyson visit. She appreciated his concern, and even more so, appreciated that he was trying to be proactive in giving Nicholas a mild antibiotic, so that his Pneumonia would not come back in full. He departed alone.

Bernie stayed to complete the list of supplies to be ordered, and she called in the antibiotic for Nicholas. Jane finished the bed bath, and both Hospice workers left together.

The following Friday, Jane and Bernie arrived together again. Gabriella could sense they both seemed to be in grouchy moods. She tried making conversation, but they did not want to partake. Having a strong sixth sense of people's moods and auras, Gabriella went into the kitchen, where she could observe them without hovering.

Bernie checked Nicholas in her usual quick fashion, but she did not have any comment to make. Gabriella walked to the round table. Of course, she was wondering how his lungs sounded, now that he was taking a mild antibiotic. She was not expecting any negative comments.

"Do his lungs sound better to you, now that he's been on the antibiotic?"

"No. About the same," Bernie replied. Then she added,

"Are you in the process of making funeral arrangements?"

"No! Why would I? Nicholas is doing fine." "I'm not thinking about death," replied a surprised Gabriella.

"You should. He's under Hospice care ... that's what Hospice means!" retorted Bernie.

"Really? No one ever gets better on Hospice? Gee, Bernie, thanks for the news! You know, you have a very negative attitude, lady, and I don't appreciate it one bit! You're not my idea of a good Nurse. You never have any encouraging words to offer Nicholas or me. I think you're in the wrong profession!"

Bernie just looked at Gabriella in shock. Jane stood by Nicholas staring in silence.

"Actually, both of you have the wrong attitude," Gabriella stated pointing to Jane. "Every time I walk you to the door when you're leaving, Jane, you say the same thing over and over... 'Let him go. He wants to go, but you're holding him back. Let him go.'

Gabriella continued,

> "I'm sick of hearing that from you, Jane. God will decide when to take Nicholas—not me, you, or anyone else. While he's here, I'm going to do everything I can to love him, make him happy, and keep him comfortable. He's my everything, ladies. So, get with the program!"

Jane and Bernie had no response, as they could see Gabriella was not going to tolerate any opposition to her goal. Bernie finished the supply sheet, and Jane put on her sweater.

> "I'll see you next week." said Gabriella as they both departed.

Gabriella gave serious thought to changing to Golden Stallion Hospice. She even called their rep, Cheryl, and asked her if it was possible.

> Cheryl replied, "Absolutely. Just say when."

Because she was so upset, Gabriella relayed to Cheryl a few conversations she'd had with Jane and Bernie. Cheryl apologized for their harshness and said,

> "That's not the way it works. We're here to reduce anxiety and offer emotional support. They should never try to diminish your optimism by saying depressing things, and they should always be supportive about doing all they can, to help the patient. I'm so sorry to hear that you're experiencing this type of negativity. Let me know when you want to make the switch. I'm here for you," replied Cheryl.

Over the weekend, Gabriella still could see that Nicholas's cough was increasing, and when she listened to his lungs, she of course could hear congestion.

I'm tired of this runaround by Bernie, Gabriella thought.

"I'm calling Dr. Yurkevich," she stated.

Gabriella placed a call with his answering service, and later that day, Dr. Yurkevich returned the call. She apprised him of her dislike for the Hospice Nurse, Bernie. She told him that Dr. Greyson had visited and prescribed a mild antibiotic, but that Nicholas was coughing more.

Dr. Yurkevich was very attentive. He said that he would prescribe a stronger antibiotic, along with cough medicine. Also, Nicholas should probably have an oxygen machine. He would take care of that immediately. Everything she needed was delivered later that evening. Gabriella could see that oxygen did relieve Nicholas's coughing. She also increased his nebulizer treatments. Both aided greatly.

As an entertainer, Nicholas had been a night owl his entire life. He came alive in the night. Gabriella had thought about that, when she noticed that he slept mostly all day, but when the sun went down, Nicholas felt the most like talking, so she tried to arrange herself to be there on the sofa, hoping he would talk. Of course, it was still the Christmas season, and his tree lights were blinking constantly all day and night, for Nicholas to enjoy.

One evening, Gabriella put Nat King Cole's *Stardust* album on. The music was so soothing. As "Stardust" played, one of Gabriella's favorite songs, Nicholas awoke.

"I love that song," he said.

"Me too, darling."

"Where are you?" he asked.

"I'm over here on the sofa. Turn your head to the left," replied Gabriella.

"Where?" he asked.

Gabriella got up and gently turned his head to the left, so he would be looking toward the sofa area, and could see her. Walking back around, she showed him where she had been sitting.

"Can you hold my hand?" he asked.

"Yes, if I move this end table over a bit, and then move the sofa closer to your bed. Let's see. Yes, now I can hold your hand. Feel my hand?"

"Yeah. I like when you hold my hand," replied Nicholas.

"I love holding your hand, Sweetie. And I love that it's just you and me here in our own home. Nice and comfortable. Just you and me."

Then Nicholas said something that surprised Gabriella,

"Who's that other lady who comes here?"

"What other lady? Do you mean Jane or Bernie? The Aide and Nurse?"

"No, I know them. The other lady."

"Honey, what lady? Is she pretty? If she is, that would be me." Gabriella laughed.

"No, not you. I know you." he chuckled.

"She comes sometimes and just stands here and stares at me, smiling. She doesn't have much to say, but I do love seeing her. It makes me feel good to see her."

"Hmmm... I don't know who she is, darling. Let me know when she's here again."

Gabriella sat there for a long time thinking about the woman who was visiting Nick.

Could it be The Blessed Mother? she pondered.

He is wearing her Scapular, and has shown her much devotion during his life.

Wow, I wonder ... she thought.

CHAPTER 51

NICK SINGS AGAIN!

Miracle #4

Tuesday, December 11, 2012, was Gabriella's birthday. She was about to receive a gift from Nicholas, that would leave her crying tears of great joy.

As the telephone rang early that morning, a sweet voice identified herself as the Hospice Chaplain, Catherine Martha. She apologized for not already having come to visit Nicholas, but asked if she could come that afternoon.

During the conversation, she mentioned that she played the guitar, and asked if it would be all right for her to bring it along. She had heard that Nicholas had his own Orchestra, so she thought music might thrill him. Of course, Gabriella agreed, and excitedly told Nick that the Hospice Chaplain was coming and bringing her guitar. Nicholas smiled.

Catherine Martha arrived at 1:30 p.m. She was a short woman, light brown hair, in her early 50's, soft spoken, smiled often, and was very warm and friendly.

Nicholas had been sleeping prior to her visit and was now awake. It was perfect timing. She pulled up a chair next to his bed, and talked directly to him, as Gabriella sat at the side round table. Catherine Martha asked him a few questions, he answered briefly, and then she mentioned that she knew he had a Big Band Orchestra, and had worked with many big-name performers in his life.

"Yes, that's true," replied Nicholas.

"I heard that you're a singer too?"

"Yes," Nicholas replied.

"I have a song I'd like to sing, and I'm sure you'll know the words, so if you would like to sing along, that would be fine with me. Okay?"

She had his full attention, which was amazing in itself. He replied, quickly,

"Yes."

Catherine Martha started to strum her guitar, which, thankfully, was not electric. Then she started to sing, in the loveliest sweet voice, "*Santa Lucia*".

Nick listened attentively, and when it came to the chorus, *Santa Lucia,* Nick automatically started singing along. Together they repeated the chorus several times, and Nick sang it till the end.

"Santa Lucia …. Santa Lucia," singing loudly and on key.

Catherine Martha started crying as she sang. Tears were also streaming down Nick' face as he sang. Gabriella sat in wonderment, and was crying uncontrollably.

Her prayers had been answered—as she had so wanted to hear Nick sing again. It was truly miraculous!

At the end of the song, Gabriella rushed to Nick's side, threw her arms around his neck, while crying and kissing his face. Nick kept crying too.

> "Thank you, my Darling. It was SO beautiful to hear you sing again. Thank you! I love you so much!" she repeated as she wiped his tears, as well as her own.

She turned to address Catherine Martha.

> "Thank you, Catherine Martha, for the miracle that you brought us today, on my birthday. It was magnificent. Thank you so much!"

Catherine Martha sat drying her tears with tissue...

> "Oh, I didn't know it was your birthday. Happy Birthday! Such a glorious present he gave both of us. I had no idea that he was capable of singing. It just goes to show that God works in wondrous ways, and we must never give up hope!"

> "You're so right, Catherine Martha. So very right...This was truly a Miracle, sent from heaven!"

Catherine Martha started to pack up, as Gabriella then offered...

> "Would you like a cup of coffee, while we chat?"

> "I'll just take a glass of water, if I may."

"Sure. Let me get it for you. How long have you been a Hospice Chaplain?" she asked as she rushed to the kitchen to retrieve the water.

"Ten years now."

"That's a long time. I bet you've seen a lot!"

"Yes. Some situations are worse than others. Some people end their lives with very little love around them. It's really very sad."

"However, I can see that's not the case here, Mrs. Carcioni. It's obvious to everyone on our staff, how much you love Mr. Carcioni."

"Yes, I do, with my whole heart. That's why I won't tolerate any negative thinking around him—and unfortunately, I've been getting that from Bernie and Jane. Sorry to relay that to you."

Catherine Martha nodded, adding,

"Both of them have been doing their jobs, for a long time. It's easy to become callous when you see death often. However, that doesn't make their behavior excusable."

Gabriella responded....

"I can understand how difficult their jobs are, but I just CAN'T have it. You understand."

"Of course, I understand. But we all know, there is an end for all of us, right?"

"Yes, of course."

Then the Chaplain added...

> "Just to be on top of things. It wouldn't hurt for you to think that God might call Mr. Carcioni home sooner than you would like, and sooner than you think. Right? I mean, it wouldn't hurt to know, what your next step will be. That's all I'm saying," stated the Chaplain.

Gabriella nodded...

> "Of course not. As a matter of fact, I did get some information in the mail the other day from Sunset Crematory. I just started reading it. Nicholas and I both want to be cremated."

> "If I may," interjected Chaplain Catherine Martha ... "I have referred several people to a Crematory in the western suburbs that I do trust, *Page Cremations*, and they are very fair in their pricing. It's about twenty-five miles from here. They do a very professional job. Would you like their card?"

> "Yes. It wouldn't hurt to have it. I'll call them and see what they provide, and if they would come this far," replied Gabriella thankfully.

> "Yes, please do. I'm sure they will be glad to help you, when you need them. Mention my name. They've known me for years."

Upon standing, Catherine Martha added...

> "Well, I must go. I have a full calendar this afternoon."

She walked over to Nicholas' bedside.

"Mr. Carcioni, it was wonderful meeting you, and thank you for singing along with me. You have a most beautiful voice, and I can see why you were so successful."

Nicholas whispered,

"Thank you!"

The two ladies walked to the front door.

"Take care, Mrs. Carcioni. I'll come visit as often as I can."

"You're always welcome here, Catherine Martha. God Bless!" she responded while hugging the Chaplain.

She then quickly returned to Nicholas' bedside, still with tears in her eyes.

"Thank You, my darling, for that precious Birthday gift. I'll remember it forever!"

Nicholas just smiled while keeping his eyes closed.

"My God, I love you so much!" she added.

CHAPTER 52

HOLY SMOKE

It had already showed signs of being a cold blustery December.

On Christmas Eve, a few inches of snow had graced the patio and was covering the ground. More snow was being predicted, along with frigid temperatures. Gabriella started to think, that she should have some firewood, just in case the electricity went out.

How would I keep my Nicholas warm? she thought.

She searched the local paper and called a few people who delivered firewood. One supplier, *Holy Smoke,* caught her eye. In speaking with the gentleman, she negotiated a reasonable rate, asking if he would include stacking it, by her garage. He agreed.

"When can you deliver it?" she asked.

"Today."

"Today? On Christmas Eve?"

"Yes. I could come over in an hour, if that's okay?" the polite voice replied.

"That would be perfect. See you then!"

Gabriella grabbed her checkbook, and shared with Nicholas what she was doing.

> "I have a man coming with a cord of firewood. It's so cold out, if we lose electricity at least we can burn wood in the fireplace, to keep us warm. You agree?" she asked.

Nicholas didn't reply. He just lay quietly with his eyes closed.

Bundled up in a warm coat and scarf, she walked outside the garage to wait for the man. He arrived soon in his truck, which he backed up onto the driveway. The man exiting the truck was about thirty years old, six feet tall, very nice looking, and friendly.

> "Hi, I'm Gabriella."

> "Hi, I'm David. I'll get started emptying the truck. Where do you want it stacked?"

> "Right here, against the bricks."

> "Okay. No problem."

When he was finished, he said that he was connected to *The Shepherd of Nazareth Church*, and they were having a Christmas play.

> "I think you and your husband would really enjoy the play."

> "Oh, Thank you, David. But my husband just came home on Hospice care."

"I'm so sorry to hear that. If there's anything I can help you with, just let me know," David offered.

"That's so very nice of you, David. Thank you so much." as she handed him his check.

"Take care. God bless!"

What a fine young man. So helpful. So friendly. I'm so glad I met him, Gabriella thought.

CHAPTER 53

FINAL CHRISTMAS AND NEW YEAR'S EVE

Gabriella was extremely grateful that she had Nicholas home, not only for Thanksgiving and Christmas, but she would also have him with her for New Year's Eve too. Every day upon arising, and every night before going to sleep, she thanked God for giving them this precious time together.

There was no need for gifts to be put under the tree on Christmas Day, because having Nicholas with her, was the only gift she desired. He was happy and very comfortable being in his own home, where there was peace and tranquility every day, all day long. He could feel her love and attention as she took care of him in every way possible, and there was nothing that could make him happier.

As his brain continued to click on and off, there were a few more times when Nicholas, all of a sudden, was on target. One afternoon Gabriella was changing him. When she leaned him on his side, he suddenly blurted,

"What are you doing!"

Gabriella, responding quickly—too quickly—

"I'm changing your diaper."

A very shocked Nicholas shouted,

"What!"

Gabriella hadn't expected him to be so aware. She had to think quickly.

"Oh! What's wrong with me? Did I say diaper? I meant to say, *"man pants."* The Doctor prescribed these *"man pants"* for you, so that you don't have to get up a hundred times to go to the bathroom, and you can get your rest."

Her voice was shaky.

Nicholas thought for a few seconds.

"Oh, Okay," replied a calmer Nicholas. "Okay."

Thank you, God! Gabriella thought, breaking into a sweat.

On Christmas Day, Gabriella was feeding him his liquid food and was talking out loud, as Nicholas lay there quietly with his eyes closed.

"First, I think I'll clean your feeding tube, just to make sure you're getting all your food and there's no blockage. Doctor said to give you only one and half cans now. Hopefully, this will ease your coughing a bit more. I mentioned to him that I thought you might be allergic to something in the Glucerna, and I suggested we try a different brand of food. Doctor said I could try it if I wanted to. So, I ordered a case. We'll start that today."

Suddenly Nicholas spoke, which surprised Gabriella, as she thought he was either sleeping or wasn't paying any attention to her.

"You mean Dr. Kastoris?" he asked.

Dr. Kastoris had been Nicholas's Primary Care Doctor for the past 30 years. Nick had always had a great rapport with "*the Doc,*" as he called him, and had visited his office at least once a month. He and Gabriella had even gone to dinner several times with Doc and his wife. Needless to say, Nick had always felt they had a close friendship, yet Dr. Kastoris never visited once, while Nick was in Asclepius Christian Medical Center Hospital or Lavender Gardens Nursing Home. He had not called to say he would like to come and visit. Gabriella was extremely upset, and deeply hurt over this for Nick's sake. Finally, she responded,

"No, I mean Dr. Yurkevich"

"Is Dr. Kastoris coming?" Nicholas asked.

Gabriella walked around the bed so that she would be looking at Nicholas' face. She knelt down and she kissed his forehead.

"No, sweetheart. He's out of town," she replied.

Nicholas just stared into her eyes for a few seconds, as though he was questioning if she was telling him the truth.

"Oh," he said softly as he lowered his eyes.

She bent down and gave him another kiss, and hugged him tightly in her arms. Shortly thereafter, he went to sleep.

It was a perfectly quiet Christmas Day with Christmas Carols playing all day on the stereo, Nicholas' colored tree lights constantly blinking, and several scented candles burning. Gabriella had washed and changed him, and all was perfect. She could tell he was comfortable from the slight smile on his face, as he lay sleeping.

Gabriella pulled a chair up next to the bed and took his hand gently as she started talking to him, hoping he would answer. She talked about the fact that it was Christmas, and then reminisced about Christmases of yesterday, that they had shared. She talked about the weather. It was cold and blustery outside, but they were warm and cozy inside. She had lit a fire in the fireplace, which added warmth to the atmosphere.

A friend, Betty from Palm Springs, had sent a small live decorated Christmas tree, covered with musical notes and red bows. It was such a lovely surprise, and Nicholas smiled upon seeing it, as Gabriella placed it on the table where he could look at it often.

"That's so pretty," he said smiling.

This opened a whole new set of memories. They discussed their friendship with Betty, and their friendship with her now deceased husband and their good friend, Pat. Yes, they shared a multitude of happy memories from their 33 years of togetherness. Today, she recounted many of them for him as he lay quietly. It was as if she was telling one bedtime story after another.

Of course, every story ended with, … "and Nicholas and Gabriella lived happily ever after."

Nicholas had entertained on New Year's Eve all his life with his Combo and Big Band Orchestra. When he stopped performing on a regular basis, it was such a pleasure just to be with

Gabriella, and to share the entire day together. They would have an early dinner at one of their favorite restaurants, dancing afterward to a Combo in the lounge.

Home by 9:00 p.m., both would get showered and change into their comfortable lounging clothes. Nick would light the fireplace, while Gabriella prepared snacks, including hot buttered popcorn, and their favorite drinks. Nicholas's favorite drink was always J&B scotch and water, with a lemon twist. Gabriella preferred Sambuca, Frangelico, or Red wine.

Finally, they would settle in to watch TV, waiting to ring in the New Year. At midnight, they would follow the Polish custom of having a piece of herring, in wine sauce, as the first morsel of food in the New Year. They had practiced this tradition for many years.

This New Year's Eve had to be altered a bit, however she still intended to keep tradition.

Just before midnight, she prepared two pieces of herring, one for her and one for Nicholas. She poured herself a glass of Cabernet. For Nicholas, she poured a very small amount of J&B scotch in a glass and added a little water and a squirt of lemon.

She went to Nicholas's bedside as the Grandfather clock in the Foyer struck midnight. Gabriella wished Nicholas a Happy New Year...she kissed him, and put the glass to his lips. He opened his mouth slightly, and she let some fall on his tongue.

He gave her a little smile, without saying a word, he could taste the Scotch.

> "Happy New Year, my darling! We've made it through another year. It's now 2013, and we both know you've

always considered 13 to be your lucky number. I love you so much!"

"Thank you, Dear God, for giving us one more holiday together!" she voiced.

CHAPTER 54

EMERGENCY!

The first few days of the new year were relatively quiet. Nicholas slept most of the day and into the night. He wasn't talking as much as he had been prior, and it seemed as if he was just content with being clean and comfortable. He never complained that he was hungry, or in any pain. Much of the day, he lay there sleeping with a little smile on his face, which Gabriella surmised was a reaction to a good dream. Perhaps he was seeing relatives or friends, who had long ago passed. It gave her much comfort to see him smile.

On January 5, 2013, at 6:00 p.m. Gabriella prepared to give Nicholas his food and meds, as was routine. She had been noticing that he had started to cough more that day. As she approached his bedside, she was shocked to find blood squirting out of his stomach (belly button), like a fountain. Blood was all over his stomach and the sheets.

Frantically, she put a towel over the area to stop the bleeding, but the blood kept gushing out. Immediately, she sent a SOS text to Dr. Yurkevich, and then she quickly dialed Hospice.

Dr. Yurkevich was quick to respond, and wanted to know if the blood was coming from his feeding tube. Gabriella responded that it was coming out of his stomach.

Bernie, the Hospice Nurse called, and said to put a belt around him and tie it tight to stop the bleeding. Gabriella responded that she did not have a belt that would go all around him, as his stomach was swollen.

Dr. Yurkevich suggested that she hold her hand over the area and apply pressure. He told her to apply a large bandage of some sort, or use bath towels, and then turn him all the way over onto his right side. Additionally, she should administer Morphine, as Nicholas was still coughing.

Quickly, Gabriella got bath towels and did as he instructed. The pressure she applied started to slow the bleeding. After about 25 minutes, Nicholas stopped coughing. Bleeding had finally ceased also.

Nicholas fell asleep. Gabriella did not give him any food or meds. She did not want to aggravate whatever had just occurred.

Later that evening, she washed and changed him, and all the bedding.

She sent a text to Dr. Yurkevich, asking what he thought had happened, but he did not respond.

Bernie offered no explanation either.

OUR LADY OF MT. CARMEL SCAPULAR

CHAPTER 55

DEATH VISITS ON SUNDAY

Sunday, January 6, 2013, started out as any other day. Cold, bitter wind blew against the patio doors of the Family room, forcing snowflakes to dance everywhere. Gabriella arose early at around 7:00 a.m., and gave Nicholas his feeding, even though she was giving him only one can of liquid food a day now, in order to ease the strain on his lungs, and lessen his coughing. That morning, she decided to wash him and change his clothes and bedding, before she went upstairs to dress herself.

"Good morning, darling. Did you sleep well?" she asked.

Nicholas did not answer. He just lay there with his eyes shut.

"I'm going to bathe you now and get you cleaned up, so you can relax and enjoy this lovely day," she said.

"I gave you only one can of food because I'm trying to make it easier on you, so you'll cough less. Doctor Greyson thought that would be a good idea."

She proceeded to do her normal hygiene procedures, even trying to brush his teeth, but Nicholas did not feel like cooperating, as he normally would. He just seemed to be enjoying being asleep, and did not want to open his mouth or his eyes. He had been like this more and more over the past few days.

Even Jane had tried to get him to talk when she was there the last time, but he looked as if he was enjoying where he was in dreamland, and did not want to be bothered with anyone.

A wide smile had graced his face on Friday as he lay there with closed eyes.

> "Look, missis, come see! He's smiling! Why is he smiling so much?" asked Jane excitedly.

> "Oh, he's probably having a wonderful dream, Jane. It's so good to see him smile," Gabriella replied, bending over and kissing his face.

Asking Nicholas....

> "Are you having a happy dream, Nicholas? With your Mom and Dad? Maybe your Brother? That's good. You enjoy visiting with them," she said happily.

When she finished caring for him on this Sunday morning, he looked clean and comfortable, but there was no smile. He was not coughing. In fact, he made no gestures or expressions at all.

Gabriella went upstairs to get herself dressed. When she came back down, she checked on Nicholas and found him sleeping, just as she had left him. He looked comfortable and contented.

Satisfied that he was taken care of, she decided to go back upstairs to call the Dell Computer Help Desk. Recently, when she was sending the update emails, her Desktop computer had started to give her problems.

As usual, it took a long time for someone to come on the line with Dell, usually located in India.

As she explained her problem to the man, he had her perform several procedures, as he tried to solve the problem.

As time went by, she noticed she had been on the phone for approximately 2 hours. She told the Technician that she had to go, saying ...

> "I have to give my husband his medicine. If you want me to, I'll leave this line open, and you can stay inside my computer, to fix it, but I'm going to leave you now."

> "Okay, ma'am. I will keep trying to fix your computer," he replied.

Gabriella brought the phone downstairs, laid it on the kitchen table, and went to Nicholas's side as she explained about her computer problems. Nicholas lay sleeping.

Gabriella then proceeded into the kitchen, and she started to mix the five medications he required at that hour, along with his liquid food. Proceeding to Nicholas, she started administering, while saying.

> "Nicholas, my love, I'm so sorry I was gone for so long. I have your medicines and your food, and I won't be leaving you again. The tech guy can fix it or forget it. I'm sick of messing with that computer."

Nicholas did not respond; he just lay there. Gabriella then started to pour the liquid food into his tube. As she administered, she noticed the sheet had moved, and that his legs were a grey color. She felt his feet and legs. They were ice cold.

Alarmed, she called out to him,

> "Nicholas, darling! What's wrong? Your feet and legs are frozen! Nicky! Nicky!"

Stopping the feeding, she hurried around to the other side of the bed. Hugging him, she grabbed for the comforter to cover him.

> "Nicky baby! Open your eyes! What's wrong? Your legs and feet are so cold. Here, sweetheart, the comforter will keep you warm. There now, that's better. I'll put this blanket on you too."

But, Nick would not open his eyes. In kissing his face, it was still warm, as was his arms.

> "You'll warm up fast, now that you're snuggled in, my li'l angel. Let's say our Rosary together, darling. Want to open your eyes for me? Come on baby, pray with me."

She held his hand, and did not let go through the entire Rosary. Giving him kisses intermediately. When she finished, she gave him more kisses.

At that moment, her Cell phone vibrated on the kitchen counter. Meanwhile, the landline phone was still live on the kitchen table, connected to the man from Dell, whom she had completely forgotten about!

She ran into the kitchen, to grab her Cell, hoping it would be from Dr. Yurkevich. However, it was not.

Instead, someone had sent a beautiful GIF of Jesus, dressed in an all-white robe, walking off the altar of a small dark wooden chapel toward her. He drew closer and closer, and finally opened his arms to embrace her. She was so shocked at this life-like image, she dropped the Cell phone on the counter, and immediately took the GIF as a sign, that Jesus was coming for Nicholas.

Running to Nicholas, she scooped him up in her arms crying.

> "Nicholas! My darling Nicholas! Jesus is coming to take you home. Don't be scared, my darling. I've got you in my arms. I won't let go of your hand until Jesus takes it from me. Oh, Nicky, I love you so much! I'm here, sweetheart."

With tears streaming down her face and onto his, she kept rocking him back and forth, in her arms, and could feel his forehead was still warm. Without hesitation, Gabriella started to tell Nick all the things, that she would miss about him.

> Oh, Nick, my love, if you leave me, I will miss so many things about you!
>
> I will miss your brilliant smile... your hugs and kisses, especially when I'm sad and worried.
>
> I will miss your Intelligence, and how you always advised, protected, and guided me.
>
> I will miss your soft velvety singing voice, that was always so romantic and soothing! And, of course, I will miss you leading your Orchestra, which delighted so many people, and made me so proud!
>
> Most of all, my darling, I will miss your jovial personality, and your endless jokes that always made me smile!
>
> "Oh my God, Nick!" she cried...barely able to continue, as her tears fell like rain down her face. "You are my

entire world, and no one will ever take your place. I love you my darling, and always will! You are, and have been, my everything...my heartbeat...my entire world! Don't be afraid. I've got you in my arms!"

Gabriella was going to miss everything about him, and she wanted him to know that, even though her tears were choking her, as she spoke, hugging him tightly in her arms.

Suddenly she thought about the Scapular of Our Lady of Mt. Carmel that they both wore. Holding Nicholas with one arm, and reaching into his pajama top with the other, she pulled out the Scapular, saying out loud, crying in desperation.

> "Blessed Mother, he has worn your Scapular all these years. You know he loves you. You said that anyone who wears your Scapular will not see the fires of hell. Please keep your promise. I need to know that you will keep your promise. Please let me know, that you have kept your promise to my darling Nicholas! *Please!*"

She laid him down and kept crying as she rested her head on his chest. His forehead was still warm, but his face was very cool. Quickly she grabbed her stethoscope, and placed it on his chest. She placed it on the right side, and then moved it over slowly to the left.

She heard his heart beating slowly and softly. But then, all of a sudden, she heard one final beat. Panicking, and wanting to hear that sound again, so she kept moving the stethoscope all over his chest, but she heard nothing more. Without realizing it at the time, she had heard his last heartbeat!

Gabriella had never been present when someone was dying, and therefore had not known what to expect. She bundled

Nicholas up even more, to keep him warm, and then thought about the oxygen tank.

> "You need oxygen! That's what you need, Nicky. Why didn't I think of this sooner? Here, let me get this going for you."

With shaky hands, she placed the mask on his face and turned the loud machine on. It was now a few minutes before 10:00 p.m. She sat on the sofa, staring at him for hours. Gabriella watched as his olive-colored skin turned a grayish color, and then it turned pure white. She fell asleep at around 1:00 a.m. and awoke at 3:00 a.m. Nicholas was still in the same spot he'd been two hours before, and his entire body was extremely white in color.

Slowly she got up, and turned the oxygen machine off. She removed the mask and felt his cold face. She kissed his cold forehead. In lowering the rail to the bed, she hugged him one more time, and kissed him gently on the cheek.

He was gone, and she knew it. With her soft voice, she said...

> "Well, my darling," she whispered with tears flowing, "I guess you're in heaven now, with Jesus!"

Gabriella stood sobbing in a paralyzed state of shock. Her heart was shattered. She did not expect Nick to leave her so soon. As though being guided, she robotically turned and ascended the stairs, leading up to the Master Bedroom.

"You will go to heaven, in style, Mr. Carcioni, as you had lived!" she whispered.

Opening his closet, she retrieved his tuxedo, white shirt, cufflinks, bow tie, socks, and underwear. She took his tux and shirt to the ironing board and started to press them. Nicholas had always liked extra starch in his collar and cuffs, and as she was pressing his shirt, she suddenly said out loud,

> "I know … extra starch." she smiled, as she could hear him coaching her.

When the shirt was pressed and the tux was free of wrinkles, she shined his black dress shoes with polish. When she was finished, she hung the shirt and tux on a hanger, and carried it down to him along with the accessories.

Standing in front of his bed, she held it up and said to him,

> "See? All pressed. You will look as handsome as ever walking into heaven, my darling."

Quickly she went upstairs and got herself dressed. When she came downstairs, she changed Nicholas, gave him a bed bath, dressed him in a clean T-shirt and pajama top, shaved him, and put clean linens on the bed.

> "There. You're nice and clean," she said as she added shaving lotion. "And now we can call Hospice."

It was 7:00 a.m. First, she called *Page Crematory* and got their answering service.

> "Hello. This is Mrs. Carcioni. My husband, Nicholas, passed last night, and I would like you to come and get him ready for Cremation. Could you have Alex give me a call?"

> "Yes. I will reach him and have him call you right away, Mrs. Carcioni."

Then Gabriella called Hospice, and got their answering service.

"Hello. This is Mrs. Nicholas Carcioni. My husband, Nicholas, passed away last night, and I have called the Crematory to come and get him. I'm waiting for a call back.

The answering service representative replied,

"Your husband died last night, and you're just calling us now?"

"Yes. I wasn't sure if he was gone until about three this morning. I have never been with someone who was dying. But he is gone. I know that now. I have already washed him, and he is ready for the Crematory, so Jane and Bernie don't even have to come over." Gabriella spoke firmly, but softly.

The Hospice rep responded quickly...

"Oh, I will call both of them immediately, Mrs. Carcioni. I'll call you back."

"Fine. But if the Crematory comes, I will let them take Nicholas." Replied Gabriella.

Within three minutes the phone rang. It was Alex from the Crematory.

"Mrs. Carcioni. First permit me to offer you my deepest condolences on the passing of Mr. Carcioni. Yes, we will come and take Nicholas. We should be there in about two hours. Then in about two days, you can come with another person and have your last viewing. He will be cremated him that day or the next. You can then come back, and select the urn for his ashes, and take him with you. Do you have his clothes ready?"

"Yes. I have it all ready for you. He will be going in his full tuxedo."

"Wonderful! We'll see you soon."

As soon as they hung up, Catherine Martha, the Hospice Chaplain called.

"I'm coming now, and should be there in twenty-five minutes. Jane is on her way and should be there in ten minutes. Bernie will be there in an hour or so."

"Okay. Fine. See you then."

The doorbell rang, and it was Jane. Immediately upon stepping in, Jane offered her condolences. She was washing her hands, when the doorbell rang again. It was Chaplain Catherine Martha, who also immediately offered her condolences once again. All three went into the Family room.

"I'll wash him, missis," Jane stated compassionately.

"No need, Jane. I already washed him and changed everything. He's all set."

"But, I normally do that, missis."

Catherine Martha looked at Gabriella and touched her arm, saying softly.

"Let her wash him again. That's what she does. Okay?"

Gabriella thought for a moment.

"Okay, Jane. You may do it. Put the same T-shirt and pajama top on him because they're clean, and button it up so he looks neat."

"Yes, missis," replied Jane.

Catherine Martha asked what had happened, and Gabriella recounted the entire Sunday for her.

"I have to call Coroner Larry now," Catherine Martha stated, as she started dialing his number.

When Catherine Martha told Coroner Larry that Nicholas had died during night, but that Gabriella hadn't been sure till this morning, he became livid.

"He died last night, and she is just calling it in today! Check that body over for abuse!" he screamed. "This is absurd!"

"You don't understand, Coroner Larry," Catherine Martha tried interjecting.

"You check every inch of his body for abuse!" He continued to shout.

Gabriella had heard enough! She snatched the phone from Catherine Martha and shouted back.

"This is Mrs. Carcioni. I did not abuse my husband! Check his entire body! Check anything and anywhere you want. I don't give a shit what you think. My husband died last night—around ten o'clock on Sunday, January sixth!"

Catherine Martha became alarmed and grabbed the phone back from Gabriella.

> "Okay, Coroner Larry, I'll check his entire body and call you back. Thank you!"

Then quickly she tried advising Gabriella.

> "Gabriella, you don't want to tick off the Coroner. Stay calm. I'm not going to check Nicholas. We all know how you adored that man. Coroner Larry has no idea about the love that you had for him. Stay calm."

Gabriella informed Catherine Martha that she did call *Page Cremation,* saying they would be coming soon to pick up Nicholas.

Gabriella had already been thinking about a Memorial Service for Nicholas, and she asked Catherine Martha if she would sing "Santa Lucia" at the Memorial, as she had sung it at the house with Nicholas.

> "I have to go and talk with one of the Catholic churches in the area," she told the Chaplain.

> "I know exactly what type of Memorial I want for him— one with lots of music. I'll let you know where and when."

Catherine Martha replied quickly,

> "Great. I'd be honored to sing at Mr. Carcioni's Memorial.

> "Let's call Coroner Larry back now." Being connected to his office, she stated, "Hello Coroner, I checked him, and there are no marks of abuse. Everything is as it should be."

"Good. The death certificate will be made out for January 7, 2013. Let the widow know that."

"Okay. I will."

Just then Nurse Bernie arrived. When Gabriella opened the door, Bernie entered. Without even offering her condolences, she came inside and headed straight for the Family room. Almost simultaneously, two people from the crematory arrived, and Catherine Martha asked them to wait in the driveway.

> "If it gets too cold out there, guys, you're welcome to come and sit in the Living room, until we're finished here," offered Gabriella.

> "That's okay. We'll wait outside," said one of the men.

Another forty-five minutes passed, during which time Catherine Martha and Bernie completed all the paperwork that documented Nicholas's death.

Up to this point, Gabriella had not shed a tear. She had handled everything in a very sedate, mature manner, somehow knowing that Nicholas was out of his suffering and in the arms of Jesus.

Catherine Martha went outside to get the men from *Page Crematory*. When they came in, they suggested that maybe Gabriella should step into another room.

> "No. I'll stay with my Nicholas," Gabriella responded.

The men took out a black leather bag with zipper.

> "Just don't cover his face. Zip it up to his waist only," Gabriella instructed while everyone looked on.

"Yes, ma'am."

The guys did so, and they placed a pink silk rose on Nicholas's chest. As they began to maneuver the gurney, Gabriella grabbed Nick' hand, and they all walked out together. Gabriella went through the door first, followed by Nicholas, then Catherine Martha, Bernie, and, finally, Jane.

> "Would you like us to stay with you, Gabriella?" Catherine Martha asked.

> "No, Thank you. But I'll be in touch," she said receiving a hug from the Chaplain.

Then Gabriella looked at Jane and Bernie,

> "Thank you, Jane and Bernie. Take care."

Gabriella turned to be with Nicholas, as the men positioned him in the van. In the meantime, the ladies got in their cars and left.

Finally, the men from the Crematory said they were set, and they closed the doors to the van, that had no windows.

Gabriella stood on the long driveway, and watched the van slowly leave the property, making its way to the end of the street. She watched until it was out of sight. No neighbors were around. Not a soul. Gabriella stood in the cold January wind with tears rolling down her face, knowing her Nicholas would never be home again. Her heart was pounding, as if it was going to jump out of her chest. She looked up into the sky and, amid her tears, she screamed out....

> "Nick! I love you!"

Gabriella made her way into the house, crying to the point of being nauseas. She collapsed on the Living room staircase, and held onto the oak banister for support. As she cried, she called out,

> "Nick ... I need you. Please don't leave me. Please Nick ... Please ...."

She lay there crying uncontrollably for about a half hour.

During that time, she heard a disturbing noise in the Family room, but felt physically unable to address it. After a while, she thought she had better go see what had fallen in that room.

She got up and as she walked into the Family room, to her shock, the bag of diapers that she always had stacked against the wall, had been *kicked across the entire room* to the fireplace!

Standing there mystified, she finally walked over to the package, fell to her knees, and hugged it tightly in her arms.

She knew this was a sign from Nick. Crying out....

> "Oh, Nicky! You're still here. You haven't left me. I know you're still here. Thank you, my darling! Thank you! I need you with me!"

CHAPTER 56

THE BLESSED MOTHER ANSWERS PRAYER

Miracle #5

On Wednesday, January 9, Gabriella received a call from *Page Crematory*. The caller told her that Nicholas was ready to be viewed for the last time before his Cremation. Gabriella could bring one family member or friend with her.

Gabriella contacted Robert, Nick's nephew. He was the only relative that Nick had been close to, in his later years.

On one occasion, Gabriella had trusted Robert to stay with Nick for a few hours, while she ran to do grocery shopping. It was the *only* time she had left Nick, while he was home. When she returned from the store, Nick and Gabriella hugged and kissed each other, as if they had been apart for days. Their love had always been unquestionably strong.

Robert was glad Gabriella had asked him to the final viewing, and met her there the next morning.

Taken to a private room in the Crematory, Nick laid dressed in his tuxedo, bow tie, shined shoes, and everything that

Gabriella had provided, including his favorite cufflinks. Gabriella kissed his forehead, hugged him, and again whispered that she loved him. She later stepped aside to give Robert time alone with Nick.

Alex, the Crematory Director, asked Gabriella if she wanted to push the button that would start the Cremation, but Robert had advised Gabriella against it. His thoughts were it just might be too much for her heart to handle, and he undoubtedly was right.

He would be cremated later that afternoon.

On Friday, January 11, 2013, Gabriella awoke around 7:00 a.m. and started to get out of bed. As she sat up on the edge of the bed, she suddenly became extremely tired. She felt a tiredness overcome her, that she had never experienced before. She fell backward onto the bed. As soon as her head hit the pillow, she was asleep.

Suddenly, she started to dream that she was standing outside in an empty parking lot. No one else was around. In the distance, about 40 yards from her, she saw a man running toward her. As he drew closer, she saw it was Nick, fully dressed in his tuxedo and bow tie.

On the *outside* of his tuxedo was the Scapular of The Blessed Mother. In Nick's hands was a blue Rosary, that bounced back and forth, as he ran toward her with outstretched arms. It was the very same Rosary that Gabriella kept by her bedside, the Our Lady of Lourdes Rosary. She owned several pairs of Rosaries in various colors, but this was her favorite.

Nick was beaming. He was smiling so brightly! Gabriella just kept staring at the Scapular outside of his tux, wondering why it wasn't inside his shirt. As he got within 10 feet from her, she outstretched her arms to hug him. She was so excited and so happy to see him, but, quickly to her dismay, he vanished.

Slowly, Gabriella came out of the dream state. As she opened her eyes, tears were running down her face. Hiding her face in her pillow, she sobbed.

"Oh, Nicky. I miss you so much!"

Sitting up on the edge of the bed, she couldn't help but think about the vivid dream she'd just experienced. And then, all of a sudden, the realization hit her.

"Oh My God!" She blurted out loud. "That was The Blessed Mother answering my prayer. The prayer that I prayed, while Nick lay dying. I asked her to let me know, that she will keep her Promise of the Scapular, to spare him from eternal fire! And she did! She kept her Promise. Through that dream, she let me know, just as I had requested."

"That's why the Scapular in the dream was on the *outside* of his tux! And that is why he was carrying my favorite blue Our Lady of Lourdes Rosary. This was definitely a message from The Blessed Mother herself...that she had kept her Promise!"

Gabriella started to cry profusely...

Thank you, Blessed Mother, for taking care of my darling Nick, and keeping your Promise! I love you!"

Gabriella sat there for a long time, reliving that remarkable dream! She would never forget it! She would never forget the smile and jubilation on Nick's face. To this day, she thanks The Blessed Mother constantly, for letting her know.

Gabriella continues to wear her Scapular daily, and encourages everyone that they, too, should wear the Our Lady of Mt. Carmel Scapular.

"Thank you so much, Oh beautiful Heavenly Mother!"

CHAPTER 57

NICK CARCIONI MEMORIAL SERVICE

Gabriella and Nicholas had not joined any particular Catholic Church, when they moved from the city to the suburbs. They went to Mass at various churches, depending upon their schedule. Likewise, since their separation from the strict adherence to the Catholic Church over the Annulment, Nicholas and Gabriella had found other ways to serve God—ways they would never have found otherwise.

Sometimes when we experience negative things happening to us, we may later learn that it is, indeed, God showing us yet another pathway to His Kingdom.

Still being Catholic, Gabriella went first to a local Catholic Church, requesting to have Nick's Memorial Service, and once again she was met with obstruction. Being that Nicholas's whole life had been wrapped around music, Gabriella wanted to incorporate his music into his Memorial.

The Office Manager at the Church quickly informed her, that there were certain songs permitted to be sung. She would have to choose from their list. Additionally, they had a format that she would have to adhere to, and there would be no deviation allowed.

Gabriella informed the Manager, that this was her husband's Memorial, not hers nor the Church's. Gabriella did not speak with any Priests, since being told this was their policy.

All in all, she contacted six Catholic Churches in a 15 mile radius, and she received the same response from all of them. It became painfully obvious that Gabriella was going to have to seek the assistance of a Non-Catholic Church, for her Nicholas's Memorial. As she sat searching through the local phone book, and on-line reviewing her options, her friend Nancy visited, bringing sandwiches to the house.

Gabriella told Nancy about her dilemma. Nancy quickly said that the Pastor at her Catholic Church, would have gone along with Gabriella, but he was away on a cruise. However, she said she could mention it to her good friend, Deacon Kevin, but, he would then have to convince the musical director.

Nancy placed the call, and later that afternoon, Deacon Kevin emailed Gabriella, saying that the musical director refused to bend the rules. But then he added, *'wherever you decide to have the service, if you want a Catholic presence involved, I'm offering you my services.'*

Gabriella was delighted. There were three non-Catholic churches on her list. Neither of the first two she visited, offered the capabilities that she sought. Upon visiting the third church, although the date was available, when she asked to see the chapel, she was in for a surprise!

As the young girl walked her toward a set of doors, she said, "Well, it's not exactly a chapel."

"Oh, what do you call it?" Gabriella asked as the girl opened the doors.

"Well, it's just a big hall." She responded timidly.

Entering, Gabriella exclaimed,

> "This is a gymnasium! Look there are the two basketball hoops, and the lines on the floor. This is a gym!"

> "Not exactly," the girl stated. "During our service, with all the chairs on the floor, you don't even see the lines, and then you forget all about the basketball nets."

Gabriella just shook her head.

> "Thank you. I'll give it some thought," said Gabriella as politely as possible." departing quickly.

Being a Channeler, she could hear Nicholas's voice saying to her,

> "Don't have my Memorial in a gymnasium, Gabriella. Don't you dare!"

She started to laugh out loud, replying,

> "Stay calm....I would never do that to you, Nicholas Rocco Carcioni!"

Standing in the parking lot, she tried to think where she should go next. As she looked down the street, the evangelical Church, "The Shepherd of Nazareth," caught her eye.

> *Let's go see what they have to offer,* she thought.

> As she walked inside, no one was around. Seeing the sign with arrows reading, *Chapel,* she began to make her way to the back of the building, only to find a small room.

"This can't be it!" she whispered aloud.

In turning the corner to walk back to the entrance, she saw a man walking in the opposite direction way in front. She called out to him.

"Hello! Hello."

Finally, he turned around and started to walk toward her. As he drew near, she recognized him. He was the firewood guy.

"Hi!" he said, recognizing her too. "How's your husband?"

"He passed away yesterday," Gabriella replied with tears in her eyes.

"Oh, I'm so sorry."

"You're, David, the firewood guy. Nice to see you again. Is firewood your job, and this your part-time gig?" Gabriella asked with a smile.

David laughed.

"Actually, *this* is my job, and the firewood is my part-time gig!" he replied laughingly.

"I'm a Pastor here," he went on to explain.

A pleasantly surprised Gabriella exclaimed...

"Oh my God, you are! How wonderful! David! I have a dilemma, and hopefully you can help me. The Catholic Church refuses to have Nick's Memorial the way I want it—as a tribute to him. What I'm asking for is not crazy. I just want to incorporate some of his singing and music into the ceremony. Of course, it will be very spiritual."

"I think that's a great idea, Gabriella. I'm sure we can make that happen for you here."

"How big is your Chapel?"

"Oh, you don't want to hold it in our Chapel. It's too small. You want our Sanctuary, which holds over 400 people. Come. I'll show you!"

They walked toward the Sanctuary, which was located at the entrance to the church, accessed through a set of double doors. It was most convenient. The front altar was like a huge stage with six steps leading up to it. It was magnificent!

Hanging above the stage, on each side, were two extremely large white screens. The balcony housed a variety of electronic equipment, that was used for holiday productions. They even had videotaping capabilities, which was a major requirement, that Gabriella wanted done. Gabriella was ecstatic! This Church had all the capabilities for hosting the Memorial, exactly the way Gabriella envisioned it in her mind.

Another Pastor joined them, and he confirmed that they could, indeed, videotape the entire Memorial for her, which was something she definitely wanted. Gabriella had found her church!

"Thank you, Dear God!" she said aloud ecstatically.

Of course, she asked Pastor David, if he would be the celebrant, and he agreed. Then she asked him if he would mind if Deacon Kevin, a Catholic Deacon could also joined the Memorial. Pastor

David welcomed the Deacon. Gabriella set up a meeting date, when all three met, as Gabriella outlined what she wanted each of them to do. She also asked for their ideas. They were very agreeable to what she wanted, and added a few suggestions, which Gabriella accepted gladly.

Gabriella set the date for January 26, 2013, which enabled her time, to prepare for what was later described by many who attended, as a quintessential tribute.

Many people remarked:

"This was the best funeral I've ever attended!"

The weather was perfect on that January day—cold but sunny, and no snow.

At the entrance to the Sanctuary, an easel, displayed a huge color poster picture of Nicholas in his tuxedo. In front of it were 33 long-stemmed red roses, marking each year that he and Gabriella had been together. Prior to the Memorial starting, the poster and flowers were moved to the stage near the piano.

For the first hour, people came to offer their condolences, as Gabriella and Robert stood next to the altar, where Nick's urn was placed. Gabriella chose a beautiful wood Howard Miller case, to house his ashes. Bouquets of gorgeous white blizzard roses, adorned each side of the altar. Large flower arrangements on floor pedestals, were positioned on the stage near 2 podiums.

During the Condolence Hour, Gabriella had worked with *Page Crematory* to produce an on-going video of pictures, with Nicholas and all the top-name performers that he had worked with, along with photos of family and friends. This was shown on the two huge screens. As the pictures flashed, a CD created by their dear friend, Dominick, with a variety of soft mellow songs, selected by Gabriella, sung by all the singers who had worked with Nicholas, created a very spiritual atmosphere within the church.

From the very beginning until the end, the church's videographers recorded everything that was happening in the Sanctuary. Gabriella wanted a remembrance, and was so very pleased with the results of the videotape. The Sound team played an integral role throughout the entire Memorial, filling the sanctuary with wondrous music, all chosen by Gabriella.

Each of the guests was provided with a colorful eight-page booklet, that contained the words to all the songs and prayers, so that everyone could participate.

The processional song was, "Let There Be Peace on Earth."

Deacon Kevin walked around the altar, showering it with incense as Frank Sinatra's recording of "Softly As I Leave You" filled the Sanctuary.

Pastor David read Psalm 23...."The Lord is my Shepherd; I shall not want. In verdant pastures he gives me repose........And I shall dwell in the house of the Lord for years to come."

Deacon Kevin led everyone in saying The Lord's Prayer, along with an Opening Prayer specifically mentioning Nicholas's name.

The First Reading was from the book of Ecclesiastes, including The Eight Beatitudes read by his dear friend, Jack.

ECCLESIASTES 3:1-2 To everything, there is a Season.

A Time to every purpose under the heavens...a Time to be born, a Time to die....

The Second Reading consisted of several specific passages from the Bible, chosen by Gabriella, and read by friend, Pamela, which also included Romans 12:19: "Vengeance is mine; I will repay, said the Lord" (St. Joseph Edition The American Catholic Bible).

Ryan, Pianist, led everyone in singing, "Holy God We Praise Thy Name."

Deacon Kevin read the Holy Gospel, John 11:25-26: "I am the Resurrection and the Life; whoever believes in Me, though he should die, will come to Life; and whoever is Alive and believes in Me, will never die."

Pastor David delivered the homily, highlighting points of Nick's life, his talent, generosity, and compassion for the underdog, and most of all, his love for Gabriella!

As the Pastor illuminated on Nicholas's deep love for her, Gabriella's mind drifted back to a *small spiritual Wedding* that cemented their love, beyond any reason of a doubt.

Several months and years had passed, since the extensive planning of Nick and Gabriella's elaborate fairytale Wedding, **that never took place***, due to the strict Annulment stipulations of the Roman Catholic Church. It was now just a painful distant memory. Gabriella's heart never completely healed from this devastation, and never would!*

Life went on, however....Nick continued as a Professional Convention Planner, servicing clients that he had for numerous years, along with being an Entertainer, performing with his Big Band Orchestra throughout the United States and Canada.

Gabriella continued her career as Hospitality Director of Sales and Marketing.

As she sat there at Nick's Memorial, she recalled a particular date, in Las Vegas. Nick had just completed over-seeing a long two-week successful convention, with Gabriella assisting as usual. That morning, he mentioned to Gabriella that he wanted them to get dressed in their finest, and celebrate that evening, over a delicious dinner at one of the most prestigious restaurants in Vegas. Gabriella was happy to oblige.

As they walked across the Resort grounds, on their way to dinner, Nicholas led the way to a small Chapel, telling Gabriella that he had to make just one fast stop. Arriving at the arched oak door, he opened it, for her to enter.

As she entered the candlelit Chapel, she heard organ music playing softly. She noticed the entire chapel was filled with the heavenly scent of hundreds of yellow roses. Numerous candles burn with a vanilla fragrance.

A tall Reverend stood on the altar, who greeted her by name, which puzzled Gabriella standing in awe. Off to the side was a well-dressed couple smiling. Nicholas followed quietly at a distance behind her.

She turned to ask him what was happening, and found him smiling, as he approached her, taking her hand, he spoke....

> "I know this is not the wedding you dreamt of all your life, but I hope that you will know it is just as loving and spiritual, as it would have been back then, Gabriella. I

love you even more today...So I ask you again, will you marry me tonight?"

Tears rolled down her face, as she could barely reply.

"Yes, my darling Nicholas. I will be honored to be your wife."

Approaching from the side, the couple came forward. The woman handed Gabriella a huge Bridal Bouquet, of yellow roses with white tips, mixed with white lilies, surrounded by several white satin ribbons.

The ceremony was intimate, loving, sacred and romantic.

At the conclusion, Gabriella smiled and whispered over and over, as Nicholas held her in his arms.

"I love you....I love you....I love you, Nicholas Rocco Carcioni."

This memory brought tears flowing down her face, at that very moment in the Memorial.

"Thank you, my darling Nicholas." She whispered sitting in the pew.

"Even though we said, till death do us part...I still need you with me, even now!"

At this moment in the Memorial, it was Gabriella's turn to speak. Composing herself, slowly she rose....

Unusual as it was, Gabriella decided that she, herself, would deliver the heartfelt and loving Eulogy, for her darling Nicholas.

Wanting to make Nick proud, she somehow was able to get through the entire Eulogy, without breaking down in tears. Albeit at the beginning, she started to choke, but then regained her composure, and proceeded as the wife of a U.S. Marine would do, speaking in a loving, sentimental manner, with much grace.

Afterward, friends took turns approaching the microphone, telling stories about Nicholas. They shared memories, highlighting what they had admired most about him.

Catherine Martha, Hospice Chaplain, once again sang "Santa Lucia," accompanying herself on her guitar.

Members of the U.S. Marine Corps conducted the Presentation of the Flag, and a bugler played "Taps."

Pianist Ryan sang "Ave Maria."

Pastor David then announced,

> "Once again, we are all going to be entertained by Nicholas Carcioni—his beautiful singing voice and playing his tenor saxophone."

Three recordings of Nick were then played:

Nick singing, "Bill Bailey," playing his sax with his Combo. Nick singing his #1 Hit, "Apples and Bananas" with his Combo. And lastly, Nick singing, what he referred to as their song, "Always Together," along with conducting his Big Band Orchestra.

Indeed, it was emotional to hear Nick's voice again, as it touched a chord in everyone's heart, bringing tears flowing.

Deacon Kevin offered the Closing Prayer.

Pastor David announced that lunch would be served at J.C.'s, their dear friend's restaurant. A few musicians from Nicholas's Orchestra asked to be part of the Memorial: Marty, trumpet; and Bill, clarinet; while Ryan on piano; and Tom on drums also joined in-- playing the recessional song, "When the Saints Go Marching In".

They led the entire congregation in singing. Everyone applauded at the conclusion, as it was a most joyous Memorial.

During the entire Memorial, a professional photograph of Nicholas, wearing his tux and smiling brightly, shown on both huge screens above, and as Gabriella looked up, he seemed to nod in approval. Gabriella could feel Nicholas smiling down in gratitude, for all that had been said and done in his honor.

It was a marvelous tribute to a most deserving man! As she clutched the vessel with his aches, Gabriella whispered, *"Someday, we'll meet again, my love."*

The following Prayer was given to Gabriella, when she was in the third grade by a Franciscan nun. She kept it for her entire life, and prayed it often. **This prayer is never found to fail! It does not matter if you are Catholic or not!** The Blessed Mother is everyone's Heavenly Mother.

Go to her with your worries and problems. She will provide guidance and tremendous comfort!

CHAPTER 58

MIRACULOUS PRAYER
To the BLESSED MOTHER
(NEVER FOUND TO FAIL!)

NICHOLAS CARCIONI
A Chicago Legend
BORN: MARCH 4, 1925
HEAVEN BOUND: JANUARY 6, 2013
Memorial Celebration: Saturday, January 26, 2013

Oh, Most Beautiful flower of Mt. Carmel,

Fruitful Vine, Splendor of Heaven, Blessed

Mother of the Son of God, Immaculate Virgin,

assist me in this my Necessity. O Star of the Sea,

help me, and show me herein you are my Mother.

Holy Mary, Mother of God, Queen of all Universes,

I humbly beseech you from the bottom of my heart,

to succor me in this Necessity.

THERE ARE NONE THAT CAN WITHSTAND YOUR POWER.

Show me, herein, you are my Mother. O Mary conceived

without sin, Pray for us who have recourse to Thee.

Sweet Mother, I place this cause in your hands. (3 times)

(ASK and YOU SHALL RECEIVE!)

CHAPTER 59

NICK RETURNS FROM THE DEAD!

Miracle #6

October 2014

Gabriella's Gift of Channeling, in speaking to the Spirits, had become even stronger over the years.

Possessing the Gifts of being a Medium, she was able to speak (Clairaudient) to deceased friends, relatives, Saints, Angels... and yes, even Jesus and The Blessed Mother! Also, there are times when they make themselves visible to her (Clairvoyant).

In most cases, when the Spirit of the deceased comes to convey a message, it is one of importance that they want delivered to their surviving loved ones.

The Spirits have a way of becoming very insistent, and as a Channeler, one cannot just say,

> "Get somebody else to deliver your message!"

> "It doesn't work that way," says Gabriella!

Spirits want messages delivered to advise, protect, warn, comfort, or just inform those, who they have left behind. They will not leave the Channeler alone, until he or she agrees to deliver their message, either written or verbal!

Gabriella always delivers the messages exactly as she hears them. She doesn't try to sweeten, soften, or rewrite it. She does not omit anything, nor change the message in any way; and she definitely does not try to explain them. Interpretation is up to the receiver, because the messages are obviously very personal.

In recording the messages, she either writes them in longhand, or uses her computer. Some Spirits talk very quickly, and she does all that she can, to keep up with them. She has found this to be true, especially within the first 5 days after they pass.

There seems to be a window between our world and theirs. It's completely open, just after passing, when they are experiencing so much, and they are so very happy to convey all that they are seeing, feeling, and knowing. They're like little excitable kids.

They talk very fast, hoping to get it all conveyed. For all Spirits, their ability to communicate, never closes completely, but for some, their energy level diminishes slightly in time. Afterwards, the frequency and length of the messages vary.

When Nick was alive, Gabriella used to try to explain Channeling to him, but his thought had always been....

"When you're dead, you're dead!"

Gabriella would respond, smiling....

"Not exactly, my darling."

He didn't believe in any metaphysical activity. He thought dying was the end. However, NOW, Nicholas has seen that, though his body has died, and *that* Nicholas Carcioni no longer exists, the Spirit inside him continues to live...perhaps it's the subconscious that never shuts down!

Yes, he has communicated with Gabriella, stating that she had been right: death is not the end; rather, it's a beginning to a whole new adventure, which, of course, varies for each soul.

In Channeling Nick on several occasions since his passing, they both totally understand that now, at this juncture, they each have different paths, that they each must follow. An entirely new Plan has been formulated for each of them. During one Channeling session, Nick relayed....

> "Although a whole new experience is awaiting me, Gabriella, I will never stop loving you! I will be available whenever you need me...just call my name. I will always watch over you, and try to protect you from harm. It's this way with all who pass on. The ones left behind, that we have loved, are not left to be alone. No one is forgotten. We are now capable of involvement in diverging roles, and can simultaneously be in several places at once! It's really remarkable and quite beautiful! And yes... of course, we can hear everything that is said about us, and to us."

Nicholas is already involved in his next assignment, adventure, or life design...call it what you will. Gabriella must also move on, to complete the rest of her life, achieving her goals, until she accomplishes her destiny, here in this lifetime. Yes, for her, that entails initiating new beginnings, meeting new people, making new friendships, and visiting new places. They each have a totally different existence, now, that they must embrace.

That does not mean that they will forget each other, or stop loving each other, but it does mean that a part of them—the part of them that was a twosome—must be left in the past. They must now, welcome new scenarios, that have been created for them to fulfill in the present.

All that being said....one evening, in October 2014, Nick decided to *show* Gabriella that he had not left her, and she was not alone.

After Nick's passing, Gabriella had been under a tremendous amount of stress. She had been selling their home, while looking for another place to live.

In the process, she was decluttering, selling items, donating, and trying to keep up with the maintenance of their large home, and was obviously missing Nicholas a great deal.

One evening, about 9:00 p.m. She was putting clean sheets on the bed in the Master bedroom where she slept. Two lamps were lit in the room. The hallway outside the room was dark, as was the Guestroom across from the Master, where Nicholas used to dress.

As she fluffed the king-size sheet in the air to settle on the bed, she glanced across the sheet to the doorway of the room. Her eyes widened in shock, as she witnessed Nicholas walking from the dark hallway into the Master Bedroom. He was dressed in black slacks, shirt and sweater vest. It was not an illusion. It was not a shadow of him. It was *him* live, and in living color. His presence was so solid, that she thought it was an intruder at first! He took about three steps into the room, and when their eyes finally met, she gasped!

"Ahhh!" as she immediately dropped to her knees by the bed.

In feeling the blood rushing instantly to her head, she came within seconds of fainting.

Nick disappeared instantly.

Gabriella cried out, begging him to come back, while apologizing for being frightened.

"Please, my darling Nick...come back!" she sobbed passionately.

Understandably, her reaction had been one of shock, as this was the *first* occurrence of such an appearance. However, her pleas went unheard.

Nicholas never returned. Well... I must add, not on **that** particular night!

Reprint Of Advocate Guidelines

Previously published by Gloria J. Yorke in "The Midas Touch, The World's Leading Experts Reveal Their Top Secrets to Winning Big in Business and Life." Coauthored with Joe Vitale, Dan Lok, and 26 talented authors.

ADVOCATE GUIDELINES USING THE **LAW OF ATTRACTION (LOA):**

1.	Trust your Intuition	LOA... DECISIVENESS
2.	Don't be Intimidated	LOA... RESPECT FOR HUMANITY
3.	Do research	LOA... SEEK AND YE SHALL FIND
4.	Be Observant	LOA... ALERTNESS
5.	Make your Presence Known	LOA... I AM
6.	Doctor Commitment	LOA... DUTY
7.	Cleanliness	LOA... UNIVERSAL HEALTH
8.	Restrict Visitors	LOA... RESTRICTIONS
9.	Take a Break	LOA... MANIFEST WELLNESS
10.	Be A Politician	LOA... UNCONDITIONAL LOVE

Current Medication Form (*Keep in your wallet*)

Name: _____

Address: _____

ZIP _____

EMERGENCY CONTACT: _____ PHONE: _____

	Doctor	Address	Phone Number	Medicine	Reason	Dose	Frequency	#Years
1.								
2.								
3.								
4.								
5.								

Allergies: _____

440

CNA DAILY ACTIVITY FORM

(Use One Sheet per Day)

Room: _____

Patient's name: _____

DAY AND DATE: _____

CNA Name	Reason	Time In	Time Out
1.			
2.			
3.			
4.			
5.			
6.			
7.			

ABOUT THE AUTHOR

Gloria J. Yorke is a notable Best-Selling Author, having co-authored *The Midas Touch: The World's Leading Experts Reveal Their Top Secrets to Winning Big in Business & Life* with Joe Vitale, Dan Lok, and 26 additional authors.

It was a #1 Best Seller on Amazon in three categories, for a prolonged period.

Ms. Yorke was born and raised in Canonsburg, Pennsylvania, to admirable Italian and Polish parents Virginia Rose (Longo) and Edward Paul Yorke. Their loving Family includes: three Siblings, Nieces, Nephews, Grandchildren, Aunts, Uncles, and several Cousins.

Ms. Yorke enjoyed a successful 30-year career in the Hospitality field, as Director of Sales and Marketing for various hotel/resort chains. Throughout her career, she earned awards for her training, leadership, public relations, sales & marketing, and journalistic abilities. Likewise, for several years, Ms. Yorke was a distinguished journalist for Chicago suburban newspapers, who featured her bi-monthly column.

An interest in Astrology and the Metaphysical, captivated her from childhood, as she developed intuitive abilities, which she refers to as Intuitive Messaging, or Channeling. Over the years, she has realized they are, indeed, Gifts from God, and had no choice but to accept them with much Gratitude. Upon doing so, she opened herself to having profound conversations with Jesus, The Blessed Mother, Angels, Saints, as well as, departed relatives and friends, all of whom occupy various dimensions in the Spirit world.

As a Tarot Card Reader, and an empowered Empath, loving Spirit Guides often relay mystical messages through her, to the querent.

Over the years, Ms. Yorke has been a dynamic featured speaker for several organizations, and is passionate to impart the information outlined within this Book. She has captured the attention of audiences everywhere, with her powerful and factual messages.

Ms. Yorke currently resides in a suburb of Chicago.

Connect with her at: MedicalManslaughter28@gmail.com

CPSIA information can be obtained
at www.ICGtesting.com
Printed in the USA
BVHW031945260219
541220BV00001B/3/P

9 781524 697129